THE
STALKER AFFAIR
AND THE PRESS

THE
STALKER AFFAIR
AND THE PRESS

David Murphy

London
UNWIN HYMAN
Boston Sydney Wellington

Published by the Academic Division of
Unwin Hyman Ltd
15/17 Broadwick Street, London W1V 1FP, UK

Unwin Hyman Inc.,
955 Massachusetts Avenue, Cambridge, Mass. 02139, USA

Allen & Unwin (Australia) Ltd,
8 Napier Street, North Sydney, NSW 2060, Australia

Allen & Unwin (New Zealand) Ltd
in association with the Port Nicholson Press Ltd,
Compusales Building, 75 Ghuznee Street, Wellington 1, New Zealand

First published in 1991

British Library Cataloguing in Publication Data

Murphy, David
The Stalker affair and the press.
1.   Northern Ireland.   Police
I.   Title
363.2

ISBN 0–04–445411–2 HB
0–04–445412–0 PB

Library of Congress Cataloging-in-Publication Data

Available on request from the Library of Congress

Typeset in 10 on 12 point Sabon and printed in
Great Britain by Billing and Sons Ltd, London and Worcester

Contents

CHAPTER ONE

Introduction: News sources and ideology

The Stalker affair: a summary

In November and December 1982 six Roman Catholics were shot dead in the Lurgan area of Armagh by specialist squads of heavily armed Royal Ulster Constabulary (RUC) officers. The killings took place in three incidents: all had the appearance of ambushes. Five of the six victims were Irish Republican Army (IRA) or Irish National Liberation Army (INLA) suspects. One was a seventeen-year-old, Michael Tighe, who had no known paramilitary connection. In each case the victims were sprayed with fire from automatic weapons. A number of RUC men were tried and were acquitted. During their trial they revealed that they had been instructed by senior officers to cover up facts and to lie on oath in court. As a result of pressure from a number of sources, including the Director of Public Prosecutions (DPP) in Northern Ireland, Sir Barry Shaw, an inquiry was set up in late 1984. The Deputy Chief Constable of Manchester, John Stalker, himself a Roman Catholic, who had successfully investigated IRA bomb outrages in and around Manchester in the early 1970s, was appointed to investigate the RUC shootings. He and his team of detectives went to Ulster to see if there was evidence of a shoot-to-kill policy by the police in the province and to recommend action against police officers if disciplinary or criminal offences had been committed.

In May 1986 Stalker himself was removed from all duties and formally suspended a month later. Allegations of misconduct had been laid against him and these were to be investigated by the Chief Constable of West Yorkshire, Colin Sampson, who also took over Stalker's role in Northern Ireland. Three months later the Greater Manchester Police Authority (GMPA) reinstated Stalker after receiving a report from Sampson which recommended that a disciplinary tribunal be held to examine ten charges against the Manchester police chief. Of these charges, nine involved giving friends lifts in police cars and one claimed that Stalker associated with known criminals. The authority rejected the Sampson report. In March 1987 Stalker retired to write his memoirs.

In early 1988 the British government acknowledged that the Stalker/Sampson inquiry in Northern Ireland had produced prima-facie evidence of a conspiracy to pervert the course of justice by RUC men, but announced that no criminal proceedings would take place. They then appointed yet another senior British mainland police officer, Charles Kelly, the Chief Constable of Staffordshire to investigate the RUC. Eventually, the only punishments handed out to any officers were reprimands.

By March 1988, when Stalker's book was published, it had become established in the British and Irish press that Stalker was an innocent, if at worst naive man who had discovered more than he should have done for his own good. The agreed question was who had caused his career to be ruined – the Cabinet, RUC or MI5. A conspiracy theory was established in which the security services were the plotters and Stalker was the victim. This theory was current even among the right-wing, pro-government press.

A version of reality had been promulgated through the established media which conflicts utterly with the conventional academic picture of a right-wing-dominated press producing an ideological justification for the status quo and the forces of control. My aim is to show how the press came to produce this version of reality through the normal processes of news production and to examine what light this throws on notions of ideological production and ideological hegemony which have become widely accepted in mass media studies. In the process of this analysis it will be necessary to refer to the occurrences of the Stalker affair, but my focus will be on the press construction of the events and not on the events themselves. There is no attempt here to provide a definitive historical record of the killings or the police inquiries which followed. Where it is necessary to tell the story of events, however, I have made every attempt to weigh the evidence and to point out doubts and inconsistencies where they arise. As a result, most of the story is open to question. On the other hand, we do have concrete evidence of what the press did in making sense of events, and it is on this that we will concentrate.

News production and ideology

The academic analysis of the mass media's role in politics has been characterized by a tension between two lines of approach which are potentially contradictory. Both lines are often combined in the same work and, in general, the potential contradiction and the actual tension go unacknowledged. The first line expresses itself in theoretical concerns with the political system as a whole and addresses such questions as why and how the mass media are pro-business, right-wing, generally anti-trade union, and how various practices of hidden and open censorship take place. In its clearest form this approach is expressed as the Marxist analysis of cultural hegemony, in which the news media in particular are characterized as an 'Ideological State Apparatus'[1] which contributes towards the social and political dominance of the capital owning class.

The second approach is to ask the question, how do the practitioners in the mass media go about the manufacture of cultural products and particularly news. News is seen as a product of a manufacturing process which like any other is the outcome of the work processes and routines of professionals, the power relationships of the workplace, and the nature of the organization of production.[2] The two approaches often inform the same work, with the implicit assumption that there is a synergy between the macro-determination of the political system for an ideology favourable to capital and the work practices of professionals who produce what is required of them by the system.

My aim here is to examine whether this synergy actually applies and, if so, whether a system of ideological compliance is produced by the work practices of journalists. The two possible alternative views are that the work practices do not match the notion of a system-driven dominant ideology, or that they do, but in a more complex way than that allowed for in mass media analysis. The means I have adopted for addressing this question is a detailed examination of the way in which the press dealt with the 'Stalker affair'. This case is particularly suitable as a source of insight into the notion of the ideological nature of news production because at no time was a conventional view of reality taken for granted. What is often accepted without question became contested, and journalists had to make sense of events that were either unexplained or for which there were competing explanations, none of which had the sanction of 'official' authority.

In this chapter I shall examine the means by which journalists normally make sense of the social and political world in the process of manufacturing news. In subsequent chapters I shall clarify this analysis by examining how over a period of four years the mass media gradually arrived at a generally accepted version of the 'truth' of the Stalker affair. In the final chapter I shall attempt to assess what significance this analysis has for a general understanding of ideological production and its relationships to the work practices of journalists.

The organization of journalistic work

In analysing journalistic work practices academics often use the products of this work, news output, to infer how journalists go about the production of news. This approach is exemplified by the Glasgow Media Group who employ a sociolinguistic methodology in a scrutiny of television news coverage of industrial relations affairs. In *More Bad News* they express their methodology in analysing the relationship between journalistic work practices and the production of ideology:

> Our concern is to look at . . . publicly broadcast news talk –
> in the attempt to show that it routinely displays features in its
> performance which can only be explained by reference to its
> trading on a given ideology. To do this we will have to utilise
> empirical generalisations generated by other kinds of linguistic
> work and in the process we hope to show that sociolinguistics

can begin to open up the study of language usage to the analysis of ideology. Ideology in our view is not some set of alien ideas imposed, propaganda-like, upon willing and unwilling hearers. Rather, it is a representation of sets of events or facts which consistently favour the perceptual framework of one group. News talk occurs within a cultural framework which stresses its balance and impartiality. Yet despite this, detailed analysis reveals that it consistently maintains and supports a cultural framework within which viewpoints favourable to the status quo are given preferred and privileged readings.[3]

The authors propose that news is a product of work practices and further that these practices involved in writing help to create and sustain a dominant ideology. The tension between the micro-level of analysis – the work processes of journalists and the macro-level – generation of an ideology is apparent, however, in their methodology. They begin with an approach which relies on an intense analysis of the news produced leading to an indication of broadcasters' ideology: 'As a working hypothesis we have assumed that close analysis of the language of the news bulletins should provide evidence of the ideological preferences of broadcasters.'[4]

This proposition that the text is capable of providing an understanding of its own meanings and origins beyond the immediately apparent is given force by the Media Group's treatment of viewer response data which show that most people find the news impartial and that those who regard it as left-biased and those who find it right-biased are more or less evenly balanced.

However, given Smith's *sine qua non* of news (credibility in the mind of the actual audience), it would be surprising to find results different from these and they are, of course, without prejudice to the examples of skewedness that can be demonstrated by close analysis of the broadcasts themselves.[5]

It is clear that if most people who view the news find it unbiased this does not disturb the Glasgow Media Group's view that it is biased or favourable to one particular ideology. Similarly, if most people were to find that television news was

biased, this would only lend support to their view. Their attitude
to the mental states of the producers is consistent with this rather
dismissive conception of the viewer:

> This representation of events is not governed by a conscious
> attempt to present ideology. The journalists and producers
> and those they allow to broadcast of course believe that
> their routines and codes merely serve to fashion the news
> into intelligible and meaningful bulletins ... However, the
> reproduction of ideology need not be, and indeed rarely is,
> intentional. The cultural framework of our society is com-
> plex and subtle. It is this framework which, together with
> professionalisation, underpins the manufacture of news. Lack
> of awareness of this framework is no bar to its application.[6]

The journalists depicted by the Glasgow Media Group are
thus seen as producing meanings of which they are not aware.
Perhaps the cultural framework of our society is too complex
and subtle for them to grasp, or perhaps they are just too
drunk to know what they are doing. There is a profound
difficulty with this mode of analysis because it relegates the
consciousness of both the producer of news and the audience
to mere epiphenomena. If their consciousness is in accordance with the analysis all well and good; if not, it is not
surprising and does not matter. Now it is perfectly valid for
the social scientist to show that some widely held belief is
not in accordance with evidence, or that professionals hold to
myths that are not in accordance with evidence. The difficulty
here is that the sociologists are not comparing commonly held
views with evidence or testing them by rigorous application of
logical analysis. They are discussing the non-apparent meanings news conveys. These 'real' meanings of news seem to be
by implication independent of the intentions or perceptions
of those engaged in the production and consumption of the
news. How we demonstrate that these meanings do underlie the news is not clear. The problem is that this approach
renders the definition of meaning problematic and potentially
contradictory.

The task the Glasgow Group have allotted themselves is to
show that what seem to be straightforward and factual accounts
of particulars convey other ideologically charged meanings of a

general nature. All is not what it seems to be, because it has other meanings than the obvious ones. But if these meanings are present in the language they can only be recognized in usage. The authors quote Ludwig Wittgenstein as their text that 'the meaning of a word is its use in the language'. But their methodological premisses precisely disregard usage. They are not looking for meaning in the conscious linguistic activities of the journalists or of the audience. Where then does the meaning inhere? The answer is in the text, in the 'examples of cultural skewedness that can be demonstrated by close analysis of the broadcasts themselves'.[7]

The text then becomes an object of study in itself out of the context of its production or its consumption. But the notion of meaning as the Glasgow Group set out their own previously sociological objectives must involve context and the activities of members of society. How otherwise do we know the meaning of terms they use, such as 'status quo'. Literally, it should include everything as it is, including, for instance, the National Executive of the National Union of Mineworkers. Or do the authors mean that some parts of the status quo are significant and others not? Does the phrase perhaps refer to the power of the state; the social background and privilege of the judiciary; the economic power of multinational corporations; the social selectivity of the military officer class; the marginality of trade unions?

We could, of course, resolve the question in the way that the Glasgow Group recommends – by an examination of their text. We could look for the 'codes and rules' involved in their writings and regard their 'conscious practices and procedures' as only partly relevant. However, to do this would involve a major logical difficulty. It would lead to a potential infinite regression of perpetual reinterpretation and reinvention of what people say and mean according to rules devised by those interpreting texts without any necessary demonstration that such rules or similar rules apply to those who create the texts or read them. Supposing we take the notion of support for the status quo as an element in the ideology which informs news production. If such a concept is meaningful there should be circumstances where news produced would be defined as in accordance with support for the status quo and others where it is not. Could a general perception that a man is hounded out of a high-ranking job in the police force by a security services' plot and covered up by a Conservative government be considered as supporting the status quo?

In the Stalker affair, for instance, how would the preference for the 'status quo' manifest itself? Over the period of nearly two years in which the story developed, a perception emerged in accounts appearing in the press that John Stalker had been 'nobbled' by government agencies. In *The Independent* of Saturday, 6 February 1988, a leader entitled 'Terrorism in the liberal state' argued baldly:

> It was wrong in 1984 to set his investigation in train and wrong in 1986 to remove him. As Mr Stalker says, 'The way in which my removal was handled has left the firm conviction in many people's minds that I was getting too close to the truth about the activities of policemen acting under cover and without control in Northern Ireland.'[8]

This was typical of the depiction of events in the press. After the initial flurry of interest in the affair before Stalker began to tell his own story, and apart from an aberrant foray by the *News of the World* (see pages 120–3), no British newspaper ever seriously entertained the idea that Stalker was investigated and eventually resigned because of any wrongdoing on his part. And the only logical alternative was that canvassed in *The Independent* leader – that he was got rid of. As I shall show in detail the press entertained as stories various conspiracies to explain who got rid of him. Plots by masons, the RUC, military intelligence, the government and the Greater Manchester Police were all floated in newspapers which either themselves made the allegations or gave prominence to others, such as MPs, making such similar claims. For reasons we shall examine, opposing views were either not given or were marginalized.

The argument I wish to propose here is that the coverage of the Stalker affair in the press cannot be understood in terms of an underlying dominant ideology with associated 'codes or rules', whether conscious or unconscious. The press, in fact, largely arrived at a consensus which challenged the legitimacy of the state in its handling of the affair. At around the same time some newspapers taking this line on the Stalker case were glorifying the achievements of the security forces in Gibraltar and vilifying Peter Wright over the '*Spycatcher*' affair. The reason for this is not that the news media are not 'really' pro-capital or anti-labour. It is that the sort of model which imposes the consistency of an underlying hidden code which when 'cracked' reveals the hidden messages in the text is not in accordance with the way in which news is produced. In order to pursue this argument it is necessary to examine how news reporters and editors make news.

News and non-news

When sociologists write about news they frequently attempt to define it by some essential quality in its nature: its content, its style, or its structure. This often leads to the embarrassingly meaningless, as is exemplified by the American sociologist Gaye Tuchman in an an article on the production of news: 'quickening urgency is the "essence of news" '.[9] Frequently such attempts are just plain wrong. 'News work thrives upon processing unexpected events, events that burst to the surface in some disruptive exceptional (and hence newsworthy) manner.'[10] A lot of news is routine, such as House of Commons debates; American presidential elections, court cases concerning petty offences; a member of the royal family has a baby. For most of the content of any newspaper or broadcast news programme, none of the events bursts to the surface or is urgent – let alone quickeningly urgent.

What is wrong with academic definitions of news is that they seek to identify some quality in the events described or in the text as the essence of the phenomena reported. This is a profoundly non-empirical way of proceeding, first, since it ignores the primary, observable characteristic of news, that it is produced by journalists and disseminated through the press and the broadcast media, and, second, it assumes without remit that this process is the result of some quality in the nature of the events described. If we take a newspaper such as, say, the *Manchester Evening News*, we find that while on one occasion the lead story is an airport disaster which involved the deaths of fifty-four people, on most days it is a proposal to build a new factory complex creating thousands of new jobs, a visit by a member of the royal family or a routine council decision. The first story does concern an event bursting to the surface but the others more typically are routine, predictable, planned. We do not need to look to a definition for an underlying essence in the nature of events. We have a simple empirical definition of news to hand. News is what is produced by journalists, published by the news media and accepted by audiences as news. A definition simply enables us to identify a phenomenon: to understand what news is we need to examine the processes by which news production is undertaken and organized.

To begin this process, it is necessary to understand that the amount of news produced is directly related to the amount of newspaper space and air time available. There is never a day when news pages are left empty or news programmes abandoned for lack of content. On some days, such as bank holidays, there may be no papers and only limited news broadcasts. One must allow that very occasionally incidents such as the Heysel or Bradford Football Stadium disasters lead to the rescheduling of broadcast news. The very rareness of such occasions shows, however, how controlled and routinized most news production is. And even in these cases it is debatable whether the disruption of normal programming is the result of the events themselves or a reflection of the fact that they were highly visual events at which cameras were present. That is to say, the initiative may still be as much with the productive capacity of the news organization as in the nature of the events reported as news.

What is certain is that in broadcasting and the press, daily and weekly, news executives and journalists face the regular necessity of filling time or space with accounts of events. There is no option to say 'nothing much happened today'. The fact that they fill up the space available to them is the result of organized work. This organization of journalistic work centres around the demands of news in a market context: first, it must be significant at the level of the community to which the news is addressed; second, it needs to be accepted socially as sufficiently accurate for all practical purposes.

The reason for the first necessity is that news relates to a social collectivity. The audience is regarded as unified, usually in terms of a community based on its locality or as representatives of a national political identity. The community is thus seen as identical with the market for newspapers in the locality and the market for goods to which the newspaper provides access for advertisers. And news about the community in question gives meaning to that community as a political, cultural, economic and social reality. The newspaper journalist sees the audience as having certain interests as readers of his or her paper as that paper relates to a particular community. When, for instance, I worked in the 1960s as a reporter on a local weekly newspaper (now defunct) in Stretford, a suburban town (now amalgamated into a larger borough) adjacent to Manchester, a plane crashed in Stockport, a town also adjacent to Manchester and about 6 miles from our office. It was also, incidentally, the home town from which the editor (now dead) daily commuted. All that was required of us as reporters, however, was to obtain a list of casualties to see if any of them were from Stretford or Urmston (which the paper also served). The same people reading the Manchester evening papers or their national dailies would be interested in the Stockport catastrophe. But they would read the *Stretford Journal* for news about Stretford, not far-off Stockport.

News stories give significance to the communal identity of an audience. They are about a society acting as a collectivity, from the level of the local council or court of petty sessions to the activities of Parliament or the high court. Or they are 'human interest' stories which in some way transcend the individual anecdotal cases they describe and typify some general human condition, such as the power of family love, or the brutality of modern society.

The second demand, that they are accepted as true for all practical purposes, is partly because newspaper personnel work according to professional norms: reporters actually want their stories to be true. Moreover, when stories are shown to be without foundation newspapers may suffer a whole range of sanctions. These will vary from the removal of co-operation by people acting as news sources, through complaints to the Press Council to full-blown libel actions. This does not mean that news always has to be true in any absolute sense. It means in general that journalists have to be able to show that they took reasonable steps to establish its accuracy. This will vary from case to case. When reporting a court case the reporter simply has to quote accurately and attribute correctly what was said, because court cases are legally privileged. When referring to generalities the need for precision is only minimal. As we shall see below, when the issue of masonic influence was raised to explain John Stalker's suspension, newspapers were able to make fun at the Freemasons' expense by general references to influence and to run small features on secret handshakes and oaths. When individuals are named in the context of wrongdoing, however, different standards of justification apply. When the *Manchester Evening News* ran a centre page spread on masonic influence in the police in the context of the Stalker suspension and named a number of senior police officers and officials as members of the secret society, they became embroiled in legal exchanges with a number of named individuals, and eventually agreed to an out-of-court settlement with the individuals concerned including a retraction nearly three years later in May 1989.

Normal news coverage uses the choice of news sources to resolve the needs to establish the significance of news at the level of community and to establish the validity of stories. Routine news sources are officials whose roles enable them to speak on behalf of the organizations and institutions who employ them. This gives them 'spokesman' status. This resolves both problems at once. The spokesman gives voice to the institutional form of the community which means that the stories purveyed are relevant to that community. And at the same time when the spokesman is speaking within the competence of his institutionally determined role an accurate account of this by the journalist is normally accepted as true for all practical purposes.

A basic example would be the police force public relations officer who provides information about, say, crime prevention policies or the promotion of senior officers. A journalist simply reproducing such information in the form of news will know that it is acceptable both from the point of view of relevance and accuracy.

Other regular sources of normal news are people whose social positions give them access to information about institutions defined as communal but who are not spokesmen. A policeman or a soldier or a Ministry of Defence (MoD) official for instance may anonymously proffer a version of events to a journalist which, if 'true', would be considered news as defined. The journalist then has to check with a spokesman or requires some other form of evidence. Confirmation by a spokesman will be sufficient to validate the story, a denial will generally kill it. If, however, the original source insists that a story is true, the journalist may persevere. The necessity of 'proof' then becomes a more complex affair. Resources will then have to be dedicated to the job of validating the story and the decision to make these resources available will be dependent on how newsworthy the editor considers the story will be if true. It also depends on whether an editor thinks that there is sufficient basis in the original tip-off to believe it might be true. The reporter may have to produce enough 'proof' then for an editor to commit more resources to the story. But this will not be the same standard of proof required for publication. If the time and manpower is then made available, the reporter will pursue the sort of proof required for publication.

The 'proof' required is either a final confirmation by the relevant spokesman, or documentation produced originally by the relevant institution. And in the absence of these sorts of evidence then newspapers require confirmation by witnesses: the sort of evidence which would stand up in a court of law if necessary.

A story from the *Daily Mirror* in August 1985 illustrates the process. A general had been questioned about an alleged shoplifting incident in a Woolworth's store. An officer in the general's corps rang up a freelance journalist to tell him that this information was being suppressed. Meetings in officers' messes at depots throughout the corps were warned that their general had been questioned by the police and officers were warned to say nothing. A rumour arose among officers that the MoD had pressured the police and Woolworth to take no further action. As in any disciplined organization, some members had themselves been subjected to sanctions (or had comrades who had been) for alleged breaches of rules; and some felt a sense of grievance that a cover-up was being mounted to save the career of the man who had previously applied the full rigours of the disciplinary system to those of lower rank.

Hence an officer contacted the freelance journalist who then approached the Manchester office of the *Daily Mirror*. All that was known was the name of the general and that the incident had happened in a Woolworth's store, probably in London. The Manchester news editor wanted first to establish whether there was any basis for proceeding with inquiries. A reporter with a senior police officer contact mentioned the case to him. The police officer, who had a long record of tip-offs to the reporter, which had all proved true, knew of the case and was able to name the general and the store. When asked how he knew, he said he had been told by a friend who now worked for the MoD. The reporter asked if this friend would ring the *Daily Mirror* and confirm the story and the police officer agreed to ask him to do so. Shortly afterwards the reporter was telephoned by an anonymous caller who said he had been asked by a friend to contact the newspaper. He gave the fictitious name the police officer always used over the telephone.

He then gave more details of the case and a number of telephone numbers of depots around the country, along with the names of duty officers who could be contacted to confirm the story. The reporter wanted to know if the information had appeared on any orders-of-the-day (since this would be 'concrete' evidence that would 'stand up', or validate, the story) but the caller would not or could not say. Given that a known, reliable police source and an anonymous MoD source, derived from the police officer, both confirmed the tip-off, there seemed enough basis to proceed.

The story was then undertaken from the London news desk. Repeated inquiries to the army and police produced denials and so the London reporter, looking for further evidence, called back to the freelance to see if he could persuade the original army officer to speak directly to him. This he did, and in a telephone interview a number of points of fact were clarified, including the exact location of the store involved. Inquiries had begun on a Wednesday. The interview with the officer took place over the weekend and on the Sunday the *Daily Mirror* reporter was able to obtain an admission from the police and Woolworth that such an incident had taken place. He also traced the general to his home address where it was discovered he was abroad on holiday.

Once the police confirmation was obtained the paper then had sufficient evidence to publish. Woolworth declined to comment on the case but did not deny it. The story, 'General quizzed by police', relied for its basis simply on the bare bones of the incident – the general's name, age and his job, the fact that the police had been called and a quote from the police that the matter was 'being reported upon', meaning that they were considering whether or not there were grounds for prosecution.[11]

What is important to note from this case is, first, the process of evidential searching, and, second, the level of investment required. In the first instance the paper personnel had to establish that the tip-off from the freelance was not an insubstantial story, and their initial inquiries led them to believe in the story as a worthwhile line of inquiry. In the face of official denials they needed further confirmation to justify continuing the search. When they obtained a formal confirmation of the incident from the police they had sufficient 'proof' to publish. When this stage is reached the verification of the story is once again established by reference to the institutional framework that defines social relevance – in this case, the police force.

This search process involved considerable outlay in staff wages and expenses as well as freelance payments. For a paper with the resources of the *Daily Mirror* these costs, perhaps totalling two weeks' wages for a reporter, are not a major obstacle. For a small weekly paper, where each reporter will be required to write a number of stories per day and will constitute a quarter or more of the staff, this level of cost would be prohibitive. For papers in the middle range, the provincial evenings, such an outlay would cause a pause for thought. But no paper posits the normal labour costs of producing news at such a level of outlay per story. Even on the big national daily newspapers most stories have to be written on the basis of a fairly fast turn around and this requires that both the factual accuracy and the significance of news can be taken for granted. And for political and crime stories this is achieved by routine reference to the institutional order for sources of material. ('Human interest' news and entertainment stories do not raise the same issues.)

Where this is not achieved through informants who are spokesmen, it is often done through the direct observation of events organized through this established institutional order: court cases; council meetings; parliamentary sittings; formal ritualistic state occasions such as royal weddings. Equally, official documents may be the source of news. Home Office crime statistics, DHSS mortality rates, the unemployment figures produced by the Department of Employment are all routinely used as sources of news which are then divided and written as news items varying from the simple summary such as 'Crimes of Violence up by six per cent' to 'angles' on some general issue such as 'North–South divide in nation's health – Northerners die youngest'.

The outcome of these processes of news source organization is that the institutions routinely described in the reporting of news are themselves the sources of news. The press rely on them because their use solves three problems of news production at one stroke: the stories are verified because they come from official sources; they are seen as socially and politically significant because they are about and come from the very institutions which define society and polity; and (because significance and accuracy can be taken for granted) such news is low cost – it avoids complex evidential search.

All of this production process is posited on the functionalist view of society that a social structure can be equated with and is embodied by institutions and by the values and hierarchies of those institutions. This is not primarily because the press is owned by capitalists who subscribe to the existing order; it is because it facilitates the continuous low cost production of news. Given the market competition among newspapers and, increasingly, cost cutting in the broadcast media, this approach to news production is likely to become more and more common. The outcome is the *apparent* more-or-less universal subscription by the news coverage in the press to the values of the established order, and by the broadcast news media where journalists work within similar restrictions and are trained in the same approaches, often coming originally from newspaper offices.

In giving accounts of themselves journalists often portray themselves as observers and recorders of events. It is true that this is sometimes the case. They sometimes witness events such as strike meetings and picketing, and sometimes fires and the aftermaths of disasters or great events, such as the students' protest in Beijing. But this is not the routine business of most journalists most of the time. It is none the less one of the ways in which news is made and this does not necessarily involve any reinforcement by sources other than the journalists. Most of the time, however, reporters cannot be on the spot. Hence their routine reliance on sources.

What I have been referring to in describing how news is differentiated from non-news is not an analysis of what guarantees a story a place in a newspaper but what differentiates that which is guaranteed exclusion from that which is potentially available for inclusion. I have been examining the process of defining the necessary, and not the sufficient conditions of acceptance for publication. It could be likened to a process whereby a university lecturer is appointed from a list of applicants. Those who have doctorates and publications and teaching experience will automatically be regarded as academics but will not be guaranteed a job; those who are non-graduates, have not published and have no teaching experience will be regarded as non-academics and immediately rejected. The choice is made from the first set. When filling news pages editors are choosing between some news and other news – the exclusion of non-news has already been made in an earlier part of the production process in the use of sources and occasionally in evidential searches.

Not all organizations of news production in this country opt for such a low-cost established institutional basis for news sources. The only anti-capitalist daily, the *Morning Star*, does, but it identifies a different, although overlapping, institutional framework, with the Labour movement as the sanctified element in the constitution. But there are areas of journalistic activity which produce news in a way which questions the validity of the institutional framework. They are concentrated mainly in journalistic activity in which the production period is longer than daily and in which costs are less pressing. Typically, television programmes such as *World in Action* and *Panorama* adopt an approach where, for at least some of their items, an examination of evidence which calls into question the reliability of sources and the exposure of official secrecy becomes the purpose of the story. *World in Action*'s exposure by Andrew Jennings of alleged corruption in the Metropolitan Police is a case in point.[12] Jennings was employed by the BBC and originally made the film for *Brass Tacks*, but after representations from the police, the film, which cost £70,000 to make, was not shown. Jennings left the BBC and negotiated as a freelance with Granada who then made the film afresh and screened it on *World in Action*.[13] Here the whole point of journalistic activity was to show that the institutional structure was at fault, and that the Metropolitan Police and its spokesmen were not to be believed.[14]

Duncan Campbell's 'Secret Society' series, which was screened by the BBC, was posited on the notion that state secrecy was not justified by a need for national security but for other less elevated motives, such as the vested interests of those in authority. In the Zircon film, which was dropped after government pressure, Campbell's main purpose was to show that secrecy was used to lie to Parliament and that a spy satellite had been purchased for a price hundreds of millions of pounds more than was admitted and for a different purpose from that intended.

In print journalism this approach is limited to specific efforts by individuals and specialized teams. This is particularly the case in the 'quality' newspapers, especially *The Guardian* and *The Independent*, and the Sunday papers where reporters routinely have a week to work on stories. The *New Statesman*, especially under the editorship of Bruce Page, pursued a policy of exposure-oriented news and there are a number of alternative news magazines, including *Private Eye*, dedicated to producing news which challenges aspects of the legitimacy of the institutional order and of the official spokesmen who are the news source for the traditional press. This mode of news production questions what is routinely taken for granted – the factual reliability of official spokesmen and the institutions they represent. Informants such as the disgruntled army officers in the *Daily Mirror* story referred to above are the normal sources in such journalism. Policemen who know about corruption by their colleagues or masonic influence, local authority officials who claim that civil engineering contracts are given in return for favours typify the contacts for such an approach to news. Since such stories are almost always denied by official spokesmen they therefore routinely require a search for evidence, the aim of which is either to make the established order 'confess' – to provide the confirmatory statements – or to produce enough witnesses to substantiate a claim against official denials.

This investigative approach will not fill daily newspapers without the employment of vast numbers of reporters. Daily papers that carry such stories restrict them to occasional investigations or campaigns or to periodic efforts by specialists. The radical press carry small specialized investigative news sections while the rest of their pages are filled with such items as feature articles, arts reviews, satirical pieces, competitions and eating-out guides. Investigative news is a marginal, minority, high-cost activity which is 'subsidized' by other market-oriented or high audience appeal output.

Overall, the mass of normal news production depends on a functionalist institutional definition of society in order to define news from non-news. This leads to the routine use of official spokesmen, official documents and formally structured institutional events as the primary sources of news – a state of affairs which is the consequence of the production of news in a market context.

In the Stalker affair, this routine production of news was impossible from the outset. As we shall see, there was an information blackout by the normal institutional news sources from the time that Stalker was taken off his Northern Ireland inquiry and sent on unplanned leave from his office in Manchester. Under these circumstances, the press had to seek elsewhere for its information.

CHAPTER TWO

The structure of news

In this chapter I begin an examination of the structure of the news story and how this reflects the newspaper's depiction of the political order within which it operates. In doing this I will suggest that structure, form and content are part of a seamless whole. Content is not something which can simply be hung on to a pre-existing structure. The structure of news depends upon the substance of the narratives which are defined as news by the professionals who manufacture it.

In order to understand the nature of this process of manufacture, it is necessary to see it as the organized exercise of skills by professionals. It may be logically satisfying for academics to produce models of the nature of news and news production which, for instance, show how it is part of a system of capitalist ideological domination, but if these models do not show also how individual journalists actually go about their business as workers they have no logical status other than speculation. My aim here is to relate the nature of the news story as a narrative form to the activities, perceptions and aims of those whose trade it is consciously to create it. To do this we need to examine the sets of needs a news story or a news feature fulfils.

The first set of needs are those which relate the story to the world it purports to describe and the second are internal to it as a narrative form. The way in which these two sets of needs are met makes news what it is. The 'essential' quality of news which both practitioners and academic analysts have sought to identify has been in those events in the world which are seen as intrinsically newsworthy as a result of some inherent interest, excitement or drama. The Armenian earthquake, the Great Train Robbery or the Wall Street Crash are all seen as the paradigm for the self-evident news event which the journalist simply 'writes up' as a story. But most news stories are not like this. In the normal business of selecting the first lead of the day there are normally several contenders. The evidence for this is visible daily in the variety of stories which are selected as front-page leads in different newspapers and in the differing inclusion and exclusion of material from one news outlet to another.

The argument which underlies this book is that seeking the nature of news in the events described by news is to put the issue precisely the wrong way round. The nature of news lies in the practices and conventions its producers use to conceptualize, categorize, describe and explain the social and political world they attend to. These workers are engaged in a production process which involves a tighter schedule and a more regular output cycle than almost any other industrial activity, other than the dairy, the bakery, or a large works canteen. This production process is also highly capitalized and complex; such a commitment of resources cannot be dependent on anything so variable as whether some paradigmatic drama has occurred that day or that week. Such a state of affairs would mean that the size of newspapers and the length of news broadcasts depended on events which were unpredictable and beyond the control of those managing the use of resources. Such occasions as the shooting of an American president, when the normal schedules of broadcast news and the normal layout and contents of newspapers are extended and altered, merely underline the fact that 'normal news' is produced and consumed to timetables defined by management.

We need to begin our examination of the structure of news by looking at how it relates to the notion of an event in the world. In the view of the traditional journalist (as in traditional empirical sociology) the event described is the starting point of an understanding of the process of mass communication. George Gerbner's 'generalised graphic model of communication',[1] like many other academic attempts to analyse mass communication, such as that of Westley and MacLean,[2] centres around the notion that the process begins when an event in the world takes place and is then transmitted through various nodes in a network of communication channels. The journalist or mass communicator as one such node in the system transmits a depiction of the event along the channel to the receiver who then decodes the message. This analysis reflected a view that was embedded in American sociology of mass media of the 1940s and 1950s, in which empiricism and functionalism were fused. This involved academics subscribing to the ideology of American pluralism and accepting the journalist's version of himself in that system: namely that he (or, rarely, she) was the impassive reporter of the facts. Studies of journalists at work at this period tended to reflect the same view.[3] In their concentration on the world described by the journalist as the source of their explanation of the nature of journalistic work these studies focused on the speed or magnitude of the event related in the news as the quintessential source of its newsworthiness.[4] And journalists themselves, in justifying their role, stress the world of 'reality' as the controlling force over their work activities: 'I just report the facts' is the reporter's standby against attacks on the grounds of bias. C. P. Scott's dictum that truth is sacred and comment free again stresses this central notion that truth is non-problematic and is clearly distinguished from comment or interpretation. In this view the 'good' journalist simply records this world in the way that an automatic camera might take a picture, without comment, distortion, invention, or bias.

The notion that 'news value' is empirically embedded in the event covered by a news story and an apparently normal and more or less universal human response to events is the central defining characteristic of news as it is expounded in *Writing for Journalists* (London: Hutchinson, 1988) by James Aitchison, a senior lecturer and course co-ordinator in journalism studies at Napier College. This usful and revealing teaching book is relevant to us because it encapsulates the professional ethics of journalists in defining what they do and how this relates to the designated 'real world' they aim to describe. Dr Aitchison is a member of the Training Committee of the National Council for the Training of Journalists (NCTJ) and a member of the council's Scottish committee. The book also bears the imprimatur of the National Council for the Training of Journalists in a laudatory foreword by the Director, Keith Hall. The NCTJ is the body formed of representatives of both employers and employees which supervises the training of journalists and certificates them as competent professionals.

Dr Aitchison defines news in terms of the events of communal life and the 'natural' response, curiosity, by members of the community to such events: 'When our lives are touched by events then it is entirely normal that we should wish to know more about these events.' He also stresses the notion of accuracy as integral to the notion of news: 'When a newspaper keeps an accurate record of events then politicians, industrialists, sportsmen and criminals will receive their due recognition'.[5] In this traditionalist, establishment view of the role of the journalist, then, accuracy is subsumed to a wider social purpose. A responsibility is being exercised: 'due recognition', whether the approval of sporting prowess or the public exposure of the criminal's guilt, is being dealt out by the dispassionate newspaper of record. 'Maintaining that record is a highly responsible and demanding task.'[6] This notion of the reporter as a dispassionate recorder of events who at the same time has a commitment to a higher purpose than merely to provide factual accounts of social life is made explicit: 'news values are not always the same as normal human values . . . in a factual and impartial news story there is no place for an account of the journalist's feelings'.[7] The reason for this priest-like adherence to a factual and impartial news is a public responsibility: 'If facts are suppressed on the grounds that their publication could cause embarrassment to the subject of the story or to the reporter then this suppression will lead to a whimsical and erratic form of censorship.'[8]

There are two reasons for abjuring censorship, Aitchison argues: first, it would deny readers knowledge which might have an effect on their lives and would be of 'legitimate interest' to them and, second, 'this whimsical censorship would wrongly protect from public accountability those persons responsible for the actions and decisions'[9] that affect people's lives. Interestingly, the particular example the author gives of a possible act of suppression is a young journalist not publishing a story about a school teacher, known to her, who was convicted of a drink driving charge. During the early 1970s when I was doing fieldwork for a doctorate on the local press an editor expressed to me a similar view of the journalist's role. The appearance of the convicted person's name in the paper was part of the punishment, he argued, and because of this he

had included in his paper a story about a relative convicted
of shoplifting.

Examples in Aitchison's book of this dispassionate submission to 'the facts' in the interests of some high social and
political duty do not include the investigation and exposure
of crooked government officials or bent judges. Indeed, the
implicit contradiction in the notion that a reporter can be at
the same time dispassionate and committed to what is clearly
an establishment view of society and politics combined with a
role in the mechanisms of social control is one which is rarely
if ever addressed by the spokesmen for the newspaper industry
and professions. This is, no doubt, because the way in which
reality is defined, is embedded, in the established political and
legal system. This is exemplified in Aitchison's account of news
sources and the news gathering process which he summarizes
thus: 'The reporter on a local newspaper must be aware of
the main sources of news in his newspaper's circulation area.
The reporter should identify reliable people who have access to
those news sources and, where possible, establish a working
relationship with these people.'[10]

Built into the traditional view of news gathering which
Aitchison exemplifies is the idea of the coincidence of the
newspaper's circulation with that of the community: 'the main
news sources of a local newspaper are of course the people and
events that make up the life and identity of the community in
which the newspaper circulates'.[11] But it is to the institutional
establishment that he lookks as the embodiment of this community
and the source of information about communal events. The first
source he quotes is the council, the second the local MP and the
third the court. 'Other important sources' are the police, the fire
brigade, the ambulance service, the hospital, local industries and
business and their representative bodies, the chamber of trade
or commerce or a traders' association, trades unions and trades
councils, and the local football club. 'Secondary sources' are
schools and colleges, churches, local clubs and societies and
local branches of national pressure groups and charities.[12]
Although I would disagree about the order of precedence of
some of the sources referred to by Aitchison, it would be hard
to add significantly to his list or to take away from it as a factual
description of the routine sources of the normal, traditional local

journalist in terms of contacts with people and attendance at meetings. He also points the young journalist to documentary sources of news from the same institutional order.

This traditional view of the role of the local and national journalists bears a strong resemblance to the traditional functionalist approach to the social sciences. Central to it is the idea of a community, a social unit of indeterminate size united by some common set of interests and world view which differentiate it from the wider social world that constitutes its environment. There is then a definitional equation between the life and events of the people in that community with its institutional structure, so that the versions of events promulgated by powerful individuals within this structure become the established truth of communal life. 'The market', in the form of the circulation area of the newspaper, is also associated with 'the community' so that even if they are not definitionally identical the two are at least in a mutually supportive relationship. And the role of the journalist is formulated precisely in functionalist terms: to provide record of the community, to make people publicly accountable who should be, to participate in the system of social control, and to do this in the context of a set of relationships with 'contacts' chosen by their roles in the institutions which they themselves and the newspaper identify as the defining structure of the community.

This version of the role of the journalist as the slave of fact and truth is part of the professional ideology of the profession expressed by their professional organizations and by newspaper proprietors since the foundation of the modern commercial press. It conceptualizes news writing as reportage, where the journalist simply records the world as it is. If we examine what such a view might mean, however, we see that it cannot logically be taken at face value. Truth, fact and reality are all complex notions, are not simply equivalent to one another and are all used with a variety of meanings. 'Truth' in particular is a normatively highly charged concept. The 'truth' of a situation will involve an act of moral evaluation for the observer. In the Stalker case the simple 'fact' that seventeen-year-old Michael Tighe was shot in an Armagh barn by police officers is not at issue. Nor is the simple 'fact' that John Stalker, the Deputy Chief Constable of Greater Manchester, went on holiday to Miami with Kevin Taylor, a property developer and former second-hand car dealer. The issue for lawyers, politicians, the participants and the journalists who covered the affair was what these 'facts' meant. In the case of the shooting of Michael Tighe the questions which became public issues in providing a 'full' picture of events (which also meant a moral evaluation) were what the police officers said before they fired, what they intended and what they knew at the time, as well as who planned the operation, who gave the go-ahead for it and who knew about it. In the case of John Stalker's holiday the questions raised were who paid for it, whether Taylor was an associate of criminals, whether he was a wrongdoer himself, and whether, if any of these things were true, it would have compromised Stalker's integrity to have had such a relationship with such a businessman. In both cases the 'truth' of the situation is inseparable from an evaluation of the morality of the actions of participants.

Individuals in either situation might well argue that a simple statement of one particular 'fact' in the absence of others which gave it context might well not be the 'truth' in the sense that it might not be a 'full' picture of the real situation, that it might be distorted, over-simplified, or 'out of context' (the politicians' frequent complaint when they are faced with a verbatim quotation of their own words which they feel distorts what they meant while accurately recording what they said). Accounts of events which include more facts, by implication, suggest they are related in constituting meaning and this in turn may produce accusations of irrelevance, bias and over-complication. 'Truth' and 'reality' are value-loaded terms whose use is often ideologically determined.

The 'simple' notion of the fact is less simple than it seems. The view taken here is that the nature of social facts is not independent of the means by which they are defined, categorized and described. This is not the same as a 'fictional' view which implies that description 'creates' fact. It is simply a statement of the position that since we do not know any reality which we cannot describe, the facts we know depend on our ability to describe them. But even if one were to take the view that the world exists entirely independently of our ability to describe it, we would still be faced with the difficulty that any act of description depends precisely upon how much precisely we can comprehend of what we see, how much is going on that we do not see, how mistaken we are and how we relate one part of what we see to another.

In order to do their job, journalists need to resolve these problems every day of their working lives. Simple observation of reporters at work will indicate that, like the rest of us, they do not go about in a state of suspended belief in the substance of the world around: expenses are a more pressing concern than existential crises. Their problems in making sense of the social world are resolved through their working practices, which are routine and taken for granted. These practices have to establish two things about the news which journalists write: first, that it is factually accurate; second, that it has significance for the audience it is aimed at.

In the normal business of news reporting these matters are taken for granted by the routine way in which the news gathering process takes place. An editor has to fill his news pages daily or weekly, without exception with stories which can be defended, because they are public and concern named individuals, as accurate and relevant to the 'community' who make up the readership. With an infinite variety of different versions of events available and finite resources in terms of time and labour available it is necessary to have a means of focusing attention on those versions of events which can be processed as news. This cannot include as a normal part of the work routine of journalists extensive searches for evidence or discourses about the relevance of stories to the audience. In exceptional cases this may be possible but the economics and logistics of news production make it impossible as a routine activity.

The use of appropriate news sources resolves the problems of both factual accuracy and significance. An appropriate source is one which, if challenged on the basis of fact, can be quoted as legitimate, that is to say, the reporter or the paper can be shown to have acted reasonably in accepting the source as an accurate factual source. Similarly, a source is appropriate if it is accepted as conferring social significance on any statement it legitimates. Such sources may be documents or meetings of organizations or court cases or individual 'spokesmen'. Each source will have an area of social or political life where its statements are considered adequately factually legitimated and significant, simply as a result of the source from which they come.

The appropriateness and legitimacy of sources derive from an acceptance of the given social order and dominant culture. Courts confer absolute protection on statements made in open session if they are accurately reported, even if they are subsequently accepted to be untrue. This is because the journalist, in reporting the events of the court case, is not simply quoting the evidence of participants, he or she is also reporting the events of the court as an eyewitness for the public. The rituals of the courtroom involve society acting as a collectivity, in which the journalist at the press desk is playing a part. Similarly, simple reportage of sessions of Parliament or of local government are generally protected and are taken for granted as socially significant by their nature. Meetings of public institutions less integral to the central political order are less protected from factual challenge and more restricted in conveying general social significance. A speech at the Trades Union Congress (TUC) or the Confederation of British Industry (CBI) is not privileged if challenged on the basis that it is libellous. And, similarly, the power of such bodies to confer significance on happenings they organize relates to their perceived areas of competence, their power, or any threat they are seen as posing.

Documents as sources of news are equally able to confer factual legitimacy and significance on stories based on them, but only according to their own origins. Government White Papers, official statistics or royal commission reports (in the days when these were produced) may be used as authoritative sources of information, and their source again is a guarantee that they may be represented as societally significant. An Amnesty report on the Stalker shoot-to-kill inquiry and the allegations of misconduct will be seen as significant, but judgements about its factual reliability will depend on other factors, such as editors' or proprietors' own political judgements and the response of the state.

Individuals who are journalists' contacts vary from those who are spokesmen to those who are 'moles'. Spokesmen are those whose position means that they are able to speak authoritatively for the social entity involved in a story. At the simplest level individuals speak for themselves. A person whose house has been burnt down is quotable as the appropriate source in a story about the incident, but when organizations are involved the situation is less obvious. To take an example from the affairs of the Manchester Police, some years ago a source suggested that a heavily armed convoy of police vehicles escorted a lorry with a container from Ardwick goods depot into central Manchester on a regular basis on Thursday at around two o'clock in the afternoon. The lorry probably contained used bank notes to be destroyed at a Bank of England depot in the city centre. If this had been the case it opened up the possibility of an attack by armed bank robbers in streets crowded with shoppers, which could have been be avoided by doing the run at dawn.

If the fact of these arrangements were confirmed by the Chief Constable, James Anderton, then the story would be 'stood up' simply by his saying it was the case because he is a person whose status automatically confers a spokesman status on him. If the claim were made by a low-ranking police officer who could not be quoted, or by a British Rail employee, or a bank official, then other evidence such as documentary 'proof' or an admission by a spokesman would be required to 'stand up' the story. Another variant of such a story might be a protest at the alleged arrangement by a councillor at a meeting of the police authority monthly meeting. Then there would be no need to check the story for it to 'stand up', because the fact of the claim having been made at a police authority meeting would itself be the story – 'Police guns pose threat to shoppers – councillor'.

Moles are informants whose occupation or social niche gives them access to information considered by journalists to be relevant to the production of news, but who either do not enjoy the status necessary to be quoted or who fear that by being quoted they would rapidly acquire a status too low to make them quotable. Low-ranking police officers may well know about matters of policing policy but could not be quoted as official spokesmen. A chief constable's staff officer with the rank of superintendent would be quotable from the journalist's point of view as a source of information about the affairs of the chief constable's office but would cease to enjoy such a post if he were quoted in a newspaper without the prior approval of the chief constable. 'Moles' provide the raw material of news: evidence to stand up their stories has to come from the sort of authoritative source referred to above.

The first stage in the production of news is the activity of journalists. On the odd days when newspapers are not produced and when broadcast news only comes in short bulletins, this is not because of a lack of events in the world, it is because of a temporary suspension of the activities of journalists. When newspapers are thin this is not because there is less news than usual. It is because either the newspaper cannot obtain enough advertising that day to finance a paper of full thickness, or because it is a day when only a skeleton staff is at work, on Boxing Day for instance. Journalists work to a schedule of production deadlines at one end of the process and to a routine of 'news gathering' at the other.

The news gathering process reflects the daily organizational discipline of producing a paper which will sell and attract advertising. News gathering depends on a regular round of contacts whom reporters talk to; a diary of events which they attend and an Amazonian rain forest's output of press handouts every year. Some reporters specialize in court reporting, others in parliamentary reporting. Such mundane labours produce a regular flow of information which the journalist reproduces as news. This is a fairly uncomplicated exercise of reportage which involves breaking down the events of the court or Parliament into viable narratives, on the basis of a formula we shall examine below. The source of this basic reportage qualifies the resultant output as both factually valid and significant.

But these requirements are only the necessary condition for a narrative produced by a journalist to qualify as a news story. News also has to be sold in a market. This requires that it relates to the readership of a particular newspaper, which means that the raw material has to be of the sort which the news editor sees as forming the basis of the sort of story which has such an appeal. The newspaper itself is also owned by a proprietor whose political views and personal quirks it may well represent. Thus if a freelance reporter finds out that a Labour-controlled local authority has banned Rudyard Kipling books from its school libraries on the grounds that they are racist he or she knows that *The Sun*, or the *Daily Mail*, or one of the other popular right-wing dailies, will use this as the basis of a story which is populist in its simple appeal and its use of stereotypes and which also complies with the right-wing predilections of the owner: 'Red race spies ban *Jungle Book* from school book shelves.'

These concerns are all expressed in the structure of the newspaper story, but the story also has to address its internal structural needs, and its needs as part of a newspaper. In a straight news story the first paragraph, or the first two, have to state in summary what the story will say. This summary is 'angled' around what the journalist sees as its central point or theme. Everything which makes the story news is compressed into this introduction or 'intro'. The rest of the story then amplifies each of the points in the intro and gives the details which have been compressed out. In this approach to news writing the intro has to answer the questions, as appropriate, who, when, what, where and how, and frequently how much, and how many. A less obvious type of news story often favoured by the tabloids is the use of the 'come hither' intro which gives no details but lures the reader on to read the story in order to discover what it is about. The secret of this method is to identify some 'sexy' aspect of the narrative which is incorporated into the intro in the form of a mystery or riddle. Such a story might begin, 'Drinkers in a Durham mining village will be in for a sexy surprise when they visit their local from now on . . . ' The readers are then drip-fed the rest of the story titillating detail by titillating detail: the number of girls; their names; their bust measurements; their ages; whether they have done it before; whether they are embarrassed; how the men feel when they have to take their trousers off, and so on. The same sort of distinction is made by Aitchison in his account of how to write news. He distinguishes the 'comprehensive' intro from the 'specific'. The first 'summarises or encapsulates the essence of the story and delivers the main outcome in the opening sentence'. The second 'spotlights a particular fact or incident – the most important, the most recent, or the most unusual – and develops the story from that point'.[13]

The normal model of a political news story is one which reports the organized activities of a political institution in which both the factual requirements of news and its need for signification are met by accepting the premises of the same political order which validates and confirms its own significance. Within the structure of the compressed intro, and a series of paragraphs filling out the detail, the source and the authority for the story will be stated in order to locate the story as legitimate within the political framework it sustains and which sustains it. As the ideology of the professionals affirms, a news story is part of the process of continual construction of order and community. That order and community are embedded in the news because of the practices of news production.

A simple example will clarify the nature of the relationship between the structure of the narrative and its location in terms of its sources. A story appeared in the *Manchester Evening News* as its main front page lead on 18 August 1987, and it concerned Kevin Taylor, a Manchester property developer who was the central figure in allegations that John Stalker had associated with criminals. Taylor was subsequently cleared of all charges against him in a spectacular case in 1990 (see ch. 11).

The story's strapline declared 'Tycoon ruined by the Stalker affair' and beneath this the headline massively announced 'I've lost £2m says Taylor'. The story's significance was thus signalled in the strapline by the term 'Stalker affair' and in the headline by the use of the name Taylor, which by that date was well established in Manchester as part of the lexicon of the drama which surrounded the deputy chief constable. The headline and strapline are free of the normal constraints of syntax but operate within different and harsher disciplines. The main pulling points of the story have to be summarized within the space permitted by the type size – which actually means a limit not on the number of words but on the number of letters. And the message has to be formulated in a way which attracts readers. Hence they favour such words as 'slams' and 'shock' and 'rap', which combine drama and impact with a minimum number of letters. The newspaper headline is the ultimate in narrative simplification. A form of shorthand enables the dash to stand in for a verb of utterance, so that 'I've lost £2m says Taylor' could be replaced by 'I've lost £2m – Taylor'. Definite and indefinite articles are completely disposable. 'Tycoon ruined by the Stalker affair' can be rewritten 'Tycoon ruined by Stalker affair'. In fact both strapline and headline could be distilled to 'Ruined! Stalker affair cost me £2m -Taylor'. The use of the dash signals that the words are attributed to Kevin Taylor, and the use of the names Taylor and Stalker by that time signalled that the Taylor

THE STRUCTURE OF NEWS

was Kevin Taylor and that the Stalker was the deputy chief
constable of Manchester. The use of additional words such as
'tycoon' is only an option if there is sufficient space: it is there to
convey a notion of wealth and power. If there were more space,
more descriptive force might be added: 'Taylor' might become
qualified by the term 'property millionaire'.

The grammatical construction of the sentences in the news
report itself and its paragraph structure are designed to pack
as much information as possible into the space available. But
available space is a variable quantity. It varies in relation to
time as the process of producing the newspaper goes on. In
the case of the front page, for instance, an editor may decide
that new stories may need to be accommodated, or a new first
lead may be found. This means that other stories may have to
be cut or moved elsewhere on the page or in the paper. Because
of this it is also necessary during the process of constructing the
page and the newspaper that the story can easily be cut without
rendering it senseless.

The means which journalists have devised for achieving this
objective is to construct the news story so that paragraphs can
be cut out or moved. This means that last-minute changes can
be made literally in a matter of seconds, without any need for
the sub-editor to think about the effect his cuts will have on the
meaning of the report. It also obviates the need to change or
remove phrases or words in sentences. Paragraphs are the building units from which news stories are constructed. The process
is at its simplest when each paragraph follows its precursor in
descending order of importance to the story. This means that the
story can simply be cut 'from the bottom up'. When we examine
the 'tycoon ruined saga' below we will see how we can alter the
story by reconstructing it, using existing paragraphs.

The compressed nature of style imposed by the requirements
of news writing is achieved by heavy use of adjectives and
adjectival or adverbial phrases in a generally simple sentence
structure. We can see how these structural and lexical characteristics manifest themselves by a closer examination of our story
about Mr Taylor's ruin. The intro to our story reads: 'Property
tycoon Kevin Taylor – a key figure in the John Stalker saga –
today walked from a rates hearing and said that the Stalker
affair had cost him £2m and ruined him.'

We now know that Kevin Taylor is a tycoon, his business is property and he is a key figure in the Stalker affair. We know that the source of the story is the happenings in and around a rates case hearing, that he is ruined and an amount of £2 million is involved in his ruination. The second paragraph continues: 'He pleaded poverty at the hearing in Bury, when he failed in an attempt to get the council to defer action over the non-payment of the £3,135.'

This takes the story further in terms of the narrative: how much he owed in unpaid rates; his failure in court; and the involvement of the council. It also locates the story in relation to the authority structure: the process of signification for this particular story as a development of the Stalker affair is established by the fact that it is a court report which also automatically validates the factual parts that are a direct court report. The parts that relate to Taylor's claims made after the case to the reporter are hung on to the court case. This gives them topicality on that particular day, while the general context of the Stalker affair provides the major angle of the story. Taylor was already established as a major actor in this drama (and we shall examine below how this was accomplished in the press), which meant that attributable quotes from him as a spokesman on his own behalf would be adequately substantiated factually, provided they did not libel some other identifiable individual.

After identifying Taylor's address on which the rates were due in the next paragraph, two paragraphs follow which are prime examples of the sentence structure of reportage:

The £400,000 converted mill, complete with indoor swimming pool, stands in five acres of ground and has an attached staff cottage.

Today 55-year-old Mr. Taylor, who has been under CID investigation without charge, sought to have a council distress warrant over his non-payment of rates deferred.

In these two short paragraphs Taylor's life-style, the scale of his wealth, the sumptuousness of his home, the servants in their quarters are all implied and his age, his plea in court and his role as target of police inquiries are stated.

THE STRUCTURE OF NEWS

Other paragraphs follow which further establish the basis of the story's factual validity and its relationship to the institutional structure:

At today's hearing before magistrates, Mr. Taylor said he had applied under section 53 of the General Rate Act for relief.

After a 20-minute retirement, the two magistrates on the bench refused Mr. Taylor's request for an adjournment and granted the council a distress warrant.

The remaining five paragraphs of the story involve a brief summary of remarks made outside the court by Taylor, a rehash of earlier troubles with rates debts and a brief summary of the Stalker affair, any or all of which could be subbed out without making the story meaningless. So could a number of earlier ones, as long as the key paragraphs with the compressed core of narrative about the substance of the court case and Taylor's claimed ruinous loss of £2 million remain.

In the ninth paragraph of the seventeen-paragraph story a different potential angle lies dormant: 'The Director of Public Prosecutions is now reviewing the police reports on the probe into the troubled tycoon's affairs and Mr. Taylor said, "I have had three years of phone tapping, mail interception and I still don't know what the outcome is with the DPP." ' The story continues: 'Mr. Taylor, a Manchester-based property developer, has always denied any wrongdoings and insisted he didn't know what the police inquiry was about.'

Because of the way in which the story is structured in paragraph units we could rewrite it with these two paragraphs as the basis of the intro and leave the rest of the story unchanged, apart from altering the order in which some of the paragraphs occur. We could provide a strapline and headline using the tags 'Stalker' and 'Taylor' to signal the nature of the story in the same way as the original, thus:

Strapline: 'Stalker probe tycoon "kept in the dark".'
Headline: 'Police bugged me for three years – Taylor.'

We might then structure the story around the ninth paragraph. Our intro might read: 'Property tycoon Kevin Taylor – a key figure in the John Stalker saga – today walked from a rates hearing and claimed that police had tapped his phone and read his mail for three years without ever telling him why or charging him.'

We can then use the existing tenth paragraph as the follow-up to the intro without altering it: 'Mr. Taylor has always denied any wrongdoings and insisted he didn't know what the police inquiry was about.'

We could then proceed with the paragraphs of the original story in the same order, referring to Bury magistrate's court to locate our story around an 'event' in the established institutional order, and summarise the biography and life-style of Taylor without this involving any alteration to the paragraphs themselves – only to the order in which they occur. As a result the ninth paragraph, instead of being the one referring to the phone tapping would now refer to Taylor's being ruined.

I am not arguing that the phone tapping story is the 'real' story, simply that it is an alternative, and that because of the way in which the original story is built up of discrete paragraph units, the central point of the story can change with only minimal changes to the wording of the introductory paragraphs and some alteration to the order in which the succeeding paragraphs occur. One of the reasons for not using the phone tapping angle as an intro was that Taylor's travails with the police, his civil rights being abused, his innocence and his having been kept in the dark had already been well aired. His financial ruin was a different angle on the story, and newness is one of the preferred characteristics of news, although, as any perusal of the coverage of the royal family or Sylvester Stallone's sex life will reveal, it is not an essential requirement. In any case the Taylor finances were obviously related to a court case involving non-payment of rates.

The paragraph structure enables us to change the meaning of the story by some minor alterations of wording and changes in the order. It is a simpler matter still to cut the story by dropping some paragraphs in order to shorten the story without destroying the narrative sense. The following extract is made up of the eighth, ninth, tenth and eleventh paragraphs of the story:

THE STRUCTURE OF NEWS

Mr. Taylor said he was seeking rates relief because he had no income at all and, asked after the hearing how much money he had lost, he said: 'Two million pounds has gone.'

The Director of Public Prosecutions is now reviewing police reports on the probe into the troubled tycoon's affairs and Mr. Taylor said, 'I have had three years of phone tapping, mail interception and I still don't know what the outcome is with the DPP.'

Mr. Taylor, a Manchester-based property developer has always denied any wrongdoings and insisted he didn't know what the police inquiry was about.

At today's rates hearing before magistrates, Mr. Taylor said he had applied under section 53 of the General Rate Act for relief.

If we were simply to remove the phone tapping paragraph and the one protesting his innocence the story would run from paragraph eight to paragraph eleven thus:

Mr. Taylor said he was seeking rates relief because he had no income at all and, asked after the hearing how much money he had lost, he said: 'Two million pounds has gone.'

At today's rates hearing before magistrates, Mr. Taylor said he had applied under section 53 of the General Rate Act for relief.

The story still makes narrative sense. This raises the question of what constitutes narrative sense in the context of a news story. There seem to be two basic requirements: that one part of the story is not contradicted or diminished by another; and that one paragraph follows another either as a logical development of its precursor or as part of a series of consequences from the introduction. In this story, as we have now edited it by removing paragraphs nine and ten, paragraph eleven, which now becomes paragraph nine, expands on eight and amplifies the intro. But similarly if nine and ten were put back in they also make narrative sense by explaining the rates story and the claim about the lost £2 million in terms of their context in the Stalker affair which was raised in the intro.

The angle of a news story serves two main purposes: first, it dramatizes the events it depicts to maximize the story's impact or 'reader appeal'; second, it focuses the story around one major issue to avoid confusion in a storytelling enterprise geared to a short concentration span and limited space.

Because of this, not only can we not have paragraphs which contradict the intro, we also have to avoid paragraphs which cast doubt on an original claim – which might 'kill' the intro. An experienced reporter will produce news without necessarily consciously considering these factors, any more than a plumber necessarily thinks consciously that it is necessary to measure his pipe runs accurately to within an eighth of an inch minus an appropriate allowance for the fittings at the ends. Such considerations are the accepted preconditions for the successful accomplishment of work. The consequence of these characteristics of the structure of the news story is that it constitutes a process of narrative simplification: the stories are short, dramatic, free of internal contradiction, doubt, or qualification.

Summary

News is structured around requirements that stem from its need to be accepted as accurate and significant at a societal level defined as the 'community', which tends to be equated with a paper's circulation area or readership. These preconditions for the successful construction of social reality govern the production of any particular story by defining the parameters within which the process of production takes place.

These external factors determine the nature of what is referred to by journalists as the 'news gathering' process. The use of the term gathering implies that news is simply picked up already in its news form, which is as self-evident an entity as a wild blackberry, and simply passed on by the journalist to the reader, suggesting that the work involved is more like packaging and retailing rather than production. Nevertheless, as we have seen, news is a product, and the versions of reality gathered by journalists are the raw material for the process of news manufacture. What determines which sources are used in this 'news gathering' activity are the needs for a socially acceptable standard of factual accuracy and significance at the level of the community. These necessities emerge from the way in which news production is conceptualized and practised by those in the newspaper industry. Thus, although the parameters referred to above are external to any particular story, they are not imposed on the news producer from some external 'real world'; rather they are part of the conceptual framework of the journalist and follow from the decision to produce news in a given way and in a given context.

These demands are satisfied by the use of sources of information from established institutions of authority, in particular from attendance at the organized events of such institutions – sittings of Parliament, ministerial briefings, council meetings, court cases, etc. – from the use of official documents and from official spokesmen. In order to produce news which is clearly grounded in such a basis of authority, a style of narrative – reportage – is devised in which references to such institutions become part of the internal requirements of the narrative. In this sort of narrative the journalist takes the role of an apparently passive recorder of facts, manifested in the constant references to sources for all factual claims. This is not the only way of relating a news story to the world it claims to describe, as we shall see in the next chapter, but it is the 'normal' routine mode of reportage of political and legal affairs.

Similarly, its mode of narration is the pattern for normal news storytelling, which is a process of constant expansion, from the ultimate compression of the headline to the intro, which puts the angle on the story, to the body of the story. This is made of paragraphs which can be moved or edited out as units, leaving the story making narrative sense within the requirements of news production.

Journalists often refer to themselves as mere slaves of 'the facts'. This diminishes the nature of their work. They have to work within the discipline of the 'facts' as defined by their sources. But what they do with these versions of reality depends upon their skills and the way in which they deal with such things as the perceived tastes and demands of readers, the anticipated response to published material of contacts and the subjects of the news themselves, the response of proprietors and how they think competitor colleagues will deal with the same material.[14]

CHAPTER THREE

Reporting and investigating

The news coverage of the Stalker affair was the outcome of processes far more complex than those involved in the production of routine news. The first stories to emerge revealed that the story posed an unusual problem for journalists. Whereas reliance on official sources of the sort referred to in the last chapter normally produces an account of events which is ordered in terms of its depictions of existing states of affairs and the explanations offered, in this case all that was on offer seemed to be a mystery. Subsequent events and news coverage, as we shall see, revealed that what was happening was not entirely a surprise to the editor of the *Manchester Evening News*, Michael Unger (pages 212–13).

On 31 May 1986, along with reporters in other papers, Tom Sharratt and Paul Johnson in *The Guardian* reported under the headline 'Police chief investigated for disciplinary offence' that John Stalker, the Deputy Chief Constable of Greater Manchester, was being questioned by police officers about serious disciplinary offences, that he was on temporary leave and that the investigation was being supervised by the Police Complaints Authority.[1] But this was the limit of the information available from institutional sources. Johnson and Sharratt reported that both the Police Complaints Authority (PCA) and the Greater Manchester Police Authority (GMPA) 'refused to comment on the nature of the allegations'. They quoted a spokesman for the PCA as saying that the 'complaint was referred from the Greater Manchester Police', and produced a statement from Roger Rees, the clerk to the Greater Manchester Police (GMP) that 'information had been received about Mr. Stalker's conduct which disclosed the possibility of a disciplinary offence'. The only 'factual' statement available from official sources apart

from this was that the inquiry was to be conducted by the
Chief Constable of West Yorkshire, Colin Sampson.

There would normally be four sources of information about
the police in Manchester that would satisfy the normal official
or spokesman criteria laid out in the last chapter. These would
be the meetings of the GMPA and its documents; the chairman
of the GMPA (then Councillor Norman Briggs); the clerk to the
authority, Roger Rees and, more than any other single figure, the
Chief Constable, James Anderton, or his press officer acting for
him. In the absence of Anderton his place as official spokesman
was taken by Stalker.

Indeed, not long before his own removal from duty, Stalker
had been prominently involved in a public defence of the GMP.
This was in relation to the 'Battle of Brittan' incident in March
1985 when Manchester police officers had been accused of
brutality on the steps of the students' union in putting down
a student demonstration against Leon Brittan, the then Home
Secretary, who had been invited to the university by the student
Conservative association. Some students claimed that in addition
to the attacks on students which were seen on newsreel film they
had been threatened, harassed and beaten up by GMP officers as
a reprisal for making official complaints against the police. These
complaints were being investigated by the Avon and Somerset
force under the aegis of the PCA. As Deputy Chief Constable,
John Stalker was responsible for the internal discipline of the
GMP. When one of the students, Stephen Shaw, complained that
he had been abused by officers in Bootle Street Police Station in
central Manchester, it was John Stalker who referred the matter
to the Avon and Somerset team.

When the BBC television programme *Out of Court* on 20
November 1985 examined the policing of the 'Battle of Brittan'
and the events that followed, John Stalker wrote to the programme and rejected any police culpability, citing an earlier
attack on Home Office immigration minister David Waddington
in support of the view that 'a core of violent students' existed
on the campus of the university. On the same day Stalker was
reported in the same vein in the *Manchester Evening News*
by their crime reporter Paul Horrocks. Under a single-column
picture of a smiling Stalker, the headline declared 'Demo police
"not guilty"' and the story followed on:

Allegations that police committed criminal offences following the 'Battle of Brittan' demo at Manchester University have been denied.

Greater Manchester Deputy Chief Constable John Stalker refuted many of the conclusions in a council-sponsored report into police tactics during clashes with students and into later incidents.

Mr. Stalker said: 'I totally reject and resent the suggestion that police officers of this force have committed criminal acts of burglary and theft.'

An independent inquiry set up by Manchester City Council into the visit of the then Home Secretary, Leon Brittan, last March at the students' union building accused the police of trying to intimidate and silence witnesses.

It is said that police tried to harass and frighten witnesses.

It is understood that if it is found that panel witnesses gave false evidence leading to unnecessary inquiries legal action might be taken for wasting police time.[2]

The formula 'it is understood' is used to convey information from a normally reliable 'spokesman' status source who does not wish to be identified. In this case, as in many others, Paul Horrocks's prescience turned out to be well-founded. In the event, at the end of the inquiry, a warrant was issued for the arrest of Stephen Shaw on exactly such grounds. He took the still comparatively rare step of fleeing abroad from the threat of oppression in the UK.

At this time, then, and until his removal from his duties at the end of May 1986, John Stalker, although not well known by comparison with his chief James Anderton, presented a public image of a loyal police chief subscribing to police values and defending the reputation of his force by rebutting an allegation of police participation in a criminal conspiracy. As such he was part of the institutional galaxy of spokesmen from whom journalists might seek thoroughly quotable and 'reliable' material. His role in Northern Ireland was not widely publicized: he was not depicted in the press or the broadcast media as a man in conflict with any other section of the police establishment.

This meant that when he was summarily and unexpectedly removed from his duties the normal, taken-for-granted assumptions behind the news gathering process were disrupted. As we saw in the last chapter, official news sources can normally be taken as guarantees of factual validity and communal significance on the basis of their official status. In this case the key figure cast in the role of potential deviant by official processes was himself a senior member of the very authority structure which validates news sources. A further problem was posed by the fact that he and other members of the police establishment were either unable or unwilling to give a public account of the reason for his removal from duties.

This meant that the routine reportage of events constructed through attendance at meetings, or court, or through reading official documents, or interviewing authority figures did not answer two central questions by which journalists might begin to make sense of the affair: why had John Stalker been removed from his duties and who had been responsible for his removal? These two questions were posed from the outset – they were the agenda for the affair set down by the journalists and no official agenda was provided as an alternative. They were posed in two ways.

To spokesmen for the various state agencies and other organizations such as the Freemasons, they took the overt form of details such as who said what or did what on given dates, or who associated with whom, but the wider underlying questions journalists asked themselves as they worked on the story were based on the idea that the state was operating with a secret agenda, and they wanted to know what this was. The question then was not only one of what disciplinary peccadillo Stalker was accused of, but what was behind the charge – what was the motive for bringing it. And the 'real' question which journalists came to ask about who made the complaint about John Stalker was who was behind it. The idea that there was some other truth behind the appearance of an official truth was established very quickly and is shown by the nature of the inquiries followed by journalists and in what they wrote. Such an approach to truth contradicts the traditional form of validating the accuracy and significance of news as outlined in the previous chapter.

But this alternative and questioning approach to authority did not characterize all news coverage of the Stalker affair either in terms of writing or collecting data, although it was the means by which the general level of revelation moved forward.

In fact the news coverage took three distinct forms depending on the particular by the nature of the relationship between the journalists and the people who were sources of news or who were depicted in it. The first and most frequent sort of coverage involved the press in the sort of passive role in the production of reportage outlined in last chapter. But whereas in that case the various agencies of the state acted as a unified source of validation, in the case of the Stalker inquiry no focus was provided by official sources. The government would say nothing; the PCA would only issue non-committal statements; there was internal disagreement on the GMP; the council was critical of the police; many MPs, including Conservative backbenchers, were critical of the government and of the actions of the Chief Constable of West Yorkshire; the Chief Constable of Manchester, James Anderton, would make no statement.

As a consequence, in that part of the news coverage which took the form of routine reportage, the agencies which initiated the discourse were often interested parties and pressure groups. Official sources such as the police authority provided a platform throughout for members who were suspicious of the motives which led to the investigation of John Stalker and in this arena as elsewhere the only response to such critical voices from official spokesmen was a bureaucratic silence. In this situation the agenda was being set by non-establishment voices and the journalist in his traditional role as a passive reporter simply processed these versions of events as news in the way we began to examine in the previous chapter.

This role of reporter, established through the coverage of Parliament and the courts, is based on the notion of the 'impartial' observer whose role is both totally non-interventionist and non-investigative. Skills in narrative reportage, in accurate note-taking, in deciding what can be left out of what is observed and in deciding on a 'good angle' are all part of the professional competence of the journalist in this context. But deciding on the validity of sources, considering whether the agenda is adequate, examining the relevance or reliability of evidence are not. Indeed, they would infringe on the notion of the reporter as dispassionate and apart from the drama he or she depicts.

In the Stalker affair this was the model which underlay the coverage of the GMPA meetings, Parliament, the courts, meetings of pressure groups or the press conferences organized by Stalker's solicitors. Among the hundreds of stories in this mode were those based on summaries of debates of the GMPA. An instance of this sort of coverage was a report in the *Manchester Evening News*,[3] headlined 'Stalker Row: Leaks Probe Is Demanded.' In this story every sentence was a direct or indirect quotation from the previous day's meeting of the authority, along with the names of people taking part in the meeting.

The story, in summary, was angled on a demand by councillors for a judicial review of the Stalker affair, including an investigation of leaks of details of a confidential report on Stalker's conduct by the West Yorkshire Chief Constable, Colin Sampson. The story referred to Stalker's presence at the meeting, to members' expressions of anger that sections of the report were leaked to the media before councillors saw their copies, and to a recommendation by the authority's clerk, Roger Rees, that future disciplinary proceedings should be sub judice with leakage of information to the press during inquiries to be made a criminal offence.

Similarly, a court case brought by Kevin Taylor was reported beneath the headline 'Anderton Accused of Conspiracy' in a page one lead in the *Manchester Evening News*.[4] Taylor's case was brought against the Chief Constable, James Anderton, Chief Superintendent Peter Topping, and Detective Inspector Tony Stephenson, who were all accused of conspiracy to pervert the course of justice. The case was an attempt to make the police justify a search warrant carried out at Taylor's home. The accusation in the headline was a reference to a statement by Taylor's barrister, Robin de Wilde, that Anderton and others had 'acted to procure and cause to lay false and improper information on oath' when the police applied for the warrant. The report also referred to claims made by Taylor that he was being financially ruined by the actions of the police. Since the whole of the time in court covered by the story was taken up by de Wilde presenting Taylor's case, no evidence on behalf of the police was included in the report.

As this case indicates, the mode of production of news based on the reportage paradigm does not necessarily involve reliance on the state or its bureaucracy or large-scale business as exclusive sources in the gathering of news. In this instance, because Taylor was the prime mover in the legal process, the presentation of his version of events put the police in the position normally occupied by the criminal defendant. This normal position derives from the fact that agencies of authority and control are organized to produce coherent versions of events as part of the process of their routine work. For instance, the prosecution of offenders must of necessity involve the organized denigration of an individual in terms of his failure to abide by the prevailing moral values enshrined in the legal system. As a consequence each prosecution becomes a vignette apologia for that legal system and those values, which in turn helps to legitimize the police and the judiciary which sustain them. As a consequence the normal situation is for those acting as part of this institutional framework to have the ideological initiative.

The argument being pursued here is that this initiative springs both from institutional power and from the work practices of journalists, and that under some circumstances, when one or other of the necessary conditions is missing, even apparently passive reporting produces a version of events that undermines rather than sustains the interests of institutions of authority and order. As we shall see, because the normal channels of official information were either confused or silent as the Stalker affair developed, voices opposed to the established view of matters were able to use the press's routine reliance on simple reportage as a way of getting their own alternative versions on to the agenda and indeed to determine the agenda itself.

Thus a story headlined 'Demand for Manchester Police Inquiry' in *The Guardian* referred to a call by Rhys Vaughan, a member of the Haldane Society of Socialist Lawyers at a public meeting organized in Manchester Town Hall by Manchester Labour Party. The whole story referred to statements made at this meeting. The intro read:

Manchester City Council was urged last night to call for an inquiry into Greater Manchester Police in the wake of the Stalker affair.

The story went on:

> Mr. Rhys Vaughan, a Manchester solicitor, and a member of the executive of the Haldane Society of socialist lawyers, said there was a need to examine alleged corruption within the force and links between organised crime, the police and the legal profession.

The report then located the meeting at the town hall and linked John Stalker's removal from duty with other problems in the city's police: the beating up of young black men, another alleged police beating and an alleged rape of a young black girl by police officers.

Graham Stringer, the leader of the ruling Labour group on the city council, was reported as saying that the media depiction of John Stalker as a saint missed the politics of what was happening, and Tony McCardell, the Chairman of the Police Monitoring Committee was quoted as declaring that Stalker had been sent to Ireland to do a whitewash and 'if we do not find out who the conspirators were, it can happen again'.[5]

Thus the whole story was made up of quotations from statements made at the meeting. The construction of events and the issues raised as constituting the raw material of news coverage were determined by the organizers of, and the participants in, the Labour Party meeting. So although the meeting had neither the absolute privilege of the court or Parliament, nor the restricted protection of local government, the form of the report and the job of the reporter are the same: to listen; to take notes; to check names and provide a summary of events structured around some angle which focuses the narrative and attracts readers.

The important characteristic of such reporting is that the content of the story and its form are derived from a debate initiated not by the journalist but by interested parties, who do not settle what is in the news story, nor how it is written, but do set down the agenda within which such decisions are made. One of the interesting aspects of the Stalker affair news coverage of this type was, as in the case of the story above and the Taylor court case already examined, that the routine form of reporting typically constituted an ideological critique of the notion of a social structure based on open, fair and benevolent authority. As in the two instances referred to agencies of the state are portrayed as secretive, corrupt, illicit in their actions and conspiratorial.

While the reporting appears to be simple and routine and to derive from the activities of those in the news rather than those making it, this, of course, is a characteristic of the form of the story and not a revelation of an underlying reality in the production of news. Editors decide to use or not to use material, to cover or not to cover meetings, or to use court cases prominently. None the less as a form of reporting and news production it is more routine and less expensive in terms of the use of manpower and time than the alternatives.

The second type of reporting in the coverage of the Stalker affair addressed itself to the mystery which was posed at the outset. This involved the journalists themselves defining the issues around which the news was structured and seeking the relevant evidence to substantiate the solution propounded in their story. Of course, the evidence which might be published in the story would almost certainly not be the same as that which led them to arrive at their own 'discovery'. The earliest stories to appear in this vein gave an account of Stalker's dismissal which was based partly on official sources and partly on an attempt to raise and resolve a question posed by the reporter.

In the *Guardian* report of Stalker's original removal, referred to above,[6] his removal from duty was reported by Tom Sharratt and Paul Johnson in a story which was a mixture of reportage based on official sources and attendance at the meeting along with speculation of their own which set up the questions which remained, throughout the next two and a half years, the nub of the mystery which was publicly addressed by participants and press alike.

As we saw earlier, the report was structured around two forms of news story. The first simply reported official statements: Stalker's removal from duties on temporary leave of absence; that he was being questioned about disciplinary offences; that Colin Sampson, the Chief Constable of West Yorkshire, was carrying out the inquiry into Stalker's conduct under the aegis of the PCA. These bare bones were combined with official statements declining further comment or explanation. The second part of the story then adopted an explanatory structure. The journalists set the 'official facts' in a context which they, as competent reporters, defined as relevant. They sought to identify in Stalker's biography the events which had led to his present plight.

They then identified Stalker's role in the shoot-to-kill inquiry in Northern Ireland as a possible explanation of his removal from duties. Their questions to officials suggested as much. Having revealed that he had been in charge of the investigation for the previous sixteen months, they reported questioning the RUC, who had nothing to say about the allegations against Stalker. They further explored the subject of Stalker's report into the shoot-to-kill allegations: there was no comment from the Director of Public Prosecutions (DPP) in Belfast 'which has been in possession of Mr. Stalker's detailed report for seven months'. They added that there was speculation in Belfast that the allegations against Stalker could further delay possible criminal proceedings over the shooting of unarmed IRA suspects.

Sharratt and Johnson also raised the Battle of Brittan inquiry. They reported that Stalker was awaiting a report from the Avon and Somerset team into allegations of police violence during Leon Brittan's student union visit, and the claims by the then medical student, now Dr Sarah Hollis, and another student, Steven Shaw, that they were 'assaulted, harassed and intimidated' by GMP officers as a result of complaints against the force. The investigators had taken 700 statements and were to report to Stalker in June, the reporters said.

Neither the résumé of the shoot-to-kill inquiry nor that of the Brittan inquiry investigation was explicitly referred to as an explanation of the mystery of why John Stalker had been removed from his duties. No words such as 'why' or 'because', or phrases such as the 'the reason for this may be' or 'this may be the result of' or even 'sources in the GMP suggest the reason for this is'. Nevertheless, in the context of the story the only logic which could be adduced for raising the topics is that they might provide an answer to the question. The story would not make sense as a story if this were not the case. My own inquiries at the time elicited the two lines of argument as reasons for Stalker's plight. The two questions being asked were what was the nature of the alleged disciplinary offences and what and who were behind the move to bring him down? Police sources in Manchester thought the second question was answered by the Northern Ireland inquiry: that their deputy chief constable might have been getting too close to the truth and embarrassing the government at a time when the support of the RUC was vital in suppressing Protestant violence against the Anglo-Irish agreement. They did not believe he had committed any disciplinary offences other than perhaps the most trivial. The favoured explanation among contacts associated with the police monitoring group and the campaign on behalf of Steven Shaw was that the disciplinary offences might be in some way associated with Stalker's role in relation to the Brittan affair. Thus, Sharratt and Johnson were making sense of the social world by offering possible explanations for questions which were left unanswered by spokesmen for the established institutions.

This activity of structuring reality by causal explanations relating different factual statements defines the second type of news reporting in the coverage of the Stalker affair. In this the journalists themselves define the issue to be addressed, the form in which the issue is dealt with and the evidence or story content to be used in the exercise. This may be the classic investigative report, which describes the process by which the reporter or several newspaper staff together examine some aspect of an affair not previously dealt with, or themselves reveal some new scandal – such as the alleged suppression of Stalker's inquiry by MI5 agents – or it may simply be a news feature reviewing past events and analysing their causes, effects and implications.

Much of this type of reporting of the Stalker inquiry and related matters had to take place in a limbo of state secrets and allegations of conspiracy. The normal means of locating news within the authority structure to validate it was not even an option, because there were no official versions of events available. Instead, journalists had to devise their own means to show that their stories were accurate and relevant. Such stories relied on the normal assumption of all political news that institutions of power are of central political importance. But these institutions were the topics of such news, not the sources. The sources had to be 'moles', nameless officials or other informants whose work or social milieu would give them access to information which would verify the claims on which stories were based.

The structure of this form of news does not underpin the authority that it describes. It is always, at least potentially, subversive. Since the story is revelatory, the journalist or the newspaper or both appear as the means of revealing the truth. The central assumption of such stories is that a mystery has arisen from some powerful individual's or group's actions. The mystery is the outcome of a deliberate use of secrecy, at best as the by-product of a benign policy, or at worst the result of malign conspiracy. The journalist's skill in this mode of reporting is to identify the question, pose an appropriate and credible answer, and produce the evidence which acceptably substantiates the answer.

In such an endeavour, naming names may involve a libel case. For instance *The Observer* was served with a writ because a story that used a formula to refer to an unnamed source was held by members of the shoot-to-kill inquiry team working under John Stalker in Ulster to refer to them, and since they constituted such a small and identifiable group the newspaper accepted responsibility and made a payment to the five officers involved of close to £20,000. A number of other publications were also served with writs and attempts were made to stop the publication of stories seen to be damaging to individuals named in them.

An obvious option in avoiding such difficulties is to employ general categories of villains and possible informants. If we are claiming to know that Stalker was the victim of a smear plot and we refer to 'MI5 officers' as the culprits, we are safe from libel, first because we have not identified any specific individual or sufficiently small group of people, and, second, because MI5 officers in the nature of their work cannot identify themselves. This also provides journalists with a certain level of fictional licence.

Numerous allegations can be made against generalized categories of people, for example the IRA, the MI5, the Freemasons, without any need of evidence. But in order to avoid the charge that such stories are based on groundless allegations, reporters have to demonstrate that their sources exist and are reliable. This is often difficult to achieve at the time, even when subsequent events seem to substantiate what is claimed.

The two best options for the journalist in this situation are either, as we saw in the case of the general in Woolworth in Chapter 1, to obtain an admission from an official spokesman speaking on the record or to obtain an official document which confirms as precisely as possible what the reporter claims. Where this is not the case, and where the newspaper editor is determined to publish, other means of substantiating the existence and validity of contacts such as the use of phrases like 'sources close to the RUC' or 'a senior Whitehall official' may be called in evidence in the story. Sometimes phrases may be used to hide the identity of a source. A civilian in a minor post in police headquarters who has passed on some gossip which turns out to be true may be referred to as a senior police officer, whereas a very senior officer may be referred to simply by a general phrase such as 'one Manchester police officer'. On the other hand, of course, such sources can be invented, and, in order to justify their claim to have an authoritative basis for their stories, journalists may refer to the fact that they have the names of such contacts but have to keep them secret to protect them from exposure, from police persecution or attack by terrorists. The problem for the reader is that such explanations may be perfectly valid or they may be a cover story for a deception, and there is never likely to be a way of telling the genuine from the false.

Such stories are structured around revelation, and whereas in traditional reportage the reporter and the paper are invisible, in this form of news the producers may appear as prominent agents in the events. In other more restrained forms of the genre the reporter may be identified only by name in the by-line and the pro-active role of the paper may be indicated by nothing more than the use of the verb 'revealed.'

The introductory section of the revelatory story summarizes the mystery and the solution, while the remainder of the story expands on the nature of the mystery, the answer and, in the dramatic form, probably the paper's or reporter's role in providing the answer. This is achieved by enlarging the details along with the evidence for such factual claims and causal inferences involved. As this process takes place the reporter is central to the narrative both as investigator and narrator. Early in the development of the Stalker affair *The Star* made a major entry into the field with a front page lead and a full inside page news feature based on an investigation by one of their reporters, Neil Wallis.

The headline declared in deafening type 'MI5 SMEAR SCANDAL EXPOSED' with an exclusive tag and a by-line for Wallis. It modestly announced,

The Star has been given substantial new evidence about the Stalker affair.

We can reveal the part played by MI5 in the campaign to smear John Stalker's name.

We can reveal the Manchester Deputy Chief Constable as 'the man who knew too much'.

We can reveal two other very senior RUC men have taken early retirement over the inquiry.

Stalker was getting too close for comfort in his investigation – not just about the activities of the RUC but also about MI5.

According to sources close to the RUC the plot to smear Stalker was organised by members of MI5.

They had Stalker removed because he would not back away from MI5's operations in Northern Ireland.[7]

Wallis claimed that Stalker had stumbled across MI5 operations including 'its own cross border shooting war deep inside Southern Ireland and even Dublin itself'.

The Star claimed it had the names of senior RUC officers involved in Stalker's investigations who had been moved, after being quizzed by Stalker, to equally high posts in a 'Whitehall-based security organisation' or who had been suspended. It would not reveal their names in case they became targets of IRA attacks.

The inside news feature by Wallis[8] summarized the case against MI5, 'the Whitehall-based security service'. They had organized a smear against Stalker 'according to sources close to the RUC' because he would not back away from MI5 activities in Northern Ireland. And, Wallis claimed, MI5 had plenty to hide:

(a) A private shooting war in Southern Ireland including Dublin.

(b) It allowed IRA operations to go ahead (so as not to break its own cover).

(c) MI5 specialists had been sent to Dublin on covert operations, including the burglary of Libyan terrorist suspects.

(d) Four lengthy tape recordings proving highly illegal MI5 activities had been spirited away from their Belfast headquarters back to London.

Wallis referred specifically to a 'top secret' summit conference two weeks previously which had ordered a 'cover-up'. The meeting was attended by officials from the Home Office, MI5, the RUC and 'other intelligence and police organisations'.

The 'angry chairman', Wallis claimed, 'lashed MI5 for causing the whole mess in the first place'. He identified the date of the meeting as 4 July and its location as Westminster. This unnamed chairman allegedly said that causing a public scandal to hide a squalid secret was like sending the entire British army to quell a back street prize fight.

Wallis claimed that the MI5 plot followed from the fact Stalker had dug deeper and deeper into the shootings of the six unarmed Catholics and that when he began to be interested in the MI5 bug which had been planted in the Armagh barn where Michael Tighe, the seventeen-year-old farmer's boy with no terrorist connections, was killed the MI5 panicked and devised the campaign against the Manchester policeman.

The claim to have the names of the RUC men along with the date and place of the top level meeting in London all helped convey the conviction that the story was based upon authoritative sources. But the only checkable fact in the story not already in the public domain (such as the details of the police shooting of unarmed Catholics) was the date of the meeting 4. July.

The 'shooting war' and the 'highly illegal activities' remained as collective terms which were never specified with instances of actual occurrences. No dates, nor addresses, nor names of the Dublin-based Libyan terrorist suspects were given. This is not to rubbish Wallis's claim that he had 'sources close to the IRA'. The difficulty with such reporting is that sources wish to retain their anonymity. Specifying details of events helps officials seeking the source of leaks because it always restricts the number of suspected moles and each added detail identifies them further.

Such investigative forays by journalists are nearly always confronted by this difficulty: if they are specific enough to demonstrate their own validity, they are likely to expose the journalist's contacts, and may provoke libel actions in response to allegations about individuals, or prosecutions if specific state secrets are revealed. On the other hand, without some degree of demonstrable specificity, they are open to disbelief.

This is not simply the result of the newspaper avoiding libel or other legal consequences by being non-specific; it is also the consequence of the attempt to find a sort of 'journalist's stone' which would provide an underlying theory to explain the whole drama, like the philosopher's stone which medieval scholars thought would explain the mystery of life. The claim that the bug was in the hayshed had already been widely canvassed in the British broadcast media and the British and Irish press by the time *The Star* revelation was published. It was now being used by Wallis as part of a theory which linked MI5, MI6 and other Whitehall agencies with the covert campaign to smear Stalker. It was not simply written as a factual story but as a causal explanation of the series of arcane events which had surfaced publicly in the previous month.

We will examine a number of such stories as they played their part in the unfolding of the Stalker affair. Not all of them were as non-specific as *The Star*'s effort. Names were sometimes mentioned with chapter and verse. Sometimes this was because the journalists risked libel action and fell victim to writs; sometimes the individuals named were dead; and sometimes the journalists had sufficient publishable evidence to stand up their story. What they have in common, though, is the notion that the story does not simply involve recounting events, but also proffering an explanation through revelation of what was previously secret.

In this exercise the agenda and the form of the story are set by the newspaper and the journalist. Indeed they both figure prominently as active participants in the drama. They project themselves in the character of the 'great detective', the *deus ex machina* who descends from above the fray and resolves the dramatic riddle for the puzzled audience. As in the case of the theatre and literature, it is, of course, the author who is the great detective and the author who sets the puzzles that beset the audience. In the previously outlined, more traditional, more conventional form of news, the institutional sources of news set the agenda and by themselves organizing news conferences, meetings, court cases, they predetermine the journalist's role as the passive observer who merely reports as a proxy for the reader without participating in what is happening. Of course, neither of these depictions is a statement about the 'real' world beyond the written story: they are aspects of the world constructed in the story.

The third sort of news story which characterized the coverage of the Stalker affair was the form which was the outcome of a compromise between the aims of the journalist and the interests of the subject of the news. There are in such circumstances rival agendas. The journalist is concerned to obtain a dramatic revelation; the subject of the story typically wants to put his or her own version of events or to remain silent. This type of coverage also involves naming names and is usually specific to a small number of factual claims.

The journalist's scope for revelatory statement is then limited by what can be 'stood up' by some quotable reference. When a story centres around a particular character's role in the drama, this need for quotable material for the journalist gives such individuals their bargaining power. The journalist's bargaining power inheres in the perceived fear by the subject of news that the journalist will find out what he or she wants to know anyway, may obtain quotes from others 'in the know'.

Two such stories appeared early in the affair in the *Manchester Evening News*, which led the field from the outset in its access to what was happening at the Manchester end of the drama. The paper's crime and police specialist, Paul Horrocks, and the editor, Michael Unger, were primarily responsible for this dominance. The first story resolved part of the mystery on which the press focused at the outset: the nature of the disciplinary offence alleged against Stalker. The rest of the press spent the first week after the announcement of his removal from all duties in speculation and searching for the cause. Various criminals, ex-criminals, aspirant criminals, near criminals and other obscure creatures of the Manchester underworld proffered unsolicited and modestly priced smears of the now-famous detective to the news rooms of the daily and Sunday press. Enthusiastic denunciations of James Anderton also became available in the form, largely, of unsigned badly spelt letters mostly written in block capitals.

Horrocks and his colleagues examined the possible associations with individuals which it was suggested had caused Stalker's apparent downfall. He had the advantage over other reporters of having grown up in the same area as Stalker. After fifteen years as a reporter in the city he had also built up a network of local contacts among the Manchester police and criminal fraternity and, perhaps more importantly, a memory bank of names.

Unger and Horrocks knew that Stalker was a friend of Kevin Taylor, also originally from Failsworth, a local property developer and former car trader who was also a former chairman of the Manchester Conservative Association. Horrocks also knew that Taylor associated at times in his business activities with men who had criminal records of varying vintages. Indeed, it became clear during the subsequent inquiry that Stalker had never kept his friendship with Taylor secret, and Taylor never denied that he had associated with some men who had previous criminal convictions. Unger had already been contacted earlier by Stalker and had spoken to him at length about the affair. Taylor's name had cropped up in conversation. The *Manchester Evening News* men decided that Taylor was associated with the case against Stalker. Horrocks telephoned Taylor and asked him for an interview.

One was arranged with Taylor's solicitor, Ian Burton, present. On 5 June 1986 the *Manchester Evening News* used the story from the interview as its page one lead. It was tagged 'exclusive' and under the strapline 'Tory in police probe' the headline declared 'My 17-year friendship'. The story was introduced with a revelation: 'The man thought to be at the centre of the allegations which have sparked off an inquiry into the conduct of police chief John Stalker was revealed today as Manchester businessman Kevin Taylor.'[9]

Taylor's history, background, age and occupation were concentrated into the revelatory story by the classic reporter's means of packing adjectival phrases and clauses around the subject of the sentence: 'Mr. Taylor, a 54-year-old property developer and former chairman of the Manchester Conservative Association spoke about his friendship with the Greater Manchester Deputy Chief Constable.'

Horrocks reported that Taylor revealed he was under police investigation but attacked 'reports suggesting that Mr. Stalker's suspension was linked to his association with a "known criminal"'. This was a theme to which Horrocks himself with Taylor's assistance was to return a fortnight later, but then taking the opposite view, and actually identifying the known criminal (see page 61). 'Talking for the first time' Taylor was quoted as making it clear he had 'no criminal connections whatsoever, and he had never been accused of any wrongdoing'. He found it outrageous that his integrity 'should be impugned in this way'.

The report summarized the removal of Stalker from duty, the police 'refusal' to disclose details of his alleged disciplinary offences being investigated by Colin Sampson, the Chief Constable of West Yorkshire, but added 'it is believed that they centre on his association with Mr. Taylor'.

'The businessman who lives at Summerseat near Bury said he had been a "close personal friend" of the police chief for 17 years,' the story continued. Taylor was then quoted as saying that he and Stalker had met at a parents' evening at the convent school their daughters attended; that they had attended social gatherings together, including functions at Chester House (the GMP headquarters); that their friendship was no secret, there being no reason for secrecy; that they had been on holiday together.

But, Horrocks wrote, Taylor denied he had paid for Stalker: 'I confirm that Mr. Stalker paid his own way in all respects as I would expect any friend to do.' He was 'saddened' that Stalker had not been told of their allegations against him and thought it 'disgraceful' that the police had only reluctantly admitted that he himself was under investigation, and that, despite numerous telephone calls and letters offering to supply the requisite information, they had 'persistently refused to disclose the nature of the inquiry'.

Taylor's solicitor Ian Burton provided Horrocks with confirmation that there was an inquiry and added the quote: 'Over the past ten months the police have persistently refused to detail the nature of the inquiry into Mr. Taylor and they have refused all offers of help which have been made unconditionally.'

Thus the outcome of Paul Horrocks's investigations was a story which was a negotiated order. He had revealed the solution to a mystery, and in doing so he had scooped every other reporter working on the Stalker story. His story, unlike *The Star* exposé of MI5, was quintessentially specific and supported by the name of the person involved, with the ultimate confirmation of any such allegation – a statement by the person himself.

It was a story which centred around one fundamental factual proposition: that Kevin Taylor was the man at the centre of Sampson's inquiries. It involved naming a name, rather than implying an underlying and all-embracing causal theory unattached to factual specifics. Horrocks had been able to validate his claim that Taylor was 'the man' by obtaining his own attributable acknowledgement that he was. By the exclusive tag, the use of the words 'revealed' and 'talking for the first time', paper and reporter were able to advertise their role as solvers of the mystery, although in a manner of incarnate and self-effacing modesty by comparison with that of The Star.

The other party in the negotiated order, Kevin Taylor, used the opportunity to clarify his own position in relation to the police inquiry into his affairs. It meant that the first public and published reference to the police inquiry into his business affairs was his own frank acknowledgement of his relationship with Stalker, his declaration that he was innocent, and his lawyer's statement.

This breakthrough led Horrocks into a further and equally successful line of inquiry. As a result of this contact with Taylor the reporter discovered that the police had seized photographs from Taylor's mansion at Woodmill Lane, Summerseat. One of these photographs showed Stalker at Taylor's fiftieth birthday party, and on the same photograph was a former Manchester CID man, Stephen Hayes, who had left the police in disputed circumstances and had subsequently been convicted of two offences: attempting to bribe a police officer and demanding money with menaces.

The ex-policeman Hayes had set himself up as a private detective operating in Wilmslow, the Cheshire commuter town, a dormitory town with one of the highest per capita income levels in the country. It had also earned a certain notoriety for exclusivity, being the only town in the country with its own credit card, the 'Wilmslow card', so wealthy are its inhabitants. This sense was reinforced by the town having had previously in charge of its police a chief superintendent of the Cheshire county force who declared publicly that anyone who was careless enough to be found in the town and who was black or who spoke with a Liverpool accent would automatically be questioned by the police on the basis that they must be strangers casing the joint with a view to housebreaking, armed robbery, bag snatching or watching television without a licence.

Hayes was not black and did not speak with a Liverpool accent and so despite his somewhat free and easy way with some aspects of the law he had managed to avoid the attentions of the Cheshire constabulary. Unmolested by them, he ran two detective agencies: Special Investigations Services and Special Inquiry Services, both known as SIS. His headquarters was a small upstairs office suite between Safeway and the railway station.

The Chandleresque inquiry agency was oddly out of place among the affluent boutiques and streets lined with parked German cars. Its existence was only coyly acknowledged by a small brass nameplate on a dusty green front door. Entrance was gained by ringing a bell and speaking into a microphone from which a female voice announced that Hayes was not in his office. Horrocks went with a colleague, James Cusick, in order to have a second note of anything Hayes might admit to. He rang the bell and was told by the disembodied female voice that Hayes was not in the office, but having a more robust attitude to the brush-off than this author he waited and eventually gained access by slipping in with a youth who had been sent out for sandwiches.

Hayes finally agreed to see Horrocks but only if he came into his office alone and left Cusick in the outer office. He acknowledged that he was in a photograph taken at Kevin Taylor's birthday party and that Stalker appeared in the same picture. But in return for his statement to the reporter about the photograph he also wanted the *Manchester Evening News* to reveal the truth as he saw it about his own departure from the GMP which he felt had been unjust. He even provided a picture of himself dressed in a white tuxedo, taken at the previous November's Manchester Conservative Association Ball, which was also attended by Taylor and Stalker. The picture showed Hayes looking massively down into the camera, his broad shoulders filling the frame and giving him the appearance of a well-dressed tough.

The story took up the whole front page of the 21 June edition[10] and was in the same form as the original revelation about Taylor. The strapline tagged 'Exclusive' said 'Ex-policeman reveals:' and beneath was a bold four-decker headline which extended to below the 'fold' (halfway down the page) and said 'I am the "criminal" in party picture'. On the right of the headline was the two-column picture of Hayes looking massively out of the page. Under a joint by-line for both reporters the story began with a revelation:

> Convicted ex-policeman Stephen Hayes is revealed today as the 'known criminal' photographed at a birthday party with police chief John Stalker.
> Mr. Hayes, who now runs a detective agency in Wilmslow, said that 'three or four other people with criminal records' attended the party thrown by Manchester businessman Kevin Taylor.

Thus the history of Hayes the ex-policeman, the criminal and the private detective in a town which is a byword in Manchester for affluence, and the photographs with Stalker at a party with other criminals in attendance are all compressed in two sentences which constitute the 'nose' of the story. The story followed the normal structure of expanding on the issues raised in the intro: Hayes's career in the police; the nature of his crimes; other biographical details and a brief résumé of the Stalker affair up to that point. The names of three or four other criminals were not given, but one other man with a criminal record did appear. He was (and is) James Donnelly, who played a role in the early dissemination of Stalker stories which appeared in some of the most creative news sections of the British Sunday press. These suffered from the minor defect that they were not supported by independent evidence, and while they may not have been smears in the sense that they were part of a deliberate campaign to blacken Stalker's reputation, they had a smear-like quality.

Donnelly was known to the Manchester underworld and police as 'Jimmy the Weed'. This soubriquet became so well known in the local press that he progressed from James 'the Weed' Donnelly and Jimmy 'the Weed' Donnelly to Jimmy the Weed until in 1988 he was finally distilled to his horticultural quintessence in a headline on a court case in which he was acquitted of a shooting offence − 'Weed cleared'.[11] Horrocks and Cusick planted the Weed in their Hayes story, in the third paragraph: 'And Mr. Hayes claimed that Salford ticket agent

Jimmy 'the Weed' Donnelly was also photographed at the party
– a claim denied by Mr. Donnelly.'

The Weed's photograph in the form of a single column block
of his face appeared in the story. The following day he was
featured in the *News of the World* as the source of a story
about Taylor's birthday party which likened some of the milder
excesses, at least, to the last days of Caligula (see pages 120–3 for
details of this story). Donnelly also featured with some modest
prominence in the confidential report to the greater GMPA by
Colin Sampson into the charges against Stalker. We will examine
this report in the following chapter. At the time of the Hayes
revelation, Jimmy the Weed's appearance in the *Manchester
Evening News* pre-empted his own bizarre recollections in the
News of the World of the following day.

After their Jimmy the Weed digression Horrocks and Cusick
then told their story by expanding the introduction. They began
with a brief 'story-so-far' paragraph: 'Mr. Taylor who has had
a 17-year friendship with Greater Manchester Deputy Chief
Constable Mr. Stalker is currently under police investigation.'

They then expanded on Hayes's biography and the details of
the photograph:

> Mr. Hayes, a former Greater Manchester detective who has
> convictions for attempting to bribe a police officer and
> demanding money with menaces, once served under Mr.
> Stalker in the drug squad before resigning from the force.
>   The photograph was one of a number of pictures seized
> by police when they raided Mr. Taylor's luxury home at
> Summerseat near Bury.

The story claimed that the photograph had 'sparked the
disciplinary investigation' into John Stalker's alleged conduct.
In this respect, as we shall see, the story was not wholly accurate.
The inquiry gathered a new momentum with the discovery of the
photograph but had actually commenced many months before.
The impression given by the claim that the picture started off the
investigation is that the police were already investigating Taylor
and the discovery of the photograph drew their attention to his
relationship with Stalker. It is clear, however, from Sampson's
report to the GMPA that it was not Stalker's friendship with

Taylor that got him into trouble, but Taylor's relationship with Stalker which got the businessman into trouble. As we shall show in the next chapter, the focus of the police inquiry from the outset was on the policeman and this was mainly as a consequence of claims by a convict, who was also a police informant, that Taylor was involved in exotic organized crime, and it was the possibility that Stalker was vicariously connected which led to the setting up of a special squad of police officers to examine Taylor's affairs. At the time that the inquiry began it was part of some unspecified line of inquiry to do with 'corrupt police officers'.[12] No crime had been alleged against Taylor nor specific disciplinary offences against Stalker.

At the time of the Hayes story, however, these were matters known only to a small number of police officers, and Horrocks and Cusick in the meantime had publicly discovered and fitted together another part of the jigsaw puzzle in their attempts to make sense of the confusion. The story was factually validated by the interview with Hayes and by the existence of the photograph. The reporters wrote that the picture showed Hayes and his wife and another couple with Stalker in the background talking to other people. They also revealed that the police had shown Hayes the picture when they had interviewed him the previous week. The story went on: 'Mr. Hayes, a 40-year-old father of two, said he had been at four functions – two at Mr. Taylor's home – which Mr. Stalker also attended. A third was the Conservative Association Ball in November.' Hayes was then attributed a statement which seemed damaging to Stalker in the context of an inquiry into his conduct which was beginning to be focused on the issue of his choice of friends and company and on whether he was behaving in a way which could damage discipline: 'He added: "Mr. Stalker came to those functions in the knowledge that there may be people there who were not in his best interests, but his friendship with Kevin took precedence."'

The story included a reference to another guest, Coronation Street actress Lynne Perrie, and there were a number of other guests there, including several MPs. They again referred to Donnelly's presence in the picture and carried a statement by him denying that he was at the party or that he was a friend of Taylor and that there was no reason for him to have been a guest. However, he was reported as making the cryptic claim that he did know who was on the guest list. Who was on it and how he might have known, given his earlier claim to a more or less encyclopaedic innocence of the whole affair, were never vouchsafed to the reader.

Donnelly's presence or absence from the party remained a matter of dispute. In the *Manchester Evening News* he denied he was there; in the *News of the World*[13] the following day he was credited in the context of an exclusive interview with a lurid description of who was doing what and with whom. According to Sampson in his report to the GMPA, Donnelly made a written statement to the inquiry team in which he claimed he had been invited to the party by Taylor and had introduced him to Stalker.[13] The Sampson report also referred to photographs of Donnelly with Mrs Stalker and another guest, Thomas Gardner Burke.

The Horrocks–Cusick story developed the Hayes account of his relationship with Kevin Taylor and John Stalker:

Mr. Hayes says he was quizzed by police for about half an hour but he refused to make a written statement.

He was asked how well he knew Mr. Stalker and how many times they had met at functions.

Mr. Hayes added: 'I told them we had only passed the time of day or just said hello. Mr. Stalker didn't want to know me because he knew about my past.

'John Stalker is not guilty of any impropriety in connection with me. As far as I know he's done nothing wrong at all.'

He said he first met Mr. Taylor at a business lunch in Manchester's Film Exchange in 1980. Later he was invited to Mr. Taylor's home.

A 50-foot yacht owned by Mr. Taylor is known to be part of the investigation into his business affairs.

Mr. Hayes revealed he had helped sail the vessel, the *Diogenes*, down the Manchester Ship Canal from Trafford Park across the Bay of Biscay to the millionaire's playground of Marbella, in Southern Spain.

As is normal in stories involved in a continuing affair, minor developments are simply tacked on at the end of a major lead:

Solicitor Roger Pannone, who is acting for Mr. Stalker, met Chief Constable Sampson yesterday. According to one report, the discipline inquiry has failed to disclose any evidence of misconduct by Mr. Stalker.

Today, Mr. Stalker would neither confirm nor deny he would be meeting Mr. Sampson next week. A statement will be issued on Wednesday.

In the case of the story based on Horrocks's interview with Taylor, the outcome of the story was a compromise in the sense that the journalist and the subject of the story each obtained some advantage from the outcome: Horrocks had his exclusive story and Taylor was given the opportunity of publicly declaring his innocence. The Hayes revelation was different. He was not under investigation except as a witness in the Stalker affair. Given that he was not going to be charged with any offence, he did not need to make any statement of innocence against any current charge. But he did want the story to include his account of the circumstances under which he left the police about which he still entertained a sense of grievance. When the story made no more than a passing reference to the matter, Hayes was not pleased and complained to Horrocks.

In such circumstances, however, there is little that the news source can do, other than refuse future co-operation. In this case this would not be a serious threat, since the only real information of moment for Horrocks which Hayes possessed was his own role in the Stalker affair, which was by then already in the public arena.

In both types of investigative news coverage, the journalist's role is to reveal solutions to mysteries. Within the structure of the news story, the activities of the reporter dominate the agenda. But that is not the same as saying that the form of the discourse or issues attended to is decided upon by the journalist. The form of the story of revelation is that the journalist answers an implied question and then tells the 'full story'. Wallis answered the implied question 'Who set up John Stalker and why?' and the answer was 'MI5, because Stalker was getting too close to their alleged illegal operations'. The rest of the story was an account of how far Stalker's inquiry into the Northern Ireland shootings had proceeded, what the MI5 were up to and how *The Star* knew.

Similarly, in the Taylor and Hayes interview stories, Horrocks was answering the questions: who were the allegedly undesirable associates of John Stalker and what was he supposed to have done? Horrocks was able to answer the questions with names and places and the identity of social gatherings and issues such as the holiday in Miami, the happenings on the yacht *Diogenes* and Stephen Hayes's criminal record. These issues turned out to be what much of the inquiry by Sampson, the West Yorkshire Chief Constable, was concerned with. On almost every count the exclusive investigative efforts by the *Manchester Evening News* team were borne out by subsequent events, in the sense that where they said an issue was the subject of a police inquiry it was, and in the sense that the people they named as those whose association with Stalker was at issue were so. They were able to do so in the two stories examined in this chapter by the use of the interview. In this form of story the journalist appears as the actor who has found the person involved in the drama. That person then appears to tell his own story, but no more does so than a sitter paints his own portrait.

What neither story includes is how the journalist comes to be asking the initial question. In the case of the *Manchester Evening News* stories, for instance, the major role in the investigative and news gathering process played by the editor Michael Unger is unacknowledged in the text. Journalism in this respect is like theatre. The journalist uses his or her skills and talents to show the audience a spectacle. The means by which it arises and the methods of construction are hidden. Unlike theatre the journalist works with the discipline that what is written has to be acceptable as truth according to social and professional norms. But in order to comprehend the Stalker affair and its treatment in the press we need to understand these hidden parts of the construction; how the form of discourse and the nature of the issues attended to are determined.

CHAPTER FOUR

Official reality:
The Sampson report

In order to understand the process which underlay the way in which the press produced their accounts of the Stalker affair it is necessary to outline the bureaucratic construction of events which was taking place in order to see how this provided one among many other versions of reality which journalists had to deal with.

Our best evidence for grasping this part of the complex set of events is the report of the West Yorkshire Chief Constable, Colin Sampson, who was appointed by the GMPA to investigate the charges of disciplinary offences against Stalker. This document is valuable not so much because of what it may reveal about Stalker, but in what it tells us about the police investigation of him. Some of this is stated explicitly and some has to be derived from logical inference. Other questions are raised by omissions from the report.

The document was a summary of a much longer detailed report including statements, documents and statistics. It was none the less 144 pages long and produced between 19 May and the end of August 1986. The actual investigation was completed on 6 August. By that time it was typed, corrected and distributed to all members of the GMPA and to the PCA in London. Shortly afterwards, despite the fact it was a private and confidential document protected under the terms of the Local Government Act of 1972, it was in the newsrooms of most of the national daily and Sunday newspapers as well as the more enterprising of those in the Manchester area.

This short investigation was undertaken by fifteen police officers (including Sampson), who carried out 335 'actions' obtained 169 signed statements, 146 documents and 50 exhibits.[1] They also interviewed a number of witnesses who refused to make statements. This was therefore a complicated and testing operation which involved a mass of information which was collected and interpreted for the purposes of the disciplinary inquiry. It arose out of a complaint which was the result, in the words of Sampson's report, of 'an internal investigation arising out of inquiries conducted by officers of the Greater Manchester Police'.[2] The date of the complaint was 19 May 1986 and the means of its receipt was 'personally by C. J. Anderton Esq., Chief Constable of the Greater Manchester Police to Sir Laurence Byford CBE QPM LLB, Her Majesty's Chief Inspector of Constabulary'.[3] The allegations which formed the basis of the charges concerned the company which John Stalker kept on social occasions over a fourteen-year period.

Disciplinary offences by police officers are normally investigated by the internal investigation department of their own force. If criminal charges are to be brought, these are dealt with by the Crown Prosecution Service. If the conduct is considered to be purely a matter of discipline the officer is brought before the chief constable who holds a quasi-judicial tribunal and gives a verdict on the basis of a 'prosecution' case put forward by officers of the Disciplinary Investigation Department and a 'defence' by the representative of the accused, usually a police officer who is an official of the relevant professional association.

Where the officer accused of a disciplinary offence is above the rank of chief superintendent the investigation has to be carried out by a chief constable from another force. If as a result, disciplinary charges are to be brought, the tribunal where they are heard has to be independent, probably sitting with a QC in charge and with the right of legal representation of the officer 'on trial'.

The decision whether or not to send the allegations against Stalker to a tribunal lay with the GMPA. Their alternatives were to find that there was no case for their deputy chief constable to answer or that the matters were not serious and could be dealt with by some minor disciplinary action such as a mild rebuke.

The main charge was that 'Between 1 January 1971 and 31 December 1985 John Stalker, an officer of the Greater Manchester Police, associated with Kevin Taylor and known

criminals in a manner likely to bring discredit upon the Greater
Manchester Police.'⁴ The main method by which Sampson went
about his task was to interview everyone who could be traced
who had attended a number of key social functions where
Stalker, Kevin Taylor and men with criminal records were present. He also referred to documentary and statistical evidence
and to evidence from witnesses who telephoned, or in some
other way volunteered allegations against Stalker. A crucial
element in understanding the affair is the Quality Street Gang
(QSG). This is a collection of now ageing professional criminals
who allegedly account for a lot of organized crime in the
Manchester area. They supposedly launder money, fence stolen
goods, bend solicitors and corrupt policemen. They have a
spectacular reputation which is not always easy to tie down
to any specific awe-inspiring criminal achievement.

One police fable concerns a bank robbery they allegedly
masterminded in the 1960s. The bank was in Derby and the
raiders fled from the scene in a Ford which was waiting outside
with its engine revving at full throttle. In the hurry to escape the
man holding the money was left on the steps of the bank. He
quickly waved down a taxi and gave the driver the orders that
all cab drivers wait for, usually in vain, for their whole career –
'Follow that car!' Outside the town the taxi driver managed to
overhaul the getaway car, the man with the money transferred
vehicles, and the whole gang set off to Manchester. The Derby
police quickly traced the taxi driver, who described the villains.
By the time they arrived back in Manchester the police there had
worked out the probable identities of their quarries and were
waiting to lock up the bank robbers and recover the money. The
purpose of this story among policemen seems to be to show the
provincial incompetence of the gang. Other stories show them
as rich, thuggish and powerful.

The allegation originally made by a police informer against
Stalker was that he was associated with Taylor, who in turn was
an associate of the QSG. The West Yorkshire team followed up
this allegation by looking at the QSG and their attendance at
social gatherings where Stalker and Taylor were present. The
Sampson report into the Stalker affair is a document like a
newspaper story in which a narrative is built around evidence
in an attempt to construct a version of social reality. But it is

also an argument – an argument about the guilt or otherwise of Stalker and, in achieving this, it is also an argument about the guilt or innocence of Taylor.

The evidence of numerous witnesses is considered in as much as it bears on these arguments. But in just the same way as the journalist is like a theatrical producer who hides the works behind the appearance, so Sampson's report leaves unattended the question of how the agenda for his inquiry ever came to be settled upon and how the inquiry team made its decisions as to who was to be interviewed and who left out.

A number of questions were raised in the news media about the allegations against Stalker while the inquiry was in progress. None of these was addressed in the report other than by a passing reference. It was claimed that Stalker was the victim of a masonic plot, for instance; it was alleged that the plot was undertaken by members of the GMP and the RUC. Another version was that Stalker was being silenced by the security services and the RUC (without benefit of freemasonry). There was a great deal of debate about the propriety of the way in which the inquiry was set up. No evidence other than chance coincidences was ever publicly adduced in support of the freemasonry hypothesis. A good deal of circumstantial evidence was produced, however, to show that there were strenuous efforts by the RUC to prevent the Stalker inquiries into the killings of unarmed Catholics. The only reference to such issues throughout the report was a single paragraph reference that the authors had no evidence of RUC involvement in the allegations.[5] But this is not surprising since there is no reference in the report to any line of inquiry having been undertaken which wouldd have produced such evidence.

There is also a lack of explanation about how the West Yorkshire team knew whom to interview in order to make their inquiries into Stalker's conduct over the years. Although West Yorkshire and Greater Manchester are adjacent counties police forces are by and large closed communities where only the higher ranking officers (superintendent and above) are likely to change forces in the course of their careers. Most police officers who work through to retirement do so within the force where they begin. Criminals are generally no more adventurous. Criminological studies show a depressing lack of enterprise in the endeavours of the law-breaking community. Most crimes are committed within a mile or two of the perpetrators' home. Again the exceptions are among the high status members of the various criminal professions.

The biographies of the alleged members of the QSG referred to by Sampson in his report bear out this general parochialism. The men in the tuxedos do not apparently venture far beyond their own range of night-club haunts, and their business enterprises are close to home. Only short visits to America and Spain for holidays (and some extended stays in the Marbella area when police inquiries at home are pressing) interrupt this home-centred pattern.

The hunt for the 'Yorkshire Ripper' also showed how closed the worlds of the two police forces were. Direct forensic links between evidence found at the Manchester murders and the killer Peter Sutcliffe were never made by the West Yorkshire CID despite the detective groundwork done by the Manchester team. One would not therefore expect Sampson and his men to come to Manchester armed with a deep knowledge of the city's underworld, such as it is. The only source of such evidence available to them to start their inquiries must have been the Manchester police. Sampson's own account of the QSG indeed bears this out:

> The Quality Street Gang is the name given to a group of Manchester criminals who are regarded by a number of senior police officers as being the organisers of incidents of major crime in the city. The membership of the gang appears to be ever changing and many criminals claim membership or association because it enhances their reputation amongst their fellows. Historically the group has its origins in the late 1960s and early 1970s and appears to have emanated amongst barrow boys, market traders and used car dealers. Of those people identified as belonging to this group in its early years only a few continue to associate and are suspected of currently being active, they include. . .[6]

This account continues to name a number of individuals who have criminal convictions, some of them in the distant past. Such a version of events could only have come from the GMP. The 'number of senior police officers' must be either serving or former GMP officers. Neither their names nor their precise account of how the QSG are the 'organisers' of incidents of major crime in the city' are vouchsafed. Nor do the West Yorkshire team say how they know that 'many criminals claim membership or association because it enhances their reputation'. Again the revelation that 'only a few continue to associate and are suspected of currently being active' is unattributed. Clearly, such claims come from the criminal intelligence files of the Manchester CID or from statements by individual officers. During the course of the document it becomes clear which part of the GMP was the major source.

The evidential basis for Sampson's estimation of the QSG is exemplified further by the following paragraph:

> As a group the Quality Street Gang acquired a considerable reputation with fellow criminals, the public and the police, for although individually they were dealt with by the courts for relatively minor offences, by reputation at least, they were making a good living from crime and were not getting caught.[7]

Clearly, judgements about individuals' characters are not being informed from actual criminal convictions but from the opinions of police officers who have investigated the QSG, either through using criminal intelligence files or through interviews with serving or retired GMP officers. It would be naive to think that an investigation of such a nature would be based on any other evidence. None the less, given its large audience, made up of all the members of the GMPA and officers of the PCA, it is interesting that the report does not contain any reference to sources for such claims. This document, unlike those news reports we have examined and those we will examine, speaks with its own voice. It constitutes its own authority without either referring to sources for factual verification or support for opinions. The news reporter on the other hand either refers to authoritative sources or argues from evidence.

Paragraph 17 of the report begins to reveal how Stalker and Taylor first came to be linked officially and how they were first subjected to police scrutiny. Much is left unsaid in this paragraph: 'During the first half of 1984 Detective

Chief Superintendent Topping of the Greater Manchester Police, Discipline and Complaints Department was involved in monitoring and collating information in respect of alleged corrupt officers.'[8]

It is not clear whether or not Topping was pursuing particular officers in relation to a complaint or was engaged in an open-ended inquiry into corruption amongst the generality of the GMP. This reticence might be explained by a policy of not referring to names or other specifics in relation to unproven allegations. This is disproved however by the sentence which follows immediately. It names Taylor: 'By July 1984 he had received information from a number of sources indicating that Kevin Taylor was involved with the Quality Street Gang. In particular one informant said he was involved in the financing of drugs trafficking.'[9]

It is important to note that Taylor was never convicted of any criminal offence. Even after more than two years of intense police investigation no charge relating him to drugs trafficking was ever brought against him. The report continues:

> The same informant, whilst making reference to another alleged corrupt police officer, who has since retired, said that there was a strong corrupt connection between Mr John Stalker, James Patrick Monaghan and Kevin Taylor. The friendship of Mr Stalker and Mr Taylor was an open one and was known to many officers of the Greater Manchester police including the Chief Constable.[10]

The report then refers to an alleged revelation by Detective Superintendent Bernard McGourlay, subsequently disputed in the press, as we shall see, (pages 181, 186), that a local businessman had said of Taylor, 'You must know him he is a pal of Monaghan and Jack Trickett' (alleged QSG members). This local businessman went on to say, according to Sampson, that 'Taylor has a house in Summerseat where he throws parties which are attended by the Quality Street Gang and that Mr Stalker had been at the parties. This information was passed to Detective Chief Superintendent Topping who on July 17th 1984 submitted a four page report to Assistant Chief Constable Mr Lees, who

referred it to Chief Constable C. J. Anderton.'[11] Sampson's
report continues: 'Mr Topping's report resulted in the formation
of a team dedicated to investigate the activities of Mr Taylor
and having regard to suggested drugs connection members of
the drugs intelligence unit formed the nucleus of that team.'

As inquiries led to financial matters fraud squad officers
were also enlisted into the inquiry.[12] It is clear that, if this
account of the origination of the police action against Taylor
is accurate, it was his association with Stalker that led to
his being investigated in the first place and this arose out of
an earlier inquiry by Mr Topping into police corruption. The
only reason that the information about Taylor could have been
passed to Chief Superintendent Topping at that time was that
it mentioned Stalker, since Topping was then operational head
of the 'Y' Department (the Discipline and Complaints Department). Superintendent Bernard McGourlay was then head of
the Serious Crime Squad and could have initiated inquiries into
Taylor's affairs on his own account, if serious crime had been
the focus of the inquiry and not the discipline issue which was
Mr Topping's province. In any event such inferential argument is
made superfluous by Sampson's own account. He says that it was
Topping's report to Anderton that led to the formation of a team
based on Drugs Intelligence Unit officers to investigate Taylor.

If Sampson's report is an accurate account of the order of
events it means that news stories which suggested that Stalker
was investigated because he associated with Taylor, who was
already the subject of investigation, were wrong, while those
that implied, as did Taylor himself, that he was only subjected
to a long drawn-out inquiry because of his association with
Stalker were correct, at least in terms of the order of events
and the logical impetus of the initial decision to undertake the
investigation.

As inquiries proceeded into Taylor's business affairs he became
aware of them and made a number of approaches to the police
requiring information. Eventually, on 15 January 1986, according
to Sampson's report, a letter dated 13 January, without the
envelope in which it arrived, was handed to Anderton by Stalker,
who reportedly informed his chief that he had opened the letter
on the previous day in his absence. The letter was addressed to
the chief constable and marked 'Strictly Private, Personal and

Confidential'. According to the report Stalker said that the letter was 'in respect of his friend Kevin Taylor and because of that he felt the matter should be dealt by Mr Anderton. Mr Stalker also pointed out that he was not mentioned in the letter but because of it and previous conversations he had distanced himself from Mr Taylor.'[13]

Later, on 28 February, Anderton attended a 'social function at The Piccadilly Hotel, Manchester at which Kevin Taylor made an approach to Mr Anderton and complained about the effect police inquiries were having on his business'. He also reportedly said that Stalker was no longer speaking to him and 'had backed off'.[14] The nub of the matter from the point of view of the focus of attention in the press and in its evidential impact on the police follows in the report. Orders of Access were issued on 12 March 1986 in respect of Taylor's bank accounts. His American Express account revealed 'that Mr Taylor had purchased tickets for himself and Mr Stalker for a flight from London to Miami on 29 November 1981'.[15]

The significance for the police was that this demonstrated the validity of the informant who had provided the initial impetus to Topping's investigation. When one part of a story by an inform-ant turns out to be true it follows (for the investigator) that he is reliable and that other parts of his story could also be true. In Sampson's words: 'Information had previously been received that Mr Stalker and Mr Taylor had been on holiday together and it had been suggested by the informant that it had been at Mr Taylor's expense.' [16] In point of fact this informant was a crimi-nal, David Burton, alias David Bertelstein, who, it later tran-spired, was also a Special Branch informer with recorded activ-ities in Northern Ireland in this role. He died in Preston prison in March 1985. Burton's career in the star-studded end of the crimi-nal world was referred to by Sampson apparently as a reason for having given him credibility as a knowledgeable witness.

'Burton's criminal career involved him in various capacities with the Kray twins to whom he was a chauffeur, and various members of the Quality Street Gang.' We may accept the strict grammatical construction that he was various members of the QSG (presumably the result of a split personality) or simply that the West Yorkshire team had misplaced a phrase and that Burton's career involved him with members of the gang. But in any event this biography is interpreted as a basis for taking the man seriously as an informer: 'As a result he built up a remarkable knowledge of criminals and their activity on both a local and national scale. Burton did not keep all his knowledge to himself and provided useful information to the police on a number of occasions.'[17]

Sampson reveals that Burton was interviewed on four occasions within a few weeks of his death by Detective Inspectors (DIs) Murray and Richardson of the Greater Manchester Drugs Intelligence Unit.[18] Burton's conversations with the two detectives were tape-recorded and transcribed. They involved allegations against Taylor of crimes with which he has never been charged, despite the fact that inquiries into his affairs continued for three years, when he was eventually charged with less serious financial offences, none of which was referred to by the informant Burton. Taylor was alleged by Burton to have taken part in a number of criminal activities, none of which has ever been substantiated. He was charged with a fraud against the Co-operative Bank, but was acquitted when the police case against him spectacularly collapsed (see Chapter 11). But even these disproved charges did not involve in any way the QSG or any of the criminal activities, such as drug trafficking and money laundering, which the police were interested in at the beginning of their inquiries.

Burton's allegations to Superintendent McGourlay, Detective Chief Inspector (DCI) Potts and Detective Inspector (DI) Patterson about the Stalker/Taylor/QSG connection are summarized in the Sampson report into eight specific 'incidents':

that Kevin Taylor was involved with the QSG who had an Assistant Chief Constable 'on a pension' as early as 1981;

that Kevin Taylor, Jimmy 'Swords' and Joseph Monaghan assisted each other financially;

that Kevin Taylor and Mr Stalker visited the Bavadage Club where they 'were spoken to by a criminal';

that Kevin Taylor and Mr Stalker 'visited Porters Wine Bar, Stalybridge, one Monday night where they spoke to Peter Jessop and Mickey Lee';

and on the same night they and others 'attended the Anglo-American Boxing Club nights at The Piccadilly Hotel';

that Mr Stalker obtained a free meal for his family at the Kwok Man Chinese Restaurant which a former policeman Derek Burgess witnessed;

and finally that James Anthony Donnelly (Jimmy the Weed) had said 'Kevin Taylor and Jimmy Swords could get things "straightened" through Mr Stalker'. [19]

The nature and source of these charges is hard to assess, since in the following paragraph most of the ground is removed from them. They are summaries of transcripts of the interviews of Burton with DIs Murray and Richardson in February and March 1985. His allegations to Superintendent McGourlay, DCI Potts and DI Patterson are only Burton's own account of events. In their statements to Sampson, Murray and Richardson said they regarded Burton 'as a good but dangerous informant who required careful handling' who was 'prone to embellish information and skip from one topic to another in conversation'. Neither could recall Burton referring to an assistant chief constable although they said he did make 'allegations in respect of Senior Officers whom he did not name'.[20] DCI Potts did not recall Burton at all.[21]

The allegations made by Burton to DCIs Murray and Richardson were examined by interviewing witnesses referred to in Burton's stories. Taylor acknowledged his acquaintanceship with alleged members of the QSG as he did his own gambling habits. None of the witness statements obtained actually confirmed Burton's allegations. Sampson's conclusion is, 'There appears to be remarkably little corroboration of what Burton has alleged.' But he adds the rider, 'yet there is evidence from other sources including Mr Taylor himself, connecting him with members of the Quality Street Gang and with Mr Stalker'.[22]

It is hard to grasp the logical status of the 'yet' here. It presumably qualifies the apparent dismissal of what Burton has said. If it means anything, it must at least mean 'and yet there may be something in what he says'. This does not follow. It appears from the rest of the report that Stalker made no secret of his relationship with Taylor and Taylor made no secret of his relationship with Jimmy 'Swords' Monaghan, his brother Joseph Monaghan, Vincent Schiavo, or other alleged members of the Jesse James Hole-in-the-Wall–Dalton Brothers car dealers' collective. Given that these relationships were no secret the fact they were acknowledged by Taylor and 'revealed' by Burton does not logically provide a reason for believing that other allegations made by the same source are likely to be more or less valid. It is the same as arguing that if Burton had alleged that Prince Charles was known to the Queen and she was known to the Duke of Edinburgh and all three were members of the Irish National Liberation Army then an admission by the Queen that she did know the other two constituted an 'and yet' caveat against disbelieving the INLA connection.

The more serious of Burton's allegations against Stalker was that he was by implication the assistant chief constable who was 'on a pension' to the QSG in the early 1980s. This was a period when Stalker held such a rank. Sampson searched Stalker's bank accounts and was unable to find any evidence of suspect or unsatisfactory deposits.[23] The weak nature of the evidence against Stalker in relation to the major charge of discreditable conduct is acknowledged by Sampson:

> The person who could be said to be principally responsible for the allegations against Deputy Chief Constable Stalker is now dead. David Burton was a professional criminal who was also a regular informant to the police and other bodies. The reliability of information gained from Burton was not easy to assess. He was devious and deceitful but he was responsible for the detection of some major crimes. As is often the case a proportion of information obtained in this way was speculative.[24]

The difficulty Sampson refers to is the necessary logical difficulty of considering the evidence of a liar. Liars are not so defined because they never tell the truth. Liars may be people who sometimes tell what they believe to be the truth and sometimes calculatedly say things they know to be untrue. Other liars are pathologically unable to know when they enter the worlds of their own fantasies. The outcome of this is that their versions of events may be reliable, fairly reliable or downright lies. Given that this is the case it is not logically possible to confirm the reliability of some of their accounts by reference to the truth of others nor to condemn some points on the basis of the falsity of others. The fact that Burton had given accurate information about some unspecified major crimes did not necessarily imply that he was giving reliable information about Stalker. If we were arguing from the principle of consistency one could equally well infer from Burton's deviousness and deceit that his information about the major crimes was false. In as much as Sampson's argument tends in this direction it tends towards contradiction.

The only way that one might substantiate the dead informant's allegations would be to see if they were substantiated by other witnesses, or by photographic, documentary or forensic evidence.

Sampson turns to corroboration:

> However his information is not totally inaccurate or uncorroborated. The information given to Detective Superintendent McGourlay on the golf course by Mr Wareing confirmed an association between Deputy Chief Constable Stalker and Mr Taylor and further corroborated the liaison between him and members of the Quality Street Gang. That information gave some credence to Burton's information and caused considerable concern to Superintendent Topping who had been very sceptical about the validity of the allegations. The crime intelligence records gave further support to the fear that Burton's information may be correct, as did the comments of Michael Roy Brown.[25]

The 'comments of Michael Roy Brown' is a reference to a reported interview between Brown and DCI Born and DI Murray of the GMP on 20 December 1985 'about other matters'. According to Sampson's report Brown then referred to knowing Taylor and 'having been on holiday in June 1981'.[26] This is then followed by two allegations against Taylor, one of which concerned drugs. Brown's comments, as reported in the Sampson report, amount to nothing more than two blanket allegations against Taylor and a comment about his relations with a police officer, none of which is substantiated with evidence or backed up by details: 'Mr. Brown also said of Kevin Taylor that he was the best of the long firm fraudsmen and that there was talk that he was into drugs ... Mr. Brown said that Kevin Taylor had a top man in the Greater Manchester Police.'[27]

Sampson's further evidential search took him to criminal intelligence records – those of the GMP Crime Intelligence Unit and the crime intelligence reports of the Regional Crime Squad. It is interesting to note how far back the references to Taylor begin. The first referred to in the report concerns the suspicions of a police officer in 1973 that Taylor was engaged in a criminal activity – receiving. This never resulted in a charge being brought against him but has remained in the records for sixteen years. It also indicates that two men with previous convictions were working with him, one being Harvey Sefton, known as 'Scouse Harry'.[28] From an unsigned statement obtained from Sefton it seems that he did work for Taylor, according to an earlier part of the Sampson report, and there is some evidence that he may have flown as a passenger in an aircraft flown by Taylor from Blackpool airport on a pleasure flight.[29]

The second entry was by a Cheshire police officer and also dates from 1973. It refers to the fact that Taylor had been to Spain four times in the previous fortnight. Later that year his business was reported as being in difficulties, and his final contribution to this one-man crime wave for the year was in December when a Detective Sergeant Boone reported that Taylor had built a shopping precinct behind Broughton Lane, Salford.[30]

A further six entries from crime intelligence records follow, covering a period from 1979 to 1984. The first five are a catalogue of allegations by police officers of associations between Taylor and men with criminal records, generally regarded as members of the QSG. The first claimed that Taylor had had a lengthy conversation with three such men. The second reported that another was living at Taylor's house. The third simply baldly asserted that Taylor was an associate of James Anthony Donnelly (already known to readers as Jimmy the Weed). The fourth claimed that Vincent Schiavo had obtained a 6. 25 ton yacht, the *Moriarty*, from Taylor in payment of a debt in 1983.[31] All of the entries so far predate any investigation linking Taylor with Stalker.

Sampson does not indicate why Taylor was being kept under surveillance, or why the surveillance seems to have lapsed between 1973 and 1979. It might be argued that the observations simply arose out of surveillance of known criminals with whom

Taylor happened to come into contact. This, however, would not explain the record of his trips to Spain, or his financial difficulties, and even less the fact that he had built a shopping centre in Salford, none of which is a crime in itself nor is recorded as involving Taylor with criminal collaborators. There is no doubt that for six months of 1973 Taylor was being recorded for crime intelligence purposes as a target in his own right.

The next information relates to information gained during the investigation of a fraudster, Mark Klappish. This man had in his possession both Taylor's home and work telephone numbers.[32] There then follows the information which formed part of the basis for beginning the investigation of Stalker. It concerns the reported conversation on the golf course between the off-duty Detective Superintendent Bernard McGourlay and a local businessman Gerald Wareing. Referring to a conversation earlier in their golfing session in which Taylor's connections with the QSG were mentioned by the businessman, McGourlay asked the name of the senior police officer who allegedly attended parties at Taylor's house which were also attended by members of the QSG. The reply, according to the Sampson report, was 'John Stalker'.[33]

Wareing was interviewed by the Sampson team and made a statement but

> declined to include in it any reference to his conversation with Mr. McGourlay. Mr. Lawlor who was with Mr. Wareing and Mr. McGourlay during the earlier part of their conversation told the West Yorkshire officers that he was not privy to the conversation and no statement was obtained from him.[34]

As we shall see (pages 181, 186), the press subsequently challenged the whole basis of the report of this conversation between the police officer and the businessman. A second senior police officer in the GMP was also referred to in the Sampson report as the source of information on which Chief Superintendent Topping based his first report to Assistant Chief Constable Ralph Lees who then passed on the information to the Chief Constable, James Anderton. The second officer was Chief Superintendent Arthur Roberts, the head of the Trafford Division of the GMP. The Sampson report here refers to a major conflict over a matter of fact between Topping and Roberts, one which the press took up subsequently. According to Sampson, 'on 15 May 1986 Chief Superintendent Roberts of the Greater Manchester Police spoke to Chief Superintendent Topping about a conversation he had had recently with Mr. Ian Burton, a solicitor who was representing Mr. Taylor.'[35] Topping's note of this conversation, says the report, indicated the following points:

(a)   Taylor is saying he has been to the USA and to parties with Mr. Stalker at Taylor's expense.

(b)   If nothing is done to squash inquiries then Taylor will blow out John Stalker and associates.

(c)   Taylor talks continually of his friendship with Stalker.[36]

Roberts's denial of this version of events could not be more emphatic. In Sampson's words he 'denies that there was any such inference as indicated in the above paragraph (a) and (b) and in respect of (c) says that there was never any doubt that Mr. Taylor and Mr. Stalker were friends'.[37]

Strangely, in the face of such a total conflict of evidence between two senior officers, Sampson has no comment to make. Whereas the reliability or otherwise of Burton alias Bertelstein was an issue because of his history as a liar we find that here the unavoidable conclusion is not drawn and the questions are not asked. Since the version of one man contradicts that of the other there are only two logical possibilities: either one is wrong or they both are. If one is wrong he must then either be mistaken or lying. If we assume that it was a mistake and not a lie, then this raises the possibility that the whole investigation into John Stalker's conduct may have been based on information laid by an officer who was capable of a complete error of fact about an issue of the utmost seriousness for the force of which he was a member. We do not know whether this was the case or not because the question was never posed.

If the account of events given in the Sampson report is an accurate one then there is no doubt that the original decision to investigate Stalker arose from the actions of Chief Superintendent Topping. After the alleged conversation between McGourlay and Wareing, Topping himself 'sought evidence of the association

of Mr. Stalker and Mr. Taylor and found it in the records
of the Greater Manchester Police Senior Officers' Mess which
Kevin Taylor had attended as a guest of Mr. Stalker'.[38] There
then follows what is a characteristic of the report, a serious
allegation against an individual, followed by a doubt cast on the
information or sometimes a denial from another source. 'Other
information and evidence was obtained which linked Kevin
Taylor with suspected drug dealers' is followed by 'although
doubtful about the quality of some of the information Mr.
Topping, rightly in my view, composed a confidential report
which he handed personally to Mr. Ralph Lees the Assistant
Chief Constable then responsible for Complaints and Discipline in the Greater Manchester Police'.[39] The allegation in
the report is not that Taylor dealt in drugs, but that 'information' linked him with 'suspected' drug dealers. It is quite
clear from other parts of the Sampson report that 'linked' in
the context of police crime intelligence files may mean nothing
more than 'met' or 'were in the same room at the same time' or
'had a drink together', while 'information' might well involve
unproven stories told by convicted criminals on trial for other
offences and in search of reduced sentences for helping the police.

In June 1984, then, Topping set in motion the inquiry into
Stalker's relationship with Taylor, by handing over his report
to Lees, who then passed it on to Anderton. No one seems to
have remarked that if Stalker had brought Taylor to the Senior
Officers' Mess and signed him in as a guest the relationship was
not a secret one and its discovery hardly ranked as a major
forensic coup.

In October 1984 Lees moved from the 'Y' Department, the
internal Investigation and Complaints section, to become head
of the Greater Manchester CID. The Sampson report gives
the following account of how he approached his new role:

> and in the subsequent two months addressed his mind to one
> of the Chief Constable's main objectives for 1985 which was
> to tackle the problem of drugs misuse with particular emphasis
> on persons concerned in trafficking. Mr. Lees and the Chief
> Constable were aware of the close links of the Quality Street
> Gang with both drugs trafficking and serious crime. They
> also had regard to Mr. Topping's report of 17 July 1984

[linking John Stalker with Kevin Taylor and the latter with the QSG].

The matter was tackled by substantially increasing the size of the Force Drugs Squad and the formation of a Drugs Intelligence Unit. The latter, as well as performing an information gathering and liaison base, was tasked with investigating the activities of the Quality Street Gang of which Kevin Taylor seemed to be part. They were not tasked to investigate Mr. Stalker or his friendship with Kevin Taylor.[40]

This is not quite the same account of events given earlier in the report, when Sampson said that the Topping report on Taylor's activities only arose out of an inquiry into corrupt police officers and referred specifically to his relationship with Stalker. As quoted earlier the account of the role of the Drugs Intelligence Unit's work is as follows: 'Mr Topping's report resulted in the formation of a team dedicated to investigate the activities of Mr Taylor and having regard to suggested drugs connection members of the drugs intelligence unit formed the nucleus of that team.'

Clearly if the formation of the team resulted from Topping's report on the relationship between Taylor and Stalker, and since this report referred to dark claims about the possibility of a very senior police officer being 'on a pension' from the QSG, it would have been perverse for the team not to look at the issue which lay behind its own formation – 'the friendship with Kevin Taylor' of John Stalker. A reasonable inference from the account of events presented is that the specially dedicated team were looking for connections between Taylor and Stalker, and this is given suggestive support by the fact that they very soon found it.

The Sampson report relates that members of the Drugs Intelligence Unit searched Taylor's home and offices and seized documents including two photograph albums. These are the albums which include the pictures of the Stalkers at functions also attended by known criminals, and which led to the suspension of Stalker from his duties including the investigation of the deaths of the six unarmed Catholics under the guns of the RUC.

What is interesting is that within four months of Lees taking over the CID, having left the 'Y' Department, his former second in command, Chief Superintendent Topping, followed in

February 1985 to become once again his second in command as the operational head of CID. As second in command in the Investigations and Complaints Department Topping had initiated the inquiry into Stalker and now, as second in command in the CID, he finished the job.

The inquiry into the Taylor/Stalker relationship moved from one department to another with Topping and Lees, but primarily with Topping. In his willingness to accept that the team was not 'tasked' to examine the Taylor/Stalker friendship Sampson simply accepted the version of events put to him by the GMP team which had done the groundwork for him, but it is difficult to understand how anyone could subscribe to such a naive view of what had transpired. The inquiry arose out of a concern that Stalker might be associating with the QSG through his friendship with Taylor, and that is what the especially formed team eventually 'discovered'. Although Taylor was himself eventually charged, it was with an offence involving obtaining overdrafts from the Co-operative Bank by dishonest overstatements of the value of land used as collateral. None of his three co-defendants was a member of the QSG and despite having had access to Taylor's papers and accounts for over three years the police were never able to bring charges for the exotic crimes that were originally being laid at his door. The dishonesty charge itself collapsed amid revelations of police malpractice and all defendants were cleared.

James Anderton's explanation, given in a statement to Sampson, of his own course of action clearly implies that his thoughts and behaviour were all predicated on the notion that Stalker's conduct was one of the subjects of the investigation. In view of the information he received in 1984 and 1985 he wrote to Her Majesty's Inspector of Constabularies, Sir Philip Myers, and subsequently discussed the issue with him.[41] The Sampson report says that Anderton decided to 'pursue inquiries into the Quality Street Gang' and Taylor 'without informing Mr. Stalker' of the inquiries or of the information he had received. He did so 'having regard to the lack of tangible evidence at that time of the direct involvement of Mr. Taylor in criminal activity'.[42]

Anderton decided to make a note of any 'future contacts he had with Mr. Taylor and of any relevant conversations with Mr. Stalker'.[43] In the event the only crumb to come out

of this surveillance was a reference to a conversation he had
had with Taylor where the latter had mentioned the name of
one of his acquaintances and a number of other people as
being involved in drugs and had offered to help the police to
pursue them.

During the course of the inquiry Sampson became aware that
on a number of occasions Stalker had used a police car for his
private use and to give lifts to friends in a way Sampson believed
was in contravention of the rules for use of police vehicles
laid down for the GMP by Stalker himself. This then became
a focus of attention of the inquiry team. When interviewed
Stalker countered this charge on two counts. First, his position
in Northern Ireland made him vulnerable to attack by the IRA,
and second, he argued that he used police cars off-duty no more
than other senior officers in the force. He also asked Sampson to
examine the use by his senior colleagues of police vehicles. This
Sampson refused to do.

In the final analysis the Sampson inquiry had to come to
a conclusion about the culpability or otherwise of Stalker's
conduct. In particular Sampson addressed himself to the discipline offence of 'discreditable conduct' which is set out in
Schedule 1 of the Police (Discipline) Regulations of 1985 which
says: 'Discreditable conduct . . . is committed where a member
of a police force acts in a disorderly manner or any manner
prejudicial to discipline or reasonably likely to bring discredit
on the reputation of the force or the police service.'[44]

Sampson concluded that Stalker's conduct had been discreditable, in that 'his continued association with Mr. Taylor and
persons with criminal convictions is directly in contravention
of the latter part of that discipline offence'.[45] In support of
this contention, that such associations might bring discredit
on the police force, he called in evidence the statements of six
witnesses, one of whom was James Anthony Donnelly (Jimmy
the Weed) and another Derek Oswald Britton, who was later
charged along with Kevin Taylor and two other defendants
with a conspiracy against the Co-operative Bank. A third was
the Conservative MP for Barrow, Cecil Franks, a Manchester
lawyer, who was quoted earlier in the report as commenting
unfavourably on Stalker's presence at a function also attended
by convicted criminals. After the report was later leaked Franks

made strenuous and public denials that he had ever made such a statement to the Sampson team.[46]

The Sampson report then moves on to the second disciplinary offence of disobedience to orders[47] and in particular that part of the definition of the offence which refers to behaviour which 'contravenes any provision of the Police Regulations containing restriction on the private lives of members of police forces'.[48] And such a restriction is contained in Schedule 2 of the Police Regulations of 1979 which bans political activities by police officers thus:

A member of a police force shall at all times abstain from any activity which is likely to interfere with the impartial discharge of his duties or which is likely to give rise to the impression amongst members of the public that it may so interfere; and in particular a member of a police force shall not take any active part in politics.[49]

Sampson contended that Stalker's 'prominent appearance' at Conservative Association functions was such, and that it was likely to give rise to the impression amongst members of the public that 'it might interfere with the impartial discharge of his duties'.[50] In addition to these charges Stalker was also found to have disobeyed orders by the private use of police vehicles in which he had given lifts to friends, including Taylor, in company with two of his co-defendants in the subsequent fraud conspiracy trial.[51] There are eight such charges which strike the lay reader of the document as technical and minor in the extreme compared with the gravity of the inquiry Stalker was engaged on: the shooting to death of six unarmed Roman Catholics by members of the RUC armed with sub-machine guns and automatic pistols.

Sampson not only had to formulate an opinion on the culpability or otherwise of Stalker, he also had to advise the GMPA on a course of action. The course of action he recommended was that 'having regard to the considerable amount of public speculation and interest it [the Stalker case] has generated, I am of the opinion that the evidence supports, indeed demands, that it be ventilated before an Independent Tribunal'.[52]

This recommendation along with all the others was rejected by the GMPA by a large majority when they met in August 1986 and reinstated Stalker. One reader of the report at least seems also to have rejected the advice in paragraph 458: 'The final matter is to remind readers of this report of the confidential nature of much of its contents . . . for the reasons I have outlined I must request that extreme caution is exercised.'

Conclusion

In examining the Sampson report and in understanding its significance it is necessary to bear in mind precisely this last point. It was intended to be confidential: that is, its audience was meant to be restricted either to those whose role demanded that they took part in the decision-making process or people whose paid work involved them directly in the investigation or administration of the affair. Had it been intended for public consumption it would not have been the same document. It is this lack of public accountability which removes the necessity for the normal reference to sources of authority to back up claims about, for instance, mere suspicions of people's criminal tendencies. The purpose of this document is to look at the allegations against John Stalker, and to assess their factual validity, assess whether *prima facie* they constitute an offence under the police discipline code and advise the GMPA on the appropriate action for them to take.

In order to do this Colin Sampson examined a number of statements from members of the public reflecting on the characters of various of the principal actors in the drama. I have not referred to these parts of the report because they are libellous, because they are distasteful and in some cases appear to be the outpourings of sick people. In all cases they were unsupported by evidence and Sampson rejected them. Some matters concerned with the private lives of indirectly involved individuals were also included. It is interesting that much of this sleazy material was ignored by the press, on the basis that it was too old or irrelevant to the story, which indicates that the apparent prurience of the press is limited by their focus of interest and the concept of what constitutes news, if not by morality or fastidiousness.

But the main body of his work was dealing with allegations which arose out of police inquiries into Stalker's relationship with Taylor and his friends and as a result of this into Taylor himself. Because the allegation against Stalker was that he associated with known criminals Sampson had to spend a lot of time establishing the criminal backgrounds of people who were at social functions, sometimes quite large affairs, attended by Stalker.

As a consequence more of the report appears to be an account of the social life and habits of Taylor than of Stalker. Much of the detail about Taylor would be regarded as irrelevant gossip if it came from members of the public, but it formed part of the police inquiry, or was lodged in crime intelligence files for a period of fifteen years. It was part of the social map of Manchester life held by the police and used by them to make sense of the criminal world as part of a process of identifying organized criminal gangs, targeting major criminals and combating such activities as armed robbery, receiving stolen property and drug trafficking. But that does not mean that all the information is so focused or purposeful: much of it will be noise in the system.

This is inevitable, because the information is collected in order to come to a conclusion about individuals – in the final analysis whether to prosecute or not. The only way to undertake this sort of process is take up whatever information is available and which taken-for-granted professional common sense also tells an officer might be useful. This is then sifted for relevance as the organization moves towards decision and action. But only some versions of reality ever enter the process and policemen like journalists are dependent on information sources for the way they make sense of the world. And just as journalists choose their sources on the basis of how they define news, so the police choose their sources on the basis of what they believe to be the criminal world and their need for prosecutions.

It is easy to make fun of the Sampson report, partly because it was meant to be secret and we are able to see what the police do when they think we are not looking. It seems to be making a big deal out of minor matters and at times crime intelligence turns out to be stories about a man being short of money and undertaking building projects. But it is important to remember that when the police are attempting to locate the men who earn profits from crime, one of the indicators might be that businessmen who seem at times to be short of money suddenly come into funds. What is strange about the information about Taylor from 1973 is that it is so weak, and could be about any businessman. For the civil libertarian what is disturbing is that without such surveillance resulting in any prosecution the record has remained unerased for fifteen years.

In providing a basis for an understanding of the Stalker affair the report makes it clear that the man who was more than any other responsible for the investigation of Stalker was Chief Superintendent Peter Topping, first as the operational head of the 'Y' Department, and then in the same position in the CID. It is also clear that a team of officers was formed and dedicated to inquiring into the affairs of Taylor because of his alleged links with the QSG and with Stalker.

Two characteristics about the report also emerge from a careful reading. The first is that it is not primarily about Stalker, but about Taylor – about his business, his politics, his social life, his gambling, his holidays, his night-club haunts, his friends with criminal convictions. Some of what is said about him is contributed by witnesses with axes to grind and is dismissed by Sampson. Much of it is based on the central allegations of David Bertelstein alias Burton, none of which has been substantiated by the police to the point where they have actually brought charges against anybody. The only charges brought against Taylor relate to an attempt to obtain bank overdrafts, and none of his co-defendants was named in the report as either a known criminal or a member of the QSG. And all the charges were thrown out in court.

The second is that the inquiry followed entirely on lines set by the original work of the Manchester 'Y' Department, CID and Drugs Intelligence Unit. The Manchester inquiries formed the data base from which the Sampson inquiry worked, and the witnesses interviewed were dictated by their presence at functions already identified by the Manchester detectives. This was largely inevitable, since the inquiry was by officers from another area who could only orientate themselves to the Manchester police and underworld originally by talking to the one comprehensive source of information available to them – the GMP. This does not imply anything sinister or conspiratorial. It is a characteristic exacerbated by the time limit on the inquiry. Within the total time taken there would only have been a fortnight for each of the complex tasks of collecting, collating and analysing hundreds of witness statements.

The final outcome is one that is difficult to believe in as an independent inquiry, because it was literally dependent on the GMP. This is highlighted spectacularly in the affair of the conflict of evidence between Chief Superintendent Roberts and Chief Superintendent Topping. Roberts's alleged evidence about his conversation with Taylor's solicitor Ian Burton is a vital building block in the foundation of Topping's case, carrying as it did the implication of a threat by Taylor to expose Stalker, which further seemed to imply some wrongdoing on his part. Roberts completely rebutted this version of his conversation with Topping, and yet in the face of a direct conflict of evidence by the two senior police officers Sampson was unable to form an independent assessment of who was speaking the truth, and simply left the unresolved contradiction in the report to the GMPA.

Indeed, Sampson seems to acknowledge the lack of fullness of his own report in the words of his call for a full independent inquiry. It is hard to see how anyone could have produced a thorough inquiry within the time and within the political constraints set about Sampson. In the chapters which follow we will examine how the press set about their inquiries in the same area and how eventually they set about the unfortunate Sampson.

CHAPTER FIVE

The Stalkers as soap opera

Colin Sampson's inquiries were a major focus of attention among the journalists covering the Stalker affair throughout the summer of 1986. As we saw in our examination of the *Manchester Evening News* revelations earlier these were entirely focused on letting the public know what the West Yorkshire team were after in their inquiries into John Stalker's private life. In their pursuit of the Sampson inquiry aspect of the Stalker affair the news hounds followed a number of lines. Most simply they wanted to know what Sampson was looking for and what he was finding. Second, they asked questions which Sampson, as we saw, did not even articulate or rejected when they were proffered as lines for his own inquiry.

They asked repeatedly where the allegation against Stalker had originated: had it come from Northern Ireland, or the Freemasons. They asked how the decision had ever been taken to send Stalker on unwanted enforced paid leave and to remove him from his RUC investigation. In particular they raised the role of James Anderton in initiating the inquiry and tried to see how far the government was involved in these proceedings.

The first problem faced by the press in dealing with the issue of the removal of Stalker from duties was an official blank wall of silence. In the absence of such an authenticated version of events journalists were faced with four possible lines of action: simply to report the silence and wait; to rely on other sources of information; to speculate or to investigate. The journalists' training primer we looked at earlier has nothing to say about situations where normal official sources of information run dry. The instruction to young reporters is to cultivate such sources as a means of gathering news, and the whole assumption of the training of reporters is that such a process will provide the necessary flow of information.

To follow such advice would imply simply waiting until someone in authority or an involved party either issued a statement, called a press conference or responded to a press inquiry. This would be the first of the four options. The press did not follow this course of action, but did take up all three other alternatives. The question arises why they did not simply wait passively for something to happen. The answer lies first in the competitive aspect of the work and of the industry. Within individual newspapers and between different newspapers journalists compete to succeed in their careers by making their paper the most successful in terms of news reporting, and finally and probably most importantly, for the satisfaction of being first and being right. In this environment any journalists or newspapers who stood still and waited for things to happen would be overtaken by events in the shape of the activities of more energetic 'competitor colleagues', and by consequent reactions of interested parties to journalistic activity. The outcome of such factors is an impetus to investigate and speculate on the questions raised in order to arrive at the answer first, and to be demonstrably first. The editor of the *Manchester Evening News*, Michael Unger, for instance, regards investigation as part of the work of all his reporters, and has a record of tackling difficult areas of news to support such a claim. Investigations and campaigns are expensive in terms of inputs of time and money, and require a managerial decision to dedicate such resources to a particular area of coverage, such as the Stalker affair. Alternatively, the *Observer* team of David Leigh, Paul Lashmar and Jonathan Foster permanently specialized in police- and security-related coverage and analysis. (Following a number of incidents within that newspaper organization this team is no longer together.)

The second sort of impetus to action in the face of official silence is in the nature of the political and legal situation. This involves politics both in the narrow party political sense and in the more general meaning of issues to do with the exercise of power and influence in a public arena. Interested parties wish to influence public decision-making, and in the absence of a public statement of an official line, which they would normally have to answer, are in a position to take the propaganda initiative. This relates not only to such individuals as Stalker and Taylor, whose reputations and careers were directly impugned by implied allegations of impropriety, it also relates to other people who saw the case as an example of various shortcomings in the nature of the state or of the government of the day (for those who can still make the distinction!). Thus lawyers, politicians and other affected parties agitated publicly about various aspects of the case: the worries it raised about Northern Ireland and the administration of justice there; concerns about the lack of accountability of the police; concerns about the behaviour of James Anderton as Chief Constable of Manchester. This resulted in public meetings, questions in the House of Commons, press conferences organized by Stalker or his lawyers, court cases brought by Taylor and public agitation of the issue by Labour members of the GMPA.

Third, not all newspapers are newspapers in the same way. Some of the lurid Sunday papers are regarded by members of the public and by other professionals as practitioners of cheque book journalism. As a consequence people with a sleazy tale to tell may proffer it to such outlets in the hope of making quick and easy money. The market in rumour requires that journalists involved check such stories, and this in turn may provoke the actors involved in the drama to issue statements and to hold press conferences to squash rumours and put over their own side of the question. And this is only part of the interaction of newspapers and actors in generating a complex game of information exchange. In general, inquiries by journalists are likely to provoke reaction by the object of such inquiries. Consequent press conferences and statements to the press, in turn, provoke the press to further action.

In this chapter and the next two I wish to begin to examine how these processes characterized the way the press made sense of Sampson's inquiry into Stalker's alleged misconduct and how the newspapers themselves covered some of the same ground as Sampson. In this chapter, I will concentrate particularly on that part of the coverage which was a response to the campaign waged by Stalker and his advisers to maximize the public exposure of the issue and to speed up the inquiry and the decision-making processes of the GMPA. In the next chapter, I shall examine how they followed Sampson in trying to establish the nature of the charges against Deputy Chief Constable Stalker, and tried to find an explanation for the whole affair by searching for the sources of the complaints against him and establishing the relationship between this and what was happening in Northern Ireland. I will examine later how they followed such lines as affairs in Northern Ireland or the behaviour of James Anderton.

As we saw in Chapter 3 when we were examining the way journalists construct revelatory news, the coverage began with a statemennt of a mystery. John Stalker, the Deputy Chief Constable of Manchester, had been temporarily sent on leave and relieved of his job in charge of an investigation of the homicides of six Roman Catholics at the hands of the RUC, and no one in authority was saying why. The first stories simply stated that this had happened, quoted the non-committal official spokesmen of the state agencies involved, and speculated as to why, as we saw in Sharratt and Johnson story in *The Guardian* (page 40).

But quickly a number of themes began to establish themselves, and as they did the interpretation of events in the press began to solidify around the idea that Stalker had been set up and that, whatever Sampson was doing, Stalker was an innocent man, a reliable and probably outstanding detective, whose worst possible crime was naivety. A major part of this early coverage took the form of the depiction of the plight of Stalker himself, first in relation to how he was being treated by the Sampson inquiry and second in the effect this was having on himself and his family.

Stalker: a man in the dark

By 2 June, three days after the first announcement of the inquiry into Stalker's conduct, the first of these themes emerged. Aileen Ballantyne in *The Guardian* reported under the headline 'Police Chief in the dark' that Stalker had spoken of his 'confusion and unhappiness at the lack of information about allegations of disciplinary misconduct against him'. He related this lack of information and uncertainty to the strain being imposed on his family by the situation. Ballantyne quoted a GMP spokesman as saying they had nothing to add to their earlier statement.[1]

The *Daily Express* was pursuing the same line on the same day. In a story headed 'Police silent over absence of chief', John Alley reported that 'a police force refused to elaborate' on the charges against the suspended Stalker. He was quoted as saying that he had not been told the 'nature or details of the allegations' himself.[2] The following day the *Daily Express* followed with another story on the same theme. It was based on matters parliamentary and in particular on the intentions of the Northern Ireland Social and Democratic Labour Party MP Seamus Mallon. Under the headline 'MPs' fury at police probe secrecy' the paper's unnamed parliamentary reporter wrote: 'MPs are to question Mrs. Thatcher about a wall of silence over a top level inquiry involving a police chief.' After a brief summary of events the report went on: 'Even Mr. Stalker himself, 25 years in the force, says he doesn't know what he has been accused of.'[3]

The story then referred to the Northern Ireland inquiry and Stalker's removal from it, in the light of his being due to return to the province for the second part of his inquiry. The paper said that 'some MPs' were suspicious about his having been sent on leave. Seamus Mallon 'is to ask Mrs. Thatcher about the coincidence of Mr. Stalker being given extended leave', the *Daily Express* said, and went on: 'Mr. Mallon said yesterday he has no evidence to link the controversial RUC report with the allegations against Mr. Stalker but added, "All my instincts tell me there is."'

In addition to portraying Stalker as a man in the dark, along with a general atmosphere of secrecy about the case, the *Daily Express* is here providing a context and an explanation for this secrecy: it is part of a process of silencing Stalker. As we shall see this theme of Stalker in the dark about the charges against him, in the manner of K in Kafka's *The Trial*, was repeatedly referred to throughout the Sampson inquiry. The Sampson inquiry therefore rather took on the quality of a cruel inquisition against an innocent man charged with an unnamed wrong.

The *Manchester Evening News*, which had already covered the story in the same light, produced a background news feature under the by-line of Ian Craig but with a major input from

the editor Michael Unger in which the idea of a government
conspiracy against Stalker was floated as a possibility and in
which Stalker as an innocent victim in the dark was integral:

> The making of unspecified allegations against the Deputy Chief
> Constable of one of Britain's major forces is unusual in itself.
> But the way it has been done – after Mr. Stalker had presented
> an explosive report on his Ulster investigation – has led one
> MP to suspect it is more than a coincidence . . .
>   But the way the affair has been handled in Manchester has
> only served to deepen the mystery. Why has this well-respected
> senior officer not been given details of the allegations against
> him . . .
>   The police authority chairman refuses to come clean, even
> to Mr. Stalker himself.[4]

The same approach is again exemplified by the *Daily Express*
of 7 June. A story appeared which was the outcome of a press
conference organized by Stalker's solicitor, Roger Pannone. The
headline was a dramatic *cri de coeur*: 'Tell me what I have
done'. The strapline above it read 'Deputy police chief attacks
veil of secrecy' and beneath the main headline a further dramatic
headline declared: 'Stalker talks of family anguish and challenges
his accusers'.

The *Daily Express* reporter, John Alley, explained the press
conference's objective to his readers thus: 'Mr. Stalker, number
two in the Greater Manchester Police – the second biggest force
outside London – called a press conference in an attempt to
force the Home Office into giving details of allegations now
being investigated in secret.'

It is important to note here that the explanation for the press
conference is given by the reporter and the newspaper. It is not
simply the reported speech of Stalker. There is a clear implication
Stalker was being kept in ignorance of the charges against him,
and this was later reinforced by a quotation from the press
conference in which Stalker was talking about his removal from
the Northern Ireland shoot-to-kill inquiry when he said, 'The
allegations are unknown to me.'[5]

In *The Star* the same press conference was reported including
a similar reference to a plea by Stalker to be told the nature of

the charges against him: 'Mr. Stalker insisted yesterday that he was totally innocent of any disciplinary or indeed any other offence and demanded to be told what the allegations against him were.'[6] Other papers reported the press conference in the same vein.

This aura of uncertainty was reinforced by speculation about the possible charges against him, exemplified by two paragraphs in a report from Paul Johnson in Belfast on 9 June in *The Guardian* which linked RUC men to the charges against Stalker. They said that

> it was being suggested in Northern Ireland last night that 'extensive irregularities' have come to light for the period when Mr. Stalker was in the province investigating six killings by the RUC.
>
> The claim was being dismissed by those who know Mr. Stalker and fear that attempts are being made to smear his name and reputation.[7]

In a leading article the following day, entitled 'Mr. Stalker's odd ordeal' *The Guardian* nicely drew the distinction between the acknowledged minor charges which were laid at Stalker's door and the serious matters he was investigating in Northern Ireland: the possibility of a shoot-to-kill policy by the police against IRA suspects in the province. Referring to the charges against Stalker, the paper declared: 'Whatever the complaints against Mr. Stalker may be – and at least until late today they remain miserably mysterious – they are said to be of a disciplinary, not a criminal kind.'

Later in the same article the paper editorialized that it had been an 'injustice to Mr. Stalker to level charges against him and then keep both him and the public in suspense about their nature'.[8] Both the news story and the leader were primarily focused on the Northern Ireland aspect of the affair. The reference to Stalker's being kept in the dark about the charges against him was referred to as part of the background assumptions of the case. It was by now a universally accepted truth that Stalker was not being told the charges against him. It was like part of the scenery of a play, helping to establish the atmosphere but no longer needing to be stated explicitly.

A similar reference was made in relation to a story about a meeting between Sampson and Stalker on 9 June, when the reporter, Tom Sharratt, stated that the meeting at the GMP's Sedgely Park training college was 'the first opportunity for Mr. Stalker, who was sent on leave on May 29 to learn what he is alleged to have done'.[9]

A week later The Star, in a story following a line about the influence of the MI5 in having Stalker removed from Northern Ireland referred again to the 'unspecified disciplinary offences' for which Stalker had been suspended.[10] The Guardian, the following day, still concentrating on the Northern Ireland angle, referred in passing again to Stalker's ignorance of the charges against him. 'Mr. Stalker', the first leader stated, 'has been shabbily treated. He has been kept ignorant of the detail of what is being investigated. He has not been suspended, merely invited to extend his holiday . . . Were Mr. Stalker a civilian the protests about his treatment would be loud.'[11]

It is interesting how by this time a sense of drama seemed to be overwhelming the leader writer of the newspaper. The comment appears to be on the basis that Stalker was being treated to a lesser level of protest than would have been accorded to a civilian similarly placed. In fact by this time the level of protest about Stalker's treatment was already considerable. And given that by that time he had only been sent on extended leave while the police investigated him, it is hard to believe that a civilian in the same position would even have been noticed by the public, let alone by the leader writer of The Guardian.

The Star, on 26 June, the day following a press conference given by Stalker with his solicitor Pannone, referring back to the start of the affair said, 'it is now four weeks since the 47 year old second in command of the Greater Manchester Police was told to go on leave without explanation'.[12] Tom Sharratt, in a front page report in The Guardian on the same day was claiming that Stalker had still not been told what he stood accused of. Reporting comments by Stalker at his press conference, Sharratt wrote: 'He called yesterday for a swift conclusion of the examination of the evidence against him – although he has yet to be told of any specific alleged disciplinary offence.'[13]

And still by 26 June, a month after Stalker had been sent about his non-business on an unscheduled and indefinite leave, the leader writer of *The Guardian* was writing:

> since then there has been no information, just rumour. Only on Monday of this week did Mr. Sampson see Mr. Stalker, according to whom no specific disciplinary allegations were put at the meeting. Mr. Stalker does not know officially that the area of investigation is his relationship with Mr. Kevin Taylor.[14]

A day later the *Daily Mirror*, in a story updating their coverage of the affair, reported that Stalker· had 'consistently claimed that he had been kept in the dark about the complaints against him'.[15]

This part of the coverage involved a relationship between actions initiated by the press and those initiated by interested parties. The most stunning part of a complex relationship of events was the total public silence of the West Yorkshire team and the GMP. This explains much about the nature of the press coverage. In the absence of an official line to follow the press did not simply go to Stalker for his reactions to what was happening, they also went to him to see if he knew what was happening. He did not reveal operational secrets about his work in Northern Ireland, or guess what the Manchester inquiry might be about, and when reporters asked him questions which suggested that there might be plots or cover-ups, or that there were extraordinary coincidences, he would reply non-commitally that that was for others to say, or, well, he couldn't comment, or point out that the journalist had said that, not he.

He did not deny generally such suggestions out of hand, however. Had he done so indeed it would have removed the ground from under his feet if he subsequently decided he needed to make such a claim in defending himself. Such a situation in the legal process in the event never happened. And, of course, such a denial would have been irrational. Without subscribing to a general conspiracy theory of history, or to the notion that Stalker is a hybrid of Dixon of Dock Green with Mother Theresa of Calcutta, it is quite possible to see a reasonable basis of evidence suggesting something more than chance in the improbable coincidence of Stalker's sudden removal on trivial discipline charges from a serious inquiry at precisely the time when he was trying to force the production of evidence which might embarrass the RUC, the MI5 and the government.

On the other hand, to have publicly connived at such conspiratorial theories might have left Stalker with a situation that would be hard to retrieve if he were reinstated and what' is probably more important would have proved a dangerous diversion from his main purpose – to identify and rebut the charges against himself as quickly as possible.

So while Stalker and his lawyers trod the delicate line of avoiding damaging commitment on the issue of plots and suppression of his Northern Ireland inquiry, they tried to focus the press coverage of the Manchester end of the coverage on a number of crucial issues to do with the Sampson inquiry and the affairs of the GMPA. In understanding this part of the campaign it is necessary to refer to Roger Pannone, one of the solicitors advising Stalker.

He was a senior partner in the solicitors Pannone Napier and Blackburn. Pannone is not in the traditional mould of English lawyers, first in that he runs his practice as a business with numerous outlets and that he treats clients as if they are paying customers. He had made a reputation for competence in taking on big corporations and government bureaucracy on behalf of individuals in the Thalidomide case against Distillers and had represented victims and relatives of the dead in the Manchester airport disaster when an airliner burst into flames on the runway at the city's airport and fifty-four passengers trapped inside because of egress difficulties died while firemen outside watched helpless, frustrated by the lack of a water supply.

Pannone would only take on the Stalker case after he himself was convinced of the policeman's innocence, and saw the main means of fighting the case in the first stages as being in the public arena. In order to avoid the long drawn-out process of an eventual independent tribunal he wanted to establish his client's innocence at the outset. And, given the press and broadcast media interest in the case, he and his client decided to provide journalists with the means to know what their side of the story was in relation to the charges of disciplinary offences against Stalker. Pannone wanted to get the information to one particular audience – the GMPA members who in the end would have to make a decision on the Sampson report.

Thus, by the use of press conferences and a general willingness to speak in particular to certain selected journalists a number of notions of the facts of the case became established in the press very early in the case. These were almost entirely 'pro-Stalker'. The first of these was that he had been kept in the dark about the charges against him. This was not just a case of the press being convinced that this was factually the case, but also that this fact was significant in understanding the case. The official silence of the West Yorkshire team investigating the charges and of the GMP where the allegations had originated was of major assistance to Stalker in convincing journalists that it was factually accurate to claim that he had not been told the precise nature of the charges against him. In as much as no information was being given to the press it was not difficult to believe what Stalker said.

Indeed, at one point there was implicit acknowledgement by the PCA that Stalker had not been told the nature of his alleged wrongdoings. In *The Daily Telegraph* of 9 June the Deputy Chairman of the PCA, Roland Moyle, was quoted as saying that Sampson had completed his preliminary inquiry, and that Stalker would normally be interviewed at a later date. But he said that in the interests of 'natural justice' Sampson would be seeing him the following day.[16]

This quote seemed in part also to substantiate the notion that this issue was significant, that it had meaning. Moyle seemed to be conceding that not to tell Stalker the nature of the charges against him would offend against natural justice. But the acknowledgement both of the fact and significance of the issue was eventually confirmed for the press by part of the official, established government structure.

Paul Horrocks reported in the *Manchester Evening News* of 27 June that the controlling Labour group on the GMPA were going to recommend the formal suspension of Stalker in an attempt to clarify the situation for him. 'Councillors believe', wrote Horrocks, 'that the move may help Mr. Stalker because once suspended, he will have to be told in writing of all the allegations and any possible disciplinary charges.' Pannone was quoted as saying that if Stalker were suspended it might 'crystallize' the situation and stop this 'trawling operation' by the police inquiry team. He was also quoted as saying, 'It might bring the situation to an end because we would then know exactly what allegations there are to answer.'[17]

The Star ran the same story the following day and quoted Pannone thus: 'While we would prefer Mr. Stalker to be immediately reinstated, if that is not possible at this stage, if he is suspended, we will be able to answer the allegations.'[18]

Stalker was duly suspended on 30 June, which seemed to confirm both that he had not been told the full nature of the charges against him and that this was a matter of some importance. The GMPA appeared to be responding to the campaign the Stalker camp had successfully waged through the press and broadcast media. And although in principle this is what occurred, there appeared to be some conflict between the GMPA and Stalker over whether he had been told the nature of the allegations and over the way they had suspended him.

For the first time, on 1 July, there appeared in the press a challenge from a representative of established authority to the claim that Stalker did not know the accusations levelled against him. Horrocks wrote in the *Manchester Evening News* that a 'row' had 'erupted' with a claim by the then Chairman of the GMPA, Councillor Norman Briggs, that Stalker had been told the nature of the allegations on the first day of the inquiry. According to this report Stalker had been told 'verbally' (a vulgarism meaning orally) that the inquiry was 'concerned with undesirable associations, including known criminals'.

Eleven days later, Briggs said, Stalker was served with a notice which stated that 'he had over a period undesirable associates to whom he could become obligated', the story went on. It said that details of the allegations were given to Stalker and his lawyers a week previously – which was a reference to the meeting between Stalker and Sampson reffered to widely in the press at the time. The GMPA chairman was quoted as saying, 'I simply cannot understand why he says he doesn't know. I am satisfied that he is fully aware of the allegations. These are my honest opinions of what is happening.' Peter Lakin, one of the solicitors acting for Stalker, complained of material inaccuracies in the statement by Briggs and was credited with the statement: 'The information given to him by Mr. Colin Sampson was that inquiries were being made into "innuendo, rumour and gossip" about Mr. Stalker's associations with people in Manchester. Mr. Sampson declined to provide further details.'[19] The acrimony between the GMPA and Stalker was further highlighted in *The Star* the following morning, in which a panel entitled 'Fury of top cop' revealed that Stalker had 'slammed' the GMPA for suspending him on full pay without 'having the courtesy to tell him before they made it public'.[20]

But these were minor and incidental diversions which were never widely attended to in the rest of the press and were never established as an issue. 'Stalker, the man in the dark' was a construction of events the press came to accept as a news theme and whenever newspapers spoke on their own behalf they seemed to accept this version of events. It has to be said that Briggs's account of the allegations made to Stalker at the beginning of the inquiry does not amount to a serious challenge to Stalker's claim that he had not been told the exact nature of the offences he was supposed to have committed, since the Briggs account seems to imply that for the first three weeks Stalker only knew the outline charges. The notion of Stalker charged with nameless offences in any case had a certain dramatic appeal which is in any case more newsworthy than the version put forward by Briggs. Values of probable truth and drama appeared to be pulling in the same direction: acceptance of the Stalker version of events.

Not everyone so enthusiastically embraced such a version of events, however, and a more acute challenge than Councillor Briggs's did appear in the *Police Gazette* from a retired police officer, Inspector P. Howard of Croydon. His letter won the magazine's star letter prize of £5 for the first issue in July 1986. The letter struck a critical and sceptical note about the self-portrait of Stalker as a victim which the writer alleged was conveyed in the media. 'Before he was formally suspended', wrote Inspector Howard, 'we were treated almost nightly to the spectacle of Mr. John Stalker, deputy chief constable of Manchester, accompanied by legal advisers saying how wrongly he was being treated by the PCA and others, being forced to go on leave while unsubstantiated allegations were investigated.'

The letter went on in a more robust vein:

Without going into the merits or otherwise of his case, I find this slightly nauseating in one who is, or was, responsible for dealing with discipline in his force, under the appropriate legislation – and who, I suspect, like others in his position, instigated the suspension of more junior ranks without giving much thought to the effect on the officer and his/her family.

The writer went on to ask what would happen to a sergeant or inspector on a discipline charge who gave 'nightly press conferences' and suggested there would be other 'nasty consequences' for such a person. Far from sympathizing with Stalker the writer concluded that he had received special treatment: 'although a lot is wrong with the system [of police discipline] the Stalker affair makes it worse, with one law for us and another for ACPO members. Come on, gents, fair play for all!' (ACPO is the Association of Chief Police Officers.)

This was a view I heard from police officers at the time and later. It is not uncommon for an officer under disciplinary investigation to wait for a period up to eighteen months before coming before the chief constable or his deputy to receive judgement. This does not necessarily involve being suspended for the whole period of waiting, but it may do.

This letter was written primarily for a police readership, where among junior ranks there is great resentment about the discipline system, and so it is not suprising that the press did not take up this line. The line the press took was a straightforward one to do with the Stalker case and not with general issues of police discipline. It was also tied up very early with the idea that the purpose of the inquiry was not to discover whether Stalker had undesirable associates but to smear his reputation and get him out of Northern Ireland. And the clear implication in this was that Stalker's innocence was either unqualified or tainted only by the merest indiscretion. Ordinary considerations to do with police discipline did not therefore apply, since it was not an ordinary matter of discipline.

The Stalker family under strain

The contention that Stalker had not been told the nature or the detail of the disciplinary charges against him directly involved other parties: the PCA, the GMPA and Colin Sampson. And part of the purpose of the Stalker campaign was to produce action from these in response to press activity. But the press depiction of the strain on the Stalkers as a family was something which could not be challenged by any other parties in the dispute. Only the Stalkers themselves could know the truth about this part of the drama. It was a theme which recurred throughout the affair. It was a means through which the Stalker campaign could expect to obtain a fund of public goodwill and sympathy. It was a theme which fitted the traditional notion of the human interest story making issues more real to readers by relating them to the day-to-day events of individuals. In such depictions 'how did you feel?' becomes a question by which emotionally charged responses enable the audience to empathize with participants. It is the same appeal as the fly-on-the-wall documentary or the soap opera. Readers can engage in feelings of support for some characters and antagonism for others.

At first the theme of the strain on the Stalker family appeared merely as an incidental to the main theme of John Stalker, the man in the dark. In Aileen Ballantyne's 2 June story in *The Guardian* which we examined earlier (pages 95–6) he referred to the strain on him and his wife and two children. The story quoted Stalker as saying, 'My family are as confused as I am because I can't tell them any more than we have all read in the newspapers.' Although this helped to paint a more graphic depiction of a man at a loss to know what he was accused of as he sat talking over his plight with his loyal family, it did not constitute a central focus of the drama the press created. Then in early July Mrs Stella Stalker appeared on a local news broadcast by Granada television, due to a coup by the Granada reporter who covered the story, Rob McLoughlin. Horrocks obtained a similar interview for the *Manchester Evening News* on 2 July.

The interview was the paper's page three lead and was trailed on page one with a photograph of the couple under the headline 'My anguish, by Mrs. Stalker'. The couple were photographed at a garden table, with Mr John Stalker resting his chin in his right hand, and the caption beneath dramatically declared:

> The long agony of waiting rests heavily on John Stalker and his wife Stella as they sit in the garden today. But now an anguished Mrs. Stalker has sprung to the defence of her husband – 'a straight man, through and through' – who has been suspended from his role as Greater Manchester's Deputy Chief Constable and removed from the inquiry into the Royal Ulster Constabulary.[21]

The page three article was structured more as a news feature than a story. The introduction simply introduced the interview: 'The wife of suspended police chief John Stalker spoke today about the family's nightmare while he has been at the centre of a discipline investigation.' The rest of the article, while angled on the family's suffering, actually articulated through Stella Stalker a number of issues which Mr Stalker, still fighting for a return to his job, could not publicly do.

The interview covered five main points: that the affair was putting a terrible strain on the family; that the inquiry against John Stalker was a tactic to remove him from the Northern Ireland investigation; that there was a high level of public support for him; that James Anderton had not treated the Stalkers well in their time of crisis, and that the relationship between Stalker and Taylor had been blown up out of all proportion.

The report of the interview was focused on strong emotions. Whereas Stalker had from the outset avoided public denunciation of any other individuals or allegations of conspiracies against him, and had eschewed any expression of feeling stronger than surprise or disappointment, Mrs Stalker, unconstrained by the delicate considerations of an official position, could declare herself openly:

> Mrs. Stalker told of her 'absolute anger' when her husband first told her of the official inquiry.
> She said: 'I felt John had been terribly let down. After 30 years of honest service in the police they do something like this to a man – there's something wrong and very sinister.'

The article depicted a strong and united family under attack and confused. Mrs Stalker described how she went to bed with a 'sick feeling in my heart' and thinking that they might hear something the next day, 'but it still doesn't make sense when I wake up in the morning'. They were a close family who all shared the name Stalker and they would all fight to clear his name.

Mrs Stalker then articulated very explicitly the conspiracy theory which was the main means by which the press came to make sense of the Stalker case as it developed over two years. She said she believed that the discipline investigation was a 'tactic to get her husband off the RUC inquiry'. The article then expanded this theme with a reference to unidentified 'sinister forces' which were at work and 'some kind of undercurrent which is trying to discredit him because of Northern Ireland'. This, she was quoted as saying, was the only explanation which made sense: 'I feel John has been treated like this because he was doing his job too well.'

In this situation of strain under attack from possibly sinister forces the family were not without allies. 'She said it gave the family a tremendous lift to receive hundreds of messages of support, including eight letters from chief constables.' It helped to know that so many people believed that John Stalker was an honest man and the support had kept them going. In the context of the humiliating experience of having his warrant card removed the deputy chief constable had had the loyalty of their two daughters, Colette, aged twenty, and Francine, aged seventeen.

But one figure was missing from this loyal group of family, Mancunians and police officers who were standing by Stalker – James Anderton. Mrs Stalker felt that 'he could have told us a little more'. Her account of Anderton's response to the Stalkers' troubles contained more than a hint of betrayal:

I considered that his wife and I were friends and when I spoke to the Chief Constable it was on the basis of Stella and Jim. My children even refer to him as Uncle Jim.

But when he telephoned on the day John first learned about the investigation he was very formal, and said he was 'sick at heart'.

Finally she referred to the Taylor/Stalker friendship around which the inquiry was directed, and which by then was in the public domain, originally from the efforts of Paul Horrocks, who was interviewing her. This had been blown up out of all proportion, she said. The two families had only met on three or four occasions, while her husband occasionally had lunch with Taylor if he was on a day off. She said she had no idea that anyone with a questionable background had been present at any of the functions which they had attended with Taylor.[22]

By the time of his suspension Stalker was then established through and in the press as a family man, in the dark about the charges against him, with his family under strain, apparently frozen out by his former boss, but receiving heart warming support from the community in which he was embedded. Thus the Sampson inquiry into Stalker's private life was being pre-empted by a public construction of that life, which was family-centred, affectionate and normal.

By opening their doors to the press in such a way it made it improbable that anyone would subsequently believe that John Stalker was anything less than wholesome. And emotions such as family affection and loyalty are effective concepts for rallying support – which is why politicians so often court publicity against the background of spouses and children (and perhaps why middle-aged bachelors seeking parliamentary seats sometimes marry late and unexpectedly).

By mid-July other members of the Stalker family were to appear in the press. Stalker's elderly parents wrote to Michael Meacher, the Labour MP for Failsworth where they lived, and asked him to help. The *Manchester Evening News* reported Mr Meacher's intention to write to Home Secretary Douglas Hurd to demand Stalker's immediate reinstatement. Meacher opined that Stalker's suspension was a major political scandal and that he did not believe it was unconnected to the alleged shoot-to-kill policy by the RUC in Northern Ireland. 'John Stalker's parents, Jack and Theresa Stalker of Tatchbury Road Failsworth, asked Mr. Meacher, Labour MP for Oldham West, to try to end their nightmare', the story went on, once again returning to the idea of the Stalker family's nightmare experience.

The story was illustrated by a three column picture of the couple standing proudly with photographs of their son in uniform with members of the royal family. It revealed that 69-year-old Theresa Stalker had just returned home after three weeks in Manchester Royal Infirmary where she had been after collapsing suddenly. The paper reported that Jack Stalker, aged seventy-two, blamed her illness on the Stalker affair: 'I am certain that this whole business has brought Theresa's illness on.'[23]

In August another generation of the Stalker family was part of this dramatic representation in the press. *Daily Express* reporters David Stokes and Frank Welsby revealed that Colette Stalker, John Stalker's 20-year-old daughter, had split up with her boyfriend Philip Owen, the son of North Wales Chief Constable, David Owen. The paper revealed that the couple were reunited and that Philip, himself a police officer in the GMP, had recently spent the night at the Stalker family home in Lymm, Cheshire.

The headline read 'Secret heartache of Stalker's girl' and a subheading explained 'Pressure led to parting with her Pc boyfriend'. 'The two year romance of John Stalker's daughter was almost ruined by the allegations against her father', the story declared, and later quoted 'a friend of the family' who said 'It's just another example of the intolerable pressure they have been under.' Colette's mother declined to make any comment at all. The story was clearly not inspired by the Stalkers. It did not include the age of Philip Owen nor the first name of his father, and used photographs of Mr and Mrs Stalker which had already been used and a portrait of Colette which was cut out of a group photograph.[24]

The theme of the strain on the Stalker family was called on again in December 1986 when his decision to retire was announced. It was then invoked as an explanation for why he had departed, along with two other explanations: one that he had not been consulted over the decision to search the moors at Saddleworth for the bodies of the Hindley and Brady child murder victims who were buried there in the 1960s, and the other that he had been 'frozen out' by Anderton or other people in positions of power. The causes were not mutually exclusive and sometimes appeared all together in the same story. A headline in the *Daily Mirror* of 20 December combined the family and the moors murders explanations: 'Stalker: I quit over Myra's trip to moors. It was the last straw says daughter.' Francine Stalker was quoted as saying that the first her father knew about Hindley going to Saddleworth was reading it in the media, which was 'a disgusting way to treat a deputy chief constable'. A local Labour politician said Stalker had been the victim of a conspiracy which had succeeded and a Tory MP said Stalker had been destroyed by the establishment, while Pannone the solicitor said, 'The pressures on his family particularly his wife and daughters have been intense.'[25]

Today, The Independent and The Guardian all related Stalker's departure to his statement that he was leaving for 'personal and family reasons'. The Daily Mail headline declared 'Stalker quits to end his family's pain', and the Daily Express ran a headline under a picture of Mr and Mrs Stalker with their daughter Francine which said 'Stalker quits over Moors snub', while the intro said he had quit 'for the sake of his wife, his daughters, and his mother'. The following day the Sunday Mirror revealed 'the real story' behind Stalker's 'shock retirement' with a story that 'auburn haired' Stella Stalker had told him he had to retire.[26]

Conclusion

In Chapter 3 we examined the idea of the narrative structure of an individual news story, but the word story is also used by journalists in a different sense. The Stalker affair as a whole is a story in this sense. It is the underlying set of events which is seen as the source of individual stories and it is also the long-term accumulation of events into a history which relates the small anecdotal occurrences so that they have some underlying and common meaning. The fact that we can refer to the Stalker affair means that such a process is taking place. But whereas for the journalist there is in fact such an underlying reality, for the purposes of this book we are only interested in the way such an underlying reality is constructed and how meanings and interrelationships are established.

There is in other words an underlying narrative structure which is gradually established and which may be referred to in order to make sense of the individual sub-narratives – the news stories. Not all journalists of course work with the same general underlying narrative, although in this particular case most did. In this chapter we have seen how part of the narrative which underlay the press coverage of the Stalker affair was the idea that Stalker was a man in the dark, and that the Sampson inquiry was an assault on his equanimity and reputation as well as that of his family. This of course presupposed he was innocent and if he was then there had to be some malign reason for his predicament and this could be found in the desire of unnamed sinister forces to silence and squash his Northern Ireland inquiry.

In the event of his retirement all these explanations were drawn together in the depiction of a man finally brought down by an establishment plot and, frozen out, leaving in order to spare his family more suffering. The main source of such stories could only be the Stalkers themselves. But this does not mean that they initiated them. From the outset Stalker was besieged by journalists and at first was very reticent about what he said. As time went on Roger Pannone and he fought a successful campaign to establish publicly Stalker's innocence where others had covertly set out to establish his guilt. The presentation of himself and his family as people in a Kafka-esque nightmare helped in this campaign. It also helped the press to construct a meaningful narrative using the images of family strain, loyalty of friends and betrayal of some colleagues very much in the manner of the soap opera, again as in individual stories relying heavily on a narrative simplification in which the audience identify with the unqualified good of the hero against the unqualified nastiness of those out to bring him down.

There was perhaps a certain ironic aptness in the story which appeared in the *Manchester Evening News* of 9 January 1987 that Stalker was to join the television company which produces the soap opera *Brookside*. None the less it is worth noting that these were narrative devices used by the press in order to tell a part of a complex story in a manner with which the public could identify. It is also probable that if anything the coverage understated the degree of strain which a family would experience in the circumstances in which the Stalkers found themselves.

CHAPTER SIX

'Tasty friends'

The agenda for the coverage of the Stalker affair was a negotiated order which was the outcome of the pursuit of the
production of news by journalists and the pursuit of other aims
by the various parties with interests in the affair. The one major
player, the government, which in other similar situations such
as the Gibraltar shooting would be a major player in defining
the agenda and proffering versions of events both publicly and
at unattributable private briefings, was officially silent, despite
some desultory if lurid smears which were put to journalists
about John Stalker early on in the development of the affair.
Representatives of state agencies from Douglas Hurd to Colin
Sampson would make no comments about the charges against
Stalker, the origin of those charges or the Northern Ireland
inquiry. Most astonishing to the journalists covering the case,
and to many of the citizens of Manchester, was the self-denying
ordinance of Trappist silence which seemed to inhibit their
normally loquacious Chief Constable, James Anderton.

Reporters responded to the mystery of what Stalker had been
charged with in two ways. First, they followed the same line of inquiry as Sampson and tried to discover the nature of the alleged
misconduct. Second, they tried to put the Sampson inquiry, the
allegations and the secrecy into a context which explained them
all. This second line of argument involved what in the more
pretentious language of academic social science would be called
three levels of analysis, but for journalists were simply different
angles or lines of inquiry. First, there was an attempt to identify
the immediate mechanisms by which the Stalker complaints had
been laid and the inquiry started. Such issues as the name of the
person making the original complaint and Anderton's role were

examined. Second, journalists pursued the Northern Ireland angle relentlessly in an attempt to find out what Stalker had been doing there, what he had discovered and what opposition he had encountered. And third, there was an attempt to discover how the the apparently trivial charges against Stalker in Manchester were related to the far more serious affairs in Northern Ireland: journalists sought to find the Northern Ireland connection, to show that some person or persons with RUC or government sympathies was responsible for the Manchester detective's difficulties. In this chapter we will examine how the press responded to the question addressed by the Sampson inquiry and how they searched for the nature of the charges against Stalker. We will look at how they examined the quality and context of the Sampson inquiry in subsequent chapters.

There was a major difference between this part of the journalistic activity and that associated with that which depicted Stalker as the family man in the dark. Stalker himself, his family and his lawyers had been the sources of the line that he had not been told the nature of the allegations against him and that this was placing an unbearable strain on his family. The press had made it an issue by both reporting his complaints and by their own references to secrecy, lack of information and mystery as established reality. Politicians then acted to suspend Stalker as a response to this state of affairs, in order both to clarify the charges and speed up the investigation.

The attempt to identify the source of the original allegations and the relationship of this to what had happened in Northern Ireland originated, on the other hand, from a number of sources. The definition of these lines of inquiry as major issues came primarily from the journalists themselves and from politicians and other interested parties who either wanted to know the answers to questions or who thought they knew the answers and wanted them made public. The investigation of what Stalker was supposedly guilty of was also the outcome of inquiries by journalists, responses by contacts who knew parts of the answer or who had been interviewed by the Sampson team, and some unsolicited stories proffered by individuals who had issues of their own they wanted to graft on to the robust root stock of the Stalker affair, which had taken such a firm hold on the consciousness of the public.

When the Sampson report was finally and unlawfully made public, journalists then turned their attention to the nature of the report. It was hardly ever regarded by reporters as a source of information about Stalker, but was subjected to severe critical attack. The press responded to cues from Stalker and his representatives, and to comments from other people who claimed to have had their evidence misreported by Sampson. In this as in all the other coverage of the affair the press treatment led to the conclusion that Stalker was for all practical purposes not guilty of any serious wrongdoing, that he had been deliberately removed from Northern Ireland because he was getting too close to the truth and that the Sampson inquiry was a trumped-up affair.

Having considered how the press responded to the idea that the Sampson inquiry was an affront to Stalker and his family I will examine how they pursued five other lines of inquiry which were intended to discover:

(a)   what Stalker was accused of;
(b)   the contents and quality of the Sampson report;
(c)   how the inquiry was set up and who was behind the original complaint;
(d)   the nature of Stalker's Northern Ireland inquiries, what he had discovered and what had happened to his work there;
(e)   the identity of the Northern Ireland connection in the form of some character or characters who could be shown to have connected those with a desire to stop the shoot-to-kill inquiry with those who made the original complaint against Stalker in Manchester.

These inquiries were often going on together in the pursuit of single stories and often along with the notion of Stalker in the dark and the family under strain. In that the incremental effect of such inquiries gave the whole underlying affair a narrative sense, these themes could be seen to relate to one another rather in the manner of a political thriller.

And as we shall see this eventually manifested itself in Stalker's own book and the press's generally favourable critical response to it, which was often to compare it to a thriller. One headline referred to Stalker's 'edge of darkness,'[1] the title of a television thriller in which a detective happens on a malign plot involving the British government and the CIA in the suppression of opposition to nuclear policy, and is consequently the victim of a government plot to eliminate him. Although much of the time we seem to be comparing what the press reported with what 'actually happened' in given instances, this is not the central point. Being able to identify that, when a newspaper said Sampson was investigating some issue, this was the case does not mean the same thing as saying that the newspaper had discovered 'the truth'. This is because the press themselves were bent on the discovery of a truth other than the pure recounting of verifiable facts: they were searching for a truth behind the appearance of reality; they were searching for what they thought the government was hiding; and they were attempting to make sense of the affair. One of the ways to make sense of it was to be able tell a coherent story about it and the first requirement of such a story is that it should make narrative sense.

One of the ways to do this and to communicate it is to formulate the story in terms of known genres: the soap opera or the thriller, for instance. Such genres constitute a method for making sense of the world in writing and in reading news. This enables the journalist to write to stereotypical forms and they provide for the reader a familiar framework for grasping what is happening. The headline in the *Sunday Tribune* of 22 June 1986, 'The man who knew too much'[2] is exactly such a usage. The sub-editor is able to encapsulate a theory of the silencing of John Stalker and the reader instantly knows what is being said by reference to numerous scenes in gangster movies in which the words are used to presage the demise of a troublesome gang member who has betrayed the syndicate to the police. Eighteen months later *The Observer* sub-editor, presented with David Leigh's review of John Stalker's book *Stalker*, opted for the same construction of reality with the headline, 'The man who saw too much'.[3]

The search for the charges against Stalker

In examining the way in which the news story is constructed we have already seen how the press in the person of Paul

Horrocks of the *Manchester Evening News* began the process of unravelling the case against Stalker by identifying first the businessman Kevin Taylor and secondly the ex-policeman Stephen Hayes as allegedly undesirable social contacts of Stalker (see pages 57–65). In both of these stories the Manchester paper was scooping the others in being able to identify more accurately and sooner what the Sampson inquiry was looking for. The programme of the Sampson inquiry was the basis of the agenda within which the investigation of news was undertaken.

At the same time, and in the same vein, the *News of the World*, with information provided by Jimmy 'the Weed' Donnelly, was suggesting that the Stalker disciplinary offences related to his attendance at orgies which are a more or less daily feature of life of the middle-aged citizenry of Cottonopolis, This revelation took up two inside pages and was flagged on page one with a come-hither trailer 'Lynne's amazing story. Street Star and the accused top cop.' This was accompanied by a photograph of Lynne Perrie, a middle-aged actress who acts a character in the Granada TV soap opera *Coronation Street*. The story headlined 'Gangland guests saw street star's party piece with top cop' was tagged 'Exclusive, the story the others couldn't get'.[4] A further headline declared that what followed was the 'Inside story of the nighht that cast cloud over crime-buster Stalker'.

Another source of information was a woman who had previously had an interest in an allergy clinic in Manchester with Taylor, and who apparently approached both the press and the police with stories about parties and holidays involving Taylor and Stalker. She was Sylvia Foster, who had broken off her business relationship with Taylor two years previously and had fought a legal battle with him over the terms of the separation. The Sampson team interviewed her and claimed to have received two telephone calls from a woman caller whose voice they recognized as Foster's both when they interviewed her and when they compared a tape-recording of her voice with that of the telephone calls. The telephone calls involved allegations of wild living and moral turpitude. Foster was also interviewed by the *Manchester Evening News* about Taylor but the paper decided against publication on the basis that the claims she was making could not be proved and would be libellous if proved untrue.

Journalists also turned to known contacts in the police. In the case of local reporters such as Horrocks of the *Manchester Evening News* or Alan Hart who wrote for the *News of the World* this simply meant referring to officers with whom they already had long established contacts. Other reporters had to find such sources. This they did in part by reference to other journalists with experience in the area. *Guardian* and *Observer* reporters made contact with the *Manchester Evening News* and in particular Horrocks and Rob McLoughlin and Mike Nally who work for Granada TV. Such journalists who were working directly on the story for their current employers would not provide such working capital as the names or telephone numbers of clandestine news sources. Their help would be in the nature of briefings about background and the names of sources who were not particular to themselves. The *Washington Post* and other overseas newspapers obtained their information initially from the *Manchester Evening News*. The normal first port of call for a journalist in tackling a story in a news area other than his or her own is the local newspaper. This is part of the process by which information exchange takes place within the news media and by which professionals within the business collectively through normal work practices arrive at a negotiated version of reality.

But journalists live and work within a complex network of acquaintances and friends who are not numerous by comparison with the vast social landscape they attempt to describe. And in particular those who specialize in the investigative coverage of police and political secrecy are in a population which probably does not exceed double figures. Certainly, those who are writing for national newspapers and the national broadcast media on the underlying generalities of the nature of government and the powers and nature of the security services, rather than with the trivial details of the private lives of individuals, are no more than a small bar-full.

So, for instance, when the *Observer* team of Paul Lashmar, David Leigh and Jonathan Foster wanted to know the name of police officers in Manchester they were able to tap the local knowledge of Andrew Jennings, a London-based Granada TV researcher who had previously worked for many years in Manchester both on national dailies and on an alternative magazine, the now defunct *New Manchester Review*. Jennings and Lashmar had worked jointly on a number of stories including an exposure of corruption among Metropolitan police officers. And Jennings had no direct interest in the Stalker coverage which meant that divulging his sources would be of no direct disadvantage to himself. A *Guardian* reporter, David Rose, also made contact with a police contact through a similar means. A number of journalists in the city also provided information on a freelance basis to national newspapers.

Not all newspapers had the remarkable success of Paul Horrocks or that of the *Observer* team or the *Guardian* reporters in identifying what Sampson was looking at and the results of his inquiries. *The Sunday Times* in particular seemed able uniquely to get things wrong with unerring skill. Their first foray into error was a page one lead story by Chris Ryder, Barrie Penrose and David Connett on 8 June 1986, three days after Horrocks had already identified Stalker's friendship with Taylor as the main focus of the Sampson inquiry. The headline alleged 'Police Chief faces lavish hospitality charge', and the story began with the revelation that the deputy chief constable of Manchester was to be accused the following morning of accepting 'lavish hospitality from known criminals'. A later paragraph quoted 'one senior Whitehall official' to the effect that the accusations did not have 'an Irish dimension'. Rupert Murdoch's other Sunday paper, the *News of the World*, also produced the same line under the elegant headline 'Top cop faces quiz over "shady friends": "He was snapped".'[5] This report claimed that Stalker was to be 'accused of accepting lavish hospitality from known criminals, it is claimed today'. It referred to photographs which which police were 'said to have' showing Stalker with 'several shady characters'.

At no point in the Sampson report was there any allegation that Stalker had actually been charged with receiving lavish hospitality from anyone. He was questioned about who paid for his holiday with Taylor, but at that time Taylor had not even been charged with an offence. The *Sunday Times* reference to the Whitehall source, however, fits in with what other reporters have said about information purportedly coming from Home Office officials at the time. Unsolicited calls were received by

The Guardian from Home Office 'old boys' volunteering lurid accounts of what Stalker was to be charged with, none of which materialized except in the allegations of Foster and none of which was ever put to Stalker as a charge. At this stage at least there was clearly an attempt, either orchestrated or freelance, from Whitehall or from individuals in the police force to discredit by innuendo and to create a climate in which journalists would dig into Stalker's private life for tasty 'revelations'.

The *Sunday Times* story appeared two days later than a similar one in the *Daily Mail* which had also reported that John Stalker had received hospitality from a 'known criminal'.[6] This report itself had been denied in other papers both by Stalker and Taylor,[7] and, in any case, the *Sunday Times* story had appeared two days later than the Horrocks story based on his interview with Taylor, which identified Taylor as the main focus of the Sampson report and provided dates and places where the disputed activities had taken place.

This early period of journalistic searching for the cause of the Sampson inquiry was characterized by a number of similar stories which focused on the alleged delicts of Stalker which the Sampson team were investigating. The *News of the World* story based on information supplied by the Weed was probably the most stark example of this early tendency in the coverage of some of the less fastidious parts of the British press. Given its pre-eminence and the fact that it was examined by Sampson, it is worth examining what the story said and how it was said.

The two page *News of the World* story promised much in the headlines in terms of scandal, crime and sex without necessarily delivering any of these commodities in the body of the story. The report was alluringly flagged and headlined using the most outrageous exaggeration and double meanings. On page one the inside revelations were trailed, as indicated above by a photograph of the actress Lynne Perrie with the legend 'Lynne's amazing story. Street star and the accused top cop.' The headline on the inside story, 'Gangland guests saw street star's party piece with top cop. Inside story of the night that cast cloud over crime buster Stalker' appeared under the strapline 'Revealed: How that "damning" picture was taken of a villain and deputy chief constable.'

The cumulative effect of this advertisement of the story uses trigger words such as a 'star', 'crime', 'gangland' to create an impression of drama, danger and the sort of high living associated with the roaring 'twenties. The headline 'Gangland guests saw street star's party piece with top cop' suggests that the predominant character of the party guests was criminal while 'saw star's party piece with top cop' suggests that the 'party piece' was visual, that it was something newsy enough to record the fact that it was seen and therefore that it was either unusual in some way or risqué. Similarly 'Night I ended up in pool' suggests the possibility of some late Roman excess, especially when it appears in the same context as the crosshead 'Naked antics in a Jacuzzi'. These crossheadings all add to the expectation of titillation and drama: 'Naked antics in jacuzzi; Quizzed by police', and 'Sordid affair'.

But when we examine what appears in the text of the story we find that the whole affair was much more tame on a number of counts than we were led to believe. First, the 'party piece' in which Stalker was allegedly involved was that he played the piano while the motherly actress sang 'a string of old standards, including the ballad of Frankie and Johnny – one of Stalker's party pieces at police functions'. Second, the wild part of the 'wild party' all took place after Mr and Mrs Stalker left. And, third, it does not seem to have been wild, except perhaps judged by the standards of a Scottish Free Presbyterian pub crawl. Fourth, the basis for believing the story is James Donnelly.

Under the crosshead referring to 'Naked antics in the jacuzzi' we find that there were no actually naked people in the jacuzzi, merely 'almost naked': 'Later some of the guests at the wealthy businessman Kevin Taylor's home frolicked almost naked in the jacuzzi.'

The informant is introduced as 'gangland character Jimmy "the Weed" Donnelly, who broke his silence exclusively to the *News of the World*'. After declaring that the singing by Lynne Perrie accompanied by John Stalker was 'one of the highlights of the evening' (which does not say much for the frolicking as a spectacle) the Weed revealed: 'after the fuddy-duddies went home things really livened up and about ten of the guests ended up nearly naked in the jacuzzi'. Lest any readers should be over-whelmed by this less than gripping intelligence the *News of*

the World reporter Nick Pritchard is ready with a cold poultice
to cool their fevered brows and quotes the Weed further: 'But
John Stalker and his wife had left by then.' The clear and
unavoidable inference to be drawn from this revelation is that
both Stalker and his wife were fuddy–duddies and had left with
the others of their ilk.

The crosshead 'Quizzed by police' in fact refers to the Weed's
own question and answer session with members of the West
Yorkshire police who interrogated him about the murder by
shooting of a police sergeant in Leeds in late 1984. According
to Donnelly he was released after the police realized that he
knew nothing about the shooting. 'Sordid affair' was equally
a reference to the paper's informant and his relationship to
crime and to the police and a claim that he was at the centre
of 'this whole sordid affair'. This followed the admission that
he had also been questioned about a kidnapping and did have
a criminal record. He added, however, 'No way am I a well
known criminal, yet that's what the police are basing it all on.'
Donnelly was presumably objecting to the notion that he was
well known. The headline 'Night I ended up in the pool, by
Lynne' was no less disappointing. The first paragraph disclosed
that she was fully dressed when the incident occurred. The rest
of the story recounted that she might have had a drop to drink,
that she subsequently changed into a swimming costume, had
not known that her piano accompanist was Stalker and did not
know if he was a good pianist.

Taylor was quoted as admitting that he had 'some tasty
friends' and claimed that he and Stalker were victims of MI5's
dirty tricks department. This quotation was the penultimate
paragraph of the main story. The final one was Stalker's own
refusal to comment until he knew what he was supposed to
have done.

In summary this story revealed that at some time in the past
Stalker had been to a party at Taylor's house where he had
played the piano while a well-known TV actress had sung a
number of perfectly respectable songs to an audience of 150
guests many of whom were fuddy-duddies, who left early along
with Mr and Mrs Stalker. Later on about ten people, who were
not naked, disported themselves in a jacuzzi and the actress fell
or was pushed fully dressed into a swimming pool where she

later bathed in a swimming costume. The story also referred
to two photographs which had been taken at the party one
of which allegedly featured Donnelly along with the Stalkers
while the other depicted Stephen Hayes. But this had already
been revealed in the previous day's *Manchester Evening News*.[8]
The line that Taylor claimed that he and Stalker were victims of
an MI5 dirty tricks campaign was relegated to a place lower in
order of importance than his reference to the fact that some of
his friends were 'tasty'.

Although this story is largely both trivial and farcical it is
possible to see it as part of a smear campaign against Stalker.
Certainly, the whole tone of the headlines and the trailing of the
story on the front page is suggestive of the idea that Stalker was
part of Manchester's criminal social high life, despite the fact
that this is not borne out by the text of the story and that the
events at the party would certainly not qualify for any excited
comment at breakfast during an academic conference. This story
simply enlarges on the earlier story by *The Sunday Times* of the
previous week claiming that the charges against Stalker were
that he had received lavish hospitality from known criminals.
The fact that this line of coverage came from the two Sundays
owned by Rupert Murdoch and that Home Office callers were
volunteering damaging claims about Stalker to the press might
suggest that there was a government-inspired conspiracy against
Stalker to which the Murdoch papers were party.

This is, however, not borne out by the evidence, since stories
subsequently appeared in both papers which were favourable
to the Stalker side of the case. The *News of the World* itself,
in a report a week after the wild party story, suggested that
Stalker was a victim of a plot by Freemasons,[9] which we will
examine below, And by 10 August the *Sunday Times* team was
incorrectly reporting that Stalker had been told unofficially that
the Sampson inquiry would clear him of any breach of police
discipline. The paper claimed that the investigation into Stalker's
conduct could be traced back to a minor and apparently trivial
incident in 1983.[10]

This apparently concerned Taylor and the convicted Hayes
and involved the repossession of a Vauxhall Nova car by Hayes
and an assistant acting as Taylor's agent. The car was in the
possession of Ms Kim Berry, who worked for the Manchester

Conservative Association and used the car as part of her work. She had left her job as a result of a dispute with Taylor and held the car in lieu of wages which she claimed were owed to her. Hayes's repossession of the vehicle was alleged to have involved unnecessary violence.[11]

Far from this incident being pivotal to the Sampson inquiry as the *Sunday Times* reporters suggested, it was only mentioned in the Sampson report as part of the background information on Taylor and his associates and was written up without any reference to Stalker, who was not involved in the matter at all. It involved six paragraphs out of the total of 460. Equally, the Sampson report did not vindicate Stalker: it recommended that he should face a tribunal charged with ten disciplinary offences, and Stalker himself denied that he had ever been told he was to be vindicated.[12] The other Murdoch Sunday newspaper, the *News of the World*, simply followed the same line and quoted the *Sunday Times* story that John Stalker was to be cleared by the Sampson inquiry and would return to work. Although this story could not be described as accurate in any meaningful respect equally it could not be regarded as part of a government inspired smear campaign, first, because it reinforced the impression that Stalker was innocent and, second, because it was wrong. No self-respecting smearer would inspire a fictitious vindication of his or her own victim.

Despite Stalker's own denials of any knowledge of his vin-dication by Sampson the *Sunday Times* news team did not acknowledge that it had erred. Far from it, the following week, in their issue of 17 August they claimed credit for having exclusively revealed that Stalker was to be vindicated and simply referred to the affair as if they had been correct all along. The writer of the Atticus diary column did, however, refer to the fact that Stalker had denied any knowledge that he was to be cleared, but in their Stalker coverage in the same issue as the Atticus disclaimer Penrose and Connett simply commented: 'As we disclosed last week, the 1,500 page report, which has now been delivered to the Manchester Police Authority clears Stalker of serious impropriety.' But the main thrust of this new venture into inexactitude, entitled 'Hot money link in Stalker report', was the claim that the Sampson team had undertaken an inquiry into the activities of Stanley Nin, an associate of Taylor, and

that 'What they discovered is one of the key parts of the report.'
The reporters claimed,

> We can now reveal, that a significant part of the report into
> John Stalker, Manchester Deputy Chief Constable, concerned
> the activities of a leading Manchester Tory and a Midlands-
> based charity used to launder hot money from around the
> world. The activities of this charity were exposed by *The
> Sunday Times* earlier this year.'

The detectives 'explored the activities of Stanley Nin, a financial
consultant and a former treasurer of the Manchester Conservative Association', they said, claiming that Nin was brought
into Manchester circles by Taylor. The lengthy report which
followed was then devoted entirely to the activities of Stanley
Nin, and within it was displayed a 'ragout' of a headline of a
previous revelation on the same story – 'British charity used
to launder "hot" money for Marcos'.[13]
The rest of the story made no reference to Stalker, and only
contained one reference to Taylor to the effect that Nin had
arranged some insurance and a house mortgage for him. The
only direct reference to the Stalker affair was a correction to
their previous week's story on Hayes when they had wrongly
stated that he had served a prison sentence. The whole re-hash
of a previous investigation relied on the original claim that Nin's
financial dealings were part of the 'ramifications' of the Stalker
affair. In fact Nin made only a brief appearance in the Sampson
report into the Stalker affair.
His contribution to the drama could hardly have been less
significant. He was only called in evidence as part of the section
on the Manchester Conservative Association and the report says
of him:

> Stanley Nin is a Financial Management Consultant who first
> met Kevin Taylor in 1981, but it was sometime later that he
> assisted him in some financial arrangements. The successful
> completion of their arrangements led Mr. Taylor to persuade
> Mr. Nin to take the post of Treasurer of the Manchester
> Conservative Association. Mr. Nin held the position for two
> years, i.e. until the Association folded. Although he attended

a number of Conservative Balls Mr. Nin did not meet Mr. Stalker.

This is the entire reference to Stanley Nin in the report summary by Sampson to the GMPA.

The Sunday Times was unique in falsely identifying the thrust of the Sampson inquiry, but there is certainly no consistent evidence that it was engaged in a systematic smear of Stalker. The apparent smearing which took place early in the press's attempt to find out what the Sampson team were looking for in Stalker's private life arose precisely from the nature of this search. The agenda that had been set was that of the inquiry initiated by Anderton and Her Majesty's Inspectorate of Constabulary, and this was based on the proposition that Stalker had been behaving in a way which raised the possibility of a disciplinary offence having been committed. It was thus inevitable that any inquiry following this assumption would focus on Stalker's behaviour in such a way that would call it into question – even if it were merely that of playing the piano and leaving with the fuddy-duddies.

Some days after the fuddy-duddy revelations in the *News of the World* this agenda was still focusing attention on Stalker's possible past lapses of behaviour as the subject of news. On 26 June the PCA issued a statement saying that the charges against him were of sufficient substance to warrant 'further careful investigation'. This was based on an interim report into the affair by Sampson and said that 'if proved to the required standard these allegations are capable of amounting to the disciplinary offence of bringing discredit upon the force'.

The following day the press reported this statement. A short story in *The Daily Telegraph*, which was headlined 'Stalker may face discredit charge' was a summary of the PCA statement and a brief résumé of the Stalker affair to that date, referring to his suspension, the Northern Ireland inquiry, his friendship with Taylor, his criticism of the Sampson inquiry's failure to tell him of the charges involved. As in all newspaper reports, however short, it also mentioned Stalker's age, forty-seven, and Taylor's, fifty-four.[14] The *Daily Mirror* of the same day focused in its intro more clearly on the possible reasons for the inquiry continuing. Under the headline 'Police chief probe "won't be dropped"' the story began, 'The probe into police chief John Stalker's friendship with a wealthy Tory is to continue.'

Having thus taken as the angle of the story questions about Stalker's behaviour in relation to his friendship with Taylor the story continued:

> The independent Police Complaints Authority decided last night that there were grounds for 'further careful investigation'.
>
> They added that if proved they could lead to a disciplinary offence of 'bringing discredit on the force'.
>
> Mr. Stalker, 47, was removed from a controversial inquiry into the Royal Ulster Constabulary's policy on terrorists four weeks ago.
>
> It was claimed that he associated with known criminals.[15]

Both newspapers had accepted the frame of reference laid down in the PCA handout as the basis for the story's angle. The *Daily Mirror* had dramatized the statement and in doing so had brought into sharper focus the issue of the allegation of associating with known criminals and the friendship with Taylor. Both, however, had included the information about Northern Ireland and some form of rebuttal of the allegations. In the *Daily Mirror* story this took the form, first, of a reference to a speech by Liberal MP Alex Carlisle who said in the Commons that Stalker had been suspended after urging the prosecution of senior RUC officers, and, second, by reference to Stalker's claim that he had been kept in the dark about the charges against him.

In both stories, this Stalker version of events was relegated to the lower part of the text where it was merely a context for the main angle. In this sense they resemble the normal crime story in which the charges and prosecution case take precedence and the form of this prosecution case lays down the agenda for the coverage of the story so long as the story remains based on the coverage of court proceedings or police activities, which in almost all cases it does.

But these were the last significant stories in the press which were based on information initiatives from the authorities where such information formed the accepted framework of news. Thereafter the press adopted as its agenda the examination of the reasons for Stalker's removal from duty not in his behaviour but in the desire of others to stop his inquiry in Northern Ireland. In so doing they accepted the picture of him as an innocent man going honestly about his work as a policeman.

The fact that the press began to examine different issues was due to a number of causes. As I suggested earlier, the normal agenda setting order for the depiction of deviance in the press was reversed. Stalker himself and his legal advisers mounted a coherent and purposeful press campaign to put across his own case, while the authorities remained silent. So the normal agenda setting process, in which those accused of deviance by the authorities have the issues decided for them did not operate. But there were other causes, arising from both the political culture and the work practices of journalists.

Let us first look to the general political culture. It is probably true that the 'normal' assumptions about politics encapsulated in news coverage and current events debates can be summarized as a consensus model of authority in which the reasonable citizen behaves in an orderly and legal way and in which the institutions of the state are benevolent and representative. These assumptions stress the notion of order and marginalize those groups which threaten that order. But it does not follow that this dominant paradigm excludes all others. In order to understand why not we need to examine what we mean by dominance in relation to an ideological formulation.

In the way in which news is structured journalists make assumptions about the meaning of the world in terms of a number of considerations which are ad hoc in terms of their purposes at hand. For instance, the policy of the news organization for which they work will influence what they see and what they say. Those newspapers owned by right-wing proprietors produce a remarkably predictable account of industrial disputes, of Northern Ireland affairs, of the activities of Labour councils' policies. It is clearly possible to attribute such dominance to the brute power of ownership. It is also possible to show, as Phillip Schlesinger does in his study of BBC news and current affairs production, that the organizations' news policies of impartiality and balance are internalized by journalists and also influence a process of self-selection and organizational selection in recruitment.[16]

But even if there were no direction from owners or from management in the way that journalists structure the world they describe, they would still have to undertake this process simply in order to produce news. And the way they would do it would be to appeal to some common-sense notions on the part of readers by which stories would be located in their assumptions about the world and in the way they make sense of the world. In this sense an ideological structuring of the political world may be dominant simply in the sense that it is most widely available as a means of interpreting versions of events. Such a formulation might be that of male dominance. In this respect we may have a news story which is favourable to workers on low pay because they are not paid enough to keep 'a wife and children'. The use of the paradigm of the credible male as responsible and effective enables the teller of the story and the audience to give it meaning. Such a depiction may fit in with a dominant view of gender that is shared or promulgated by the owners of capital in general or the proprietor of a given newspaper in particular, but its use in a given story does not necessarily derive from such causes. It may simply be called on ad hoc as a way of explaining some depicted state of affairs in terms which will have significance for the audience as perceived by the journalist. In this sense it is necessary to see the way in which a story is structured as contingent on its context.

It is also necessary to understand that an analysis of what a sociologist may define as the dominant ideology does not constitute an exhaustive account of the framework within which journalists and others concerned with producing accounts of reality operate. Not the least of the weaknesses of such an approach is that it makes it difficult to provide an account of how the Glasgow Media Group or the Birmingham Centre for Cultural Studies, for instance, ever came to produce accounts which are themselves a critical analysis of such dominance. Thus, even if we might agree that some version of events in general constituted a dominant ideology, unless it were the only one available it would be necessary to know how and when such an ideology was relevant and when not, how it might be modified and under what circumstances and what other ideologies were available as part of the means of making sense of the world.

We would also need to have a clear definition of what we meant by ideology, because a number of factors, as has been suggested above, also play a part in the construction of news, such as the necessity of making narrative sense, the process of narrative simplification and the ready reference to fictional genres which are familiar to readers as a means of enabling them to make sense of stories. The view taken here is that ideology refers to ways of constructing and evaluating the social world that relate to the justification of the exercise of power. This may be concerned with macroscopic explanations of economic and political power or the lack of it. Or it may be to do with accounts of work practices and their justification as technical competence. In this sense it seems that a number of factors which are relevant to the production of news are only ideological in the most attenuated use of the term.

The question of why the press opted for an explanation of Stalker's removal from duty which challenged a view of the authorities as benevolent, law-abiding, honest and representative is however central to the notion of ideology. The explanation relates to the existence and availability of other ideological formulations than the 'dominant' capitalist view of the world. It also relates to the work practices of journalists, the social context of those practices and to the way they make sense of the world. Let us examine both of these sets of considerations.

The suspension of John Stalker took place in Manchester, which has a more overwhelming Labour vote than Scotland. The dominant political organizations in Manchester are Labour, and the opposition is fragmented between the centre parties and the Conservatives. The main local press tends to reflect this situation. The *Manchester Evening News*, although still often vilified by those on the left as a pro-Tory paper, has changed greatly since the 1960s when it was edited by Tom Henry, a traditional Roman Catholic who supported hanging and was sympathetic to the Franco regime in Spain. The paper constantly criticizes the Thatcher government, gives prominence to such issues as the National Health Service and opposes hanging. New initiatives by the Labour-controlled council to renovate the city centre are well-publicized in the news columns. The paper is owned by Northern Newspapers who also publish *The Guardian*. The same company also produces a weekly free sheet, *Metro News*, in which Labour and trades union news, and issues to do with the threat of nuclear war enjoy considerable prominence. It has now taken over the local alternative magazine, *City Life*, which has become primarily an arts and listings magazine, but could not be regarded in any way as a bastion of the right.

The city council had also instituted a Police Monitoring Committee which operated a unit of researchers and journalists who produced a monthly magazine, *Police Watch*. The unit had undertaken extensive work on the 'Battle of Brittan' campaign and similarly examined the Stalker affair. On a number of occasions they were prime sources of information in generating news stories. They were also routinely contacted by journalists seeking information on the Stalker affair. The Chairman of the Police Monitoring Committee at the time was Councillor Tony McCardell who was also a member of the GMPA where he was a focus of much of the criticism of the Chief Constable, James Anderton.

The issue which Stalker had been concerned with in Northern Ireland had equally occurred in a context in which a number of competing ideological constructions were constantly being canvassed as ways of making sense of events. And while it is true that the press did not seek the opinions of IRA spokesmen or those of Sinn Fein, the Social Democratic and Labour Party (SDLP) MPs in Westminster, in particular Seamus Mallon, were frequently referred to. Mallon made it clear from the outset that he considered that 'sinister forces' were behind Stalker's removal from the Northern Ireland shoot-to-kill inquiry.

This meant that there were available for journalists examining the story alternatives to the agenda for inquiry set down by the authorities in the remit of the Sampson inquiry. This ideological background of speculation was also available to Stalker and his solicitor Roger Pannone in their media campaign to vindicate the Deputy Chief Constable. It meant that if journalists raised questions at press conferences suggesting that Stalker was a victim of a plot to cover up malpractice in the RUC he could simply refrain from contradicting them.

There were in fact a variety of available alternative explanations of the Stalker affair which emerged as the debate developed.

The Marxist and radical left version was that it was a mistake to regard Stalker as a saint who had been traduced by the system. Martin Lee, writing in *The Militant*, explained why the Tories were 'gunning for Stalker'. Stalker, he alleged, had refused to whitewash the RUC, but averred that 'we' should have no truck with this 'honest cop' nonsense. Stalker, Lee told his readers, was the person who was responsible for refusing to do anything about tracing the two police officers who had allegedly 'hounded two students in Manchester for 18 months', a reference to the 'Battle of Brittan' incidents.[17]

Graham Stringer, now leader of the controlling Labour group on Manchester City Council, writing in the February 1987 issue of *New Socialist*, ridiculed Stalker's canonization: 'As Greater Manchester's Chief Constable, James Anderton, prepared to join the Roman Catholic Church, his deputy, John Stalker, went one better. He became a saint, canonised by the media politicians and pundits.' Stringer attempted to locate the issue not in terms of an individual wrongdoing but 'within a political perspective'.[18]

In doing so Stringer related the point made earlier in this book that Stalker had previously been a publicly loyal police officer and a fully paid up subscriber to conventional ideology to the political nature of modern policing.

His friendship with Manchester businessman, Kevin Taylor, was ill-advised. Taylor hasn't a criminal record, but his circle of personal friends was not ideal company for a senior police officer. More disturbing is the arrogance of senior police officers who, like Stalker, attend money-raising functions for the Conservative Party. And attend them in an official capacity with absolute impunity. This kind of 'acceptable' behaviour demonstrates the transparency of the claim that the police are politically neutral. Can anyone imagine any chief constable anywhere attending a fund-raising function for the disqualified Lambeth councillors?

Stringer related this behaviour to the lack of democratic control over chief police officers in the 1964 Police Act, which precluded control over police policy by police authorities and reduced democratic control by the introduction of appointed magistrates as members. A statement by Anderton on BBC TV, he argued, encapsulated this:

> From a police point of view, my task in the future . . . basic crime such as theft, burglary, even violent crime, will not be the predominant police feature. What will be the matter of greatest concern to me will be the covert and ultimately overt attempts to overthrow democracy, to subvert the authority of the state and, in fact, to involve themselves in acts of sedition designed to destroy our parliamentary system and the democratic government of this country. (BBC's *Question Time*, 16 October 1979)

This formulation of the police role mainly in the political field was redefined by Stringer as 'the police protect the state and are in turn protected by the state'. This analysis applied to the Stalker affair explained the shoot-to-kill inquiry being set up by reference to the British government's attempt to 'appease Dublin in the run-up to the Anglo-Irish agreement' while that same Anglo-Irish agreement accounted for his removal from the inquiry:

> Two years later, faced with the hostility of the Paisley-led Protestant community to the agreement, the last thing the British government needed was a report which revealed the activities of counter-insurgency units engaged in cross-border operations and killing 'terrorists'.

Stalker was removed either because the government 'hurriedly conspired' against him to prevent him finding the bug, or alternatively his 'domestic enemies' in the Manchester police used his two-year absence from base to finish his career.

The central contradiction of the left position was that while it argued it was wrong to regard Stalker as a saint, they still credited him with the extraordinary strength of mind and moral purpose to stand out against the pressure from those who wanted a whitewash and to carry out a thorough investigation of the RUC killings and associated matters. However they might resist the notion, the exponents of the left arguments were still left with Stalker as at least the 'honest cop' if their arguments were to hold up.

Other positions taken up by politicians across the spectrum tended in the final analysis to accept that Stalker had been silenced and discredited as a result of a conspiracy. They took the cue from Mallon's 'sinister forces' formulation, and tended not to identify the source of the conspiracy. Cecil Franks, the Conservative MP for Barrow and a former Manchester City Council Tory group leader, on a number of occasions went as far as to identify 'the establishment' as being responsible for Stalker's removal. At the October conferences of the opposition parties there were numerous calls for answers to questions which were raised by the affair, and repeated allegations that Stalker had been silenced by some part of the government system.

Unlike the Marxist and radical left these political voices were unstinting in their praise for Stalker, and were happy to subscribe to the idea that he was an honourable man, a superb detective and a family man who had been brought low by his devotion to duty. The advocates of this view did not attempt to address the question of Taylor and his tasty friends in the official agenda, any more than the radical and Marxist left could account for the problem that if Stalker were not unusually honourable in some way as a person why had he not simply succumbed to pressure and given up his search and performed the requisite whitewash. In Chapter 7 we shall examine how the work practices of journalists, when combined with these available ideological constructions, produced an examination of the nature of the Sampson report and an analysis of how the Stalker affair arose in the first place. In doing so we will confront a remarkable uniformity of view across the political spectrum which involves a conception of the state, or at least some of its well-placed agents, as the source of a conspiracy to pervert the course of justice and in doing so to destroy the reputation of an honest man.

CHAPTER SEVEN

Investigating the investigators

Journalistic investigation of the shortcomings of the Sampson report and of the relationship between the allegations of disciplinary offences by Stalker, the Northern Ireland investigation and the circumstances under which the Sampson inquiry was set up were inextricably interwoven. A major aspect of the implicit explanation which underlay much of the journalistic coverage of these matters was that a single cause underlay the answers to all these issues, and accounted for the plight of Stalker as the man in the dark and the stress on his family. In order to see how the press explained these complex issues we need to disaggregate the issues and examine how each was dealt with before examining how they were then reassembled into an overarching theory.

In the last chapter I suggested that the press followed five lines of inquiry in their follow up of the Sampson inquiry which were intended to discover:

(a) what John Stalker was accused of;
(b) the contents and the quality of the Sampson report;
(c) how the inquiry was set up and who was involved;
(d) the nature of Stalker's inquiries in Northern Ireland, what he discovered and what had happened to his work there;
(e) the connection between the Northern Ireland affair and the investigation of John Stalker's private life in Manchester.

The issue of what Stalker was accused of was the first issue addressed by the media, but the possibility of relating this issue to events in Northern Ireland was a hare which began to run also from very early in the affair. The journalists then began to seek the connection and for more information about who set up the Sampson inquiry and how they went about it, and pursued this along with the related question of the Northern Ireland–Manchester nexus. All the themes raised continued in four-part harmony, until the unintended publication of the Sampson report led to the fifth theme, the examination of the contents of this document, which I will examine in the next chapter.

The issue of the relationship between Stalker's removal from duty and his inquiries in Northern Ireland was raised within days of the announcement of his extended leave on 30 May. By 2 June John Alley in the *Daily Express* was reporting that Stalker had been involved in serious rifts with the RUC Chief Constable, Sir John Hermon, that he had completed his interim report on the RUC inquiry and had already sent it to the DPP and was due to begin the second stage of the Northern Ireland inquiry when he was told to take time off. Alley quoted an unnamed source 'close to the row' as saying, 'Someone wants him off the investigation for their own reasons. It's all become a bit sinister.'[1]

On the same day the *Manchester Evening News* ran a story which opened up the issue of the inquiry in a way which other papers did not take up for another fortnight. A short report without a by-line on page four, in fact written by the editor Mike Unger and headlined 'Stalker dropped from probe team', identified the crux of the inquiry dispute in the revelation that it was expected that charges were to be brought against at least four senior RUC officers by Stalker on his return to the province. The story also revealed that the 'controversial Ulster report' centred on three incidents which concerned secret operations by an RUC group known as E4A. The details of the incidents, which had been investigated over sixteen months, had 'rocked the RUC'. The article said that claims had been investigated that senior RUC men drafted a cover story to conceal events leading up to six deaths.[2]

Two days later the *Manchester Evening News* carried a long news feature by Ian Craig. Unger was also heavily involved in writing and providing the background to this article, since his decision to begin the process of revelation was a major act of policy by the newspaper, which could have had repercussions especially for a local paper, whose journalists have to deal with local police spokesmen on a continuing basis as part of the normal news producing process. The article asked whether Stalker's move from accuser to accused which had caused 'deep suspicions in many quarters' meant that he had been the victim of an establishment attempt to gag him. It went on: 'Whatever emerges from Mr. Sampson's inquiry, the effect has been to shelve Mr. Stalker's damning report on Ulster's alleged "shoot to kill" policy. The report on the shooting of six unarmed terrorist suspects by RUC marksmen is believed to recommend the prosecution of several top RUC officers.'[3]

Un-named police sources in Manchester were prepared to say off-the-record early on that they suspected that Stalker's de facto suspension was associated with his having got too close to the truth in Northern Ireland, and the *Daily Express* report typified the sort of coverage given to these allegations. The *Manchester Evening News* from this early stage manifested a detailed knowledge of the nature of the Stalker inquiry in Northern Ireland which came from the specific knowledge which the editor had acquired. (We will examine how he acquired this knowledge later (pages 212–13).) But another source of information became available in the shape of MPs who used the established institution of the House of Commons and the conventional accessibility of the MP as a news spokesman to give credence to the plot theory as an explanation of Stalker's removal from the Northern Ireland inquiry. Mr Seamus Mallon, the leader of the SDLP in Parliament, let it be known that he would question the Prime Minister in the Commons about the 'coincidence' between the charges being brought against Stalker at the point where he was about to bring his inquiry in Northern Ireland to a crucial stage.

The Ian Craig article in the *Manchester Evening News* reported that 'one Northern Ireland MP, Mr. Seamus Mallon' intended to ask the Prime Minister if she agreed that it was 'highly coincidental' that Stalker should be forced to take leave of absence while charges against him were investigated. Mallon was quoted from an interview in which he linked the inquiry into Stalker's personal life to the devastating effect his inquiry might have in Northern Ireland. He said he had no evidence of any link between the controversial RUC report and the allegations against Stalker but added that 'every instinct in my body tells me there is'. The article also revealed that Mallon had been questioned by the Stalker team and had been impressed by their professionalism and their respect for the law and for people.[4]

The press reported his questions and statements in Parliament but also trailed them with stories that he was going to ask questions along with quotations from interviews with him. Mallon, the Roman Catholic SDLP MP for the Newry and Armagh constituency in which the three shooting incidents took place, was widely quoted in the press without being labelled as militant or republican or anti-police. And by the second week of June the issue of what had happened in the course of the Northern Ireland inquiry had become established as a major issue in understanding the Stalker affair. Paul Johnson, in *The Guardian* of 9 June, referring to the charges against Stalker, wrote: 'The claim [that Stalker had accepted questionable hospitality] was being dismissed by those who know Mr. Stalker and fear that attempts are being made to smear his name and reputation.' He added with extraordinary certitude: 'Whatever the exact case against him, it seems certain that RUC officers have played a part. Forces in Northern Ireland have confirmed that at least some of the information on which the inquiry is based came originally from the province.'

Johnson referred to Mallon's belief that there had been deliberate attempts to get Stalker's report quashed, and then went on to outline what was thought to be in the Stalker report. The information could only have come from someone who had had sight of the report or was a member of the investigating team. The reporter claimed that Stalker believed that there was sufficient evidence to bring seven officers to trial on charges ranging from attempting to pervert the course of justice to conspiracy to murder. Among the officers were a superintendent and a chief inspector, Johnson claimed.

He then went on to explain what Stalker's report meant in the context of Northern Ireland. He wrote that the proposal to charge officers with crimes had angered 'some senior elements in the RUC' because Stalker refused to understand or appreciate the difficulties of fighting republican paramilitaries. Two serious consequences would follow if the DPP decided on the basis of the interim report to prosecute, he argued. First, loyalist politicians could be expected to extract the maximum advantage, exploiting discontent among the RUC ranks and blaming Dublin for the prosecutions. Second, any consequent court cases would reveal the activities of undercover security operations, including cross-border incursions into the Irish Republic, the covert role of British Army intelligence, and the activities of E4A, the RUC deep surveillance team. And, he argued, it would call into question the policy decision to set up the police unit which carried out the shootings.

The underlying inference, bearing in mind the reference earlier in the article to the suggestion that Stalker had been subject to a smear campaign, was clear. The Stalker report would be an embarrassment to the government and needed to be rubbished. Johnson wrote: 'At a time when the situation in Northern Ireland is delicately balanced with slow progress of the Anglo-Irish deal it would be in the interests of many people that the Stalker report be allowed to gather dust or simply be not acted on.' After summarizing the circumstances in which the five IRA and INLA members and Michael Tighe were killed Johnson concluded his article: 'Sir John Hermon, chief constable of the RUC has always vigorously defended police tactics. However, last year the Armagh coroner, Mr. Gerry Curran, resigned over what he called grave irregularities in the police files on some of the killings and the inquests have yet to be held.'[5]

The implication of the article was clear: that Stalker was being smeared in order to stifle his inquiry. The strapline 'Shoot-to-kill prosecutions would pose serious problems for politicians' and the headline 'RUC men linked to Stalker claims' made this clear. A week later Johnson and Peter Murtagh further examined the relationship between the Northern Ireland inquiry and the allegations of misconduct by Stalker. In a front page story, in which the most crucial information was from Stalker or a police source in sympathy with him, Murtagh revealed that prior to the announcement of his removal from duties the RUC had attempted to block the inquiry by preventing him from returning to Northern Ireland.

Murtagh revealed that Stalker had planned to concentrate on the killing of Tighe, the seventeen-year-old who was killed in November 1982 and who had no connections with any paramilitary organization. Stalker had already concluded that at least one officer among the higher echelons of the RUC might have to face charges of conspiracy to pervert the course of justice. 'After Mr. Stalker expressed a determination to carry on his investigation and insisted that he would return to Northern Ireland, the moves which resulted in his effective suspension from duty four days before he planned to arrive in Belfast came to a head.'[6]

Had Stalker gone back to Belfast, the story went on, he had intended to confront Sir John Hermon about certain 'evidential matters' which 'according to sources' related to officers of a very senior rank. This was a reference to the transcript of the tape-recording of the bugged sounds of the shootings of the two youths in the barn, but no one had yet revealed that such a tape had existed. 'Stalker's team finally obtained the information early last March. When it was first requested Sir John refused but the Northern Ireland Director of Public Prosecutions, Sir Barry Shaw, ordered that it be handed over.'

Murtagh then went on to indicate the involvement of the government in the shape of the security services in the events surrounding the shooting of Tighe which by implication meant that they also had a motive for wanting the Stalker inquiry stopped:

According to some sources close to the investigation, Stalker's team believed that MI5 was involved, actively or as a back-up surveillance unit, when Michael Tighe was killed. In the course of their inquiries the team concluded that the intelligence service had become deeply involved in many aspects of security in Northern Ireland.

After a short biographical summary of Stalker's career there then followed a section of the story in which new and detailed information on the inquiry was made public for the first time including, most startlingly, the names of two of the senior officers against whom Stalker wanted disciplinary action initiated:

His brief was to investigate the killing of Tighe and the wounding in the same incident of Martin McCauley, the killing of the three IRA men, Gervais McKerr, Eugene Toman and Sean Burns, at a road block near Lurgan in County

Armagh on November 11 1982 and the killing of two INLA men, Seamus Grew and Roddy Carroll, who were shot dead in Armagh on December 12.

Tighe had no criminal record and was not known to have links with paramilitary organisations. The RUC branch had no intelligence file on him. He was shot in the chest at point blank range. Each of the incidents involved members of special squads, the Mobile Support Unit, commanded from RUC headquarters in Belfast, and E4A, a covert surveillance unit.

Both were established in such a way that their command structures led rapidly to officers at senior rank in RUC head-quarters.

Part of Mr. Stalker's brief was also to examine the structure of the system of operational command within the RUC.

The attempt to deny the Stalker team access to information, which was resolved by the intervention of the DPP was only one of a number of similar incidents which illustrated to members of the team their efforts were not welcome

Not long after he began his investigation in 1984, Mr. Stalker threatened to resign from the task because of the lack of co-operation from the RUC.

In April 1985, Mr. Stalker asked that two officers in the Special Branch, Superintendent George Anderson and a Chief Inspector Flannagan, be suspended while inquiries were made. Sir John refused, and Mr. Flannagan has since been promoted to superintendent.

Twice when Mr. Stalker booked flights and hotel accommodation to return to Belfast this year he was persuaded not to by RUC headquarters. He was given various excuses to the effect that it was not convenient or that certain officers he wished to interview would not be available.

The story then linked this chain of events to Stalker's own suspension. Murtagh reported that when a third attempt was made to return to Belfast 'efforts were made to prevent him. Nonetheless, he insisted that he would arrive on June 2 but on May 30 the announcement was made that he himself was under investigation.' The RUC were asked to comment but a spokesman declined because the investigation by Stalker's team was continuing.[7]

On the main feature page in the same issue of *The Guardian* Johnson and Murtagh developed further their analysis of the relationship between the Northern Ireland inquiry and the allegations of misconduct against Stalker in Manchester. In doing so they put together the framework of an explanation of events which eventually became the received wisdom of most of the British press. Murtagh's feature was entitled simply 'Stalker's RUC inquiry', and Johnson's 'Killings that put public gaze on covert security'. They went into some detail in their description of the killings Stalker had been investigating, and in their account of the opposition he encountered from the RUC and other security forces in Northern Ireland. Murtagh also outlined the disciplinary charges against Stalker and raised a new issue – Anderton's role in setting up the Sampson inquiry.

In the front page story the implication was clearly conveyed that Stalker's removal from the Northern Ireland inquiry was explained by the desire of the RUC top brass to be rid of him. The refusal of Hermon to suspend the two officers and the subsequent promotion of Flannagan were quoted to show how the inquiry was baulked. In the longer inside features the general picture of distrust was further reinforced with details from 'sources' about the nature of Stalker's inquiry, and at the same time the questions were raised of how the allegations against Stalker were made and how the investigation of his behaviour was set up. This was again done in the context of seeking explanations in terms of both the aims of the Northern Irish establishment and of the policy needs of the British government.

Murtagh's article began by depicting the intensity of the lack of trust between the RUC and Stalker, by means of a description of the interim report he submitted to Hermon in September 1985. Instead of the separate pages being held together in a spiral binder they were bound as a book with the pages numbered, so that there could be no tampering between the submission of the report to the RUC chief constable and its submission to the Northern Ireland DPP Sir Barry Shaw, Murtagh explained. The bound covers bore the report's title in gold lettering, including the word 'interim', Murtagh reported. This description conveyed the level of distrust, it raised the possibility that the report might have been tampered with by officers in the RUC, and it showed that this report had been seen by Murtagh and was interim, not complete. This point was important, as we shall see.

The article went on to say that Hermon had insisted, as was his right, that the DPP's copy of the report should be given to him as chief constable to be passed on to the DPP rather than it being given directly. 'Sources say that Mr. Stalker thought it rather unusual', but this was perhaps not surprising since the report recommended prosecution of several RUC officers and contained serious criticisms of the way the force was organized and structured – namely, that due to the rapid expansion of manpower in the 1970s many senior officers had been over-promoted and had asked lower ranks to undertake duties which would not be acceptable in the rest of the UK, and 'that when those officers were exposed to court proceedings their superiors had not stood by them'.

The bulk of the report, said Murtagh, concentrated on the killings in November and December of 1982, referred to above, and recommended that charges of conspiracy to pervert the course of justice and conspiracy to murder should be laid against other police officers than those who were tried and acquitted of murder.

The article then began to articulate an explanation of the affair in which the way Stalker had been blocked in his investigation of the six RUC killings was related to his being removed from duty in Manchester. The factual account went as follows.

John Stalker was appointed to investigate the killings in Northern Ireland in response to pressure put on Hermon by Shaw, the Northern Ireland DPP, after an internal inquiry by the RUC Deputy Chief Constable, Michael McAtamney, had failed to satisfy him. Stalker had been appointed as a result of talks between Sir Philip Myers, Her Majesty's Inspector of Constabulary for the North West of England and Northern Ireland, first with Hermon and then with Anderton. From the outset Stalker met strong resistance from Hermon, who had been dismissive of his work. Not long after he had arrived in Northern Ireland Stalker had it made clear to him that the RUC 'had more than a passing interest in his personal life'. An RUC officer remarked that it was known that Stalker was a Catholic and that his mother was born in County Westmeath, in the Republic.

Murtagh then turned to the background to the charges of disciplinary offences being laid against Stalker. The events leading to this had begun long before he knew about them, and related to his friendship with Taylor and in particular to his attendance at the fiftieth birthday party and Conservative Party functions. About a year previously, the article alleged, inquiries had begun into Taylor and the then head of the CID section in charge of the investigation was also a member of the Stalker team in Northern Ireland. This was a reference to Detective Superintendent John Simons, who was head of the Fraud Squad in 1985 and was part of the team which went to Northern Ireland with Stalker, but whose name was not at that time known to Murtagh as a potential 'common denominator' between Manchester and the province.

A further element in the agenda of issues to which the press attended was also raised in this article. It was the circumstances under which the inquiry into Stalker's personal conduct was set up. This referred to meetings which took place in May 1986, first, between James Anderton and Colin Sampson at the conference of the Police Federation (the representative body of officers below the rank of superintendent) at Scarborough, and, second, between Anderton and the then Chairman of the GMPA, Councillor Norman Briggs, at the authority's office in Swinton, in the northern suburbs of Salford.

Murtagh said that Anderton discussed the position of Stalker with Sampson at the Scarborough conference between 19 and 22 May. A few days later, on 27 May, Stalker and Anderton dined together with Peter Taylor, a TV reporter, and Colin Cameron, the executive producer of the BBC's Manchester-based investigative current affairs programme, Brass Tacks. The meal was intended to clear up relations between the programme and the police, which had been strained. According to Murtagh, no mention was made of the impending action to be taken against Stalker within a matter of days. This clearly must relate to conversations between the two police chiefs since one would not expect Anderton to raise the matter of the proposed removal from duty of his deputy in such company.

Murtagh then referred to the meeting between Anderton and Briggs which took place the day after the dinner with the BBC men. Anderton telephoned Briggs and asked him to come to the office as a matter of urgency. When he arrived he was ushered into a library annexe where Anderton told him that Stalker had to be investigated, taken off the Northern Ireland inquiry and replaced by Sampson. Briggs agreed and Anderton telephoned Sampson, Murtagh's story went on.

The relationship between these events and some causal framework was suggested in two paragraphs that followed:

> Some members of the Stalker team suggest that while elements within the RUC have long wanted to do down Mr. Stalker, it was only relatively recently that Government had seen the need to stop his work reaching a conclusion.

> The second stage of Mr. Stalker's investigation, due to begin on June 2, was directed at the higher echelons of the RUC. The Government would not be anxious to have RUC morale – already low and facing a summer of discontent on the streets – tested further. The survival of the Anglo-Irish Agreement was more important to both London and Dublin.[8]

Peter Murtagh had raised a series of issues in the *Guardian* front page story and on the inside feature. He had revealed how far the Stalker inquiry had gone in investigating the killing of the six Roman Catholics and had gone as far as naming the two senior officers whom he wanted to see suspended. He had also attempted to show that there was a high level of bitter opposition to Stalker's inquiry from within the RUC. The last two paragraphs quoted imply that when to this was added a government motive for silencing the inquiry – the preservation of the Anglo-Irish agreement – then Stalker was silenced. The depiction of the events involving Anderton which led to the removal of Stalker from duty and the appointment of Sampson imply two things clearly: that Sampson and Anderton had set up their own solution at Scarborough and that Briggs was simply doing what Anderton told him to. Although, if true, this would not prove that this had been done at the behest of the government it would certainly be consistent with the hypothesis that the government organized Stalker's removal from the shoot-to-kill inquiry.

Murtagh did believe and still does that this is the only sensible explanation of events. The coincidence of Stalker's removal from the inquiry at the point where he was about to reveal damning evidence makes it impossible for him to accept that there was no intention to remove a difficulty for the RUC and the government. He was also convinced of the honesty of Stalker through their meetings and unimpressed by the trivial nature of the disciplinary charges against him. At the same time the telephone calls to *The Guardian* from Whitehall suggesting that Stalker had been steeped in naughtiness of the sort which would have turned the average Borgia's hair white confirmed for him that the government was out to 'get Stalker'. After the publication of the names of Superintendents Flannagan and Anderson, Murtagh said he heard from other reporters that the RUC Public Relations Department had done their best to silence further revelations by veiled threats about what was to happen to *The Guardian* as a result. Nothing did.

In the same edition on the same page Paul Johnson examined in more detail the nature of the six killings and their context in Northern Ireland. Under the headline 'Killings that put public gaze on covert security' he amplified further the motives that a number of interests had in silencing the shoot-to-kill inquiry. He contrasted the attitude expressed by the Rev. Ian Paisley, the hardline Democratic Unionist MP, with the general blandness of official statements, and the secrecy of leaks and rumours. The Rev. Paisley had dared to say given the removal from duty of the author of the shoot-to-kill report, it would now be discredited, and should therefore be dropped and started again completely afresh. This, Johnson wrote was what the majority of the community really thought and hoped, while the nationalist politicians led by Seamus Mallon feared that Sampson would take a different line from Stalker in his inquiry or that the DPP would decide against action when he received the report.

But a trial of the seven officers for conspiracy offences, as Stalker was known to have recommended, would have effects far beyond the individual careers of the men charged: it would lead 'to the top of the force, and beyond by exposing the philosophy, strategy, and tactics behind covert security operations in Northern Ireland'. Johnson then proceeded to analyse the organizational structure of the surveillance and specialist SAS-type attack groups involved in the shootings, whose activities would be exposed by such a trial. 'Public gaze would suddenly be upon' the Headquarters Mobile Support Unit (HQMSU) which carried out the killings; E4A, the Special Branch 'deep surveillance' and undercover squad; the Special Branch itself; army intelligence; and teams of soldiers who 'operate covertly in a highly unorthodox manner'. But, Johnson argued, the repercussions would go much further, into the political arena, unsettling relations with the Irish Republic, because any court case would reveal at least one, and probably more, unauthorized crossings into the Republic by Special Branch men.

Johnson then went on to outline the circumstances of the killings in a level of detail in relation to the Stalker affair which was new. He went through the incidents chronologically. The first incident was the shooting of the three unarmed Provisional IRA men Gervais McKerr, Eugene Toman and Sean Burns at a road block near Lurgan on 11 November 1982. The RUC said the men tried to escape and were shot. 'The police fired 109 bullets into the car . . . Three HQMSU men accused of murder were cleared by a Belfast judge who said they should have been commended rather than brought to trial.'

The second incident was the shooting dead of the seven-teen-year-old Tighe and the wounding of Martin McCauley on 24 November of the same year. The HQMSU unit said it came across two men pointing rifles at them from a hayshed at the rear of an unoccupied farm in a remote country lane. The officers spattered the building with gunfire from the rifles, machine-guns, semi-automatic pistols and a pump-action shotgun they carried. Tighe had no paramilitary connections. The rifles were more than fifty years old, were without bolts and had no ammunition. In a nearby outhouse, sixty cigarette butts were later discovered, implying a security force stake-out. At the subsequent trial of McCauley it was revealed that the officers had lied in statements. They claimed this was on the orders of senior officers who wanted to conceal the part played in the operation by the Special Branch and an informer.

The third incident, on 12 December, took place on the out-skirts of Armagh city when two members of the Irish National Liberation Army (INLA) Seamus Grew and Roddy Carroll were killed by one HQMSU officer who fired nineteen bullets into the car 'killing them both outright, because he said he feared his life was in danger. Both men were unarmed.' The constable

was cleared of murder but at his trial an attempted cover-up
was again revealed in which senior officers told the constable
to lie in court and threatened him with the Official Secrets Act
'to conceal the extent of the security operation that night, a
cross-border trip by the Special Branch, the involvement of a
British army team and the safety of an informer'.[9]

Johnson's article was not simply a factual account of the
squads who did the killings and the way they were organized: it
was an explanation of why other interests in the province would
be as eager as the Rev. Ian Paisley to see the Stalker inquiry
discredited. In describing the undercover world of the HQMSUs
and deep surveillance teams, E4A, he was not simply telling a
good yarn, he was showing a need amongst those organizing
these squads for a cover-up, which was already established by
the falsification of evidence in the murder trials by the acquitted
policemen and by the officers in the trial for illegal possession
of firearms by McCauley.

Johnson interwove in the story his explanation of why those
in charge of these operations would want Stalker silenced:

Action on the basis of the Stalker report would open up the
history and the thinking behind the HQMSU. These were set
up between 1981 and 1982, containing about 30 members
each, split into quick action squads, under a sergeant, and
each unit having its own small surveillance team.

There are at least 12 such HQMSUs, trained under simu-
lated fire and in tactics which abandon the basic concept
of minimum force. It has been said that the emphasis is on
'speed, firepower and aggression' with members, many of
them ex-soldiers, taught to aim at the trunk to permanently
incapacitate.

The shadowy E4A would also have been dragged in. This
was set up in 1980 with between 25 and 30 members. E
stands for Special Branch, four is that department's number
and A means undercover.

E4A was a deep surveillance unit, trained but not specifically meant for contact situations – although some members
received instruction in England from the Parachute Regiment.
There had been rumours that E4A had been broken up to be
absorbed into the surveillance team carried by each HQMSU.

But this was contradicted by recent claims that E4A officers were involved in tracking Patrick Magee, the man convicted of the Brighton bombing.

The role of the Special Branch and its inclination to cut corners – by, for instance, making trips into the Irish Republic and trying to concoct statements – would also begin to emerge. And there would be those who would be anxious to keep the British Army out of the affair – not only Army intelligence but teams of specially trained soldiers, operating in a manner akin to the SAS but not as part of that regiment. They use unorthodox weaponry, wear plain-clothes and employ old, unmarked but high-powered cars.

Mr. Stalker was concerned about the whole set-up. Not only the attempts by senior officers to pervert justice, but the broader question of the philosophy behind such groups and the control exercised over them from the top.

In the grand words of the Anglo-Irish agreement . . . 'there is a need for a programme of special measures in Northern Ireland to improve relations between the security forces and the community, with the object in particular of making the security forces more accepted by the nationalist community.'

That was one step forward. If there is no action taken on the basis of the Stalker report that will be the equivalent of two steps backward because nationalists will never be convinced that Mr. Stalker was other than nobbled.[10]

Johnson's article posed the contrast between the 'shadowy world' of covert security operations and the opening up which would follow from Stalker's report being acted on. Things the authorities wanted hidden would be 'dragged in' and these would include illegalities. Like Murtagh he showed the motives of people in Northern Ireland who would have liked to see John Stalker 'nobbled'. What took the article further forward than the speculation which had already begun to appear in the press generally was the detailed background information about the six deaths, and the way this was related not simply to groups of policemen but to the structure of undercover operations and surveillance. This did not prove that there was a shoot-to-kill policy, in the sense that the government or the RUC had a policy of finding and executing without trial suspected terrorists, but it did seem to show that at least there was a policy of counter-terrorism which included shooting to kill if groups of heavily armed policemen thought their lives were in danger from unarmed seated suspects who had been under surveillance for some time and who were being ambushed. It seemed to show that the means for a shoot-to-kill policy existed.

It certainly showed that events which led to the Stalker inquiry were characterized by a fairly rough and ready approach to the finer points of the law relating to the rights of individuals – such as allowing them to stay alive for questioning – and of the niceties of international law – to whit not straying into another sovereign state on police business. The implication was clear: that there were many in the province who wanted Stalker silenced, and in Peter Murtagh's article the government was put forward as the prime suspect: '... elements in the RUC have long wanted to do down Mr. Stalker, it was only recently that Government had seen the need to stop his work reaching a conclusion.'[11]

It was clear from the articles and the front page news story that while some information could have come from files on reports of court cases one or both reporters were remarkably well briefed on the findings of the Stalker report, and most of what they said then and later in this regard is generally confirmed by Stalker's own subsequent book, Stalker.[12] They were clearly briefed by someone who had been involved in the inquiry. Indeed, Murtagh had seen the report and had glanced at some of its contents, but like other reporters had not actually been able to get hold of a copy.

This was moving the focus of journalistic inquiry away from the issue of what Stalker had been up to in Manchester – the agenda set by the Sampson disciplinary inquiry – and the Home Office chatline gossip. It was placed instead on the reasons behind the allegations against him. It was questioning the whole basis of the Sampson inquiry. And in raising the circumstances under which the Sampson inquiry was set up through the Scarborough meeting between Anderton and Sampson with the apparent subsequent railroading of Briggs into accepting a fait accompli another issue was placed on the agenda – the role of Anderton in the affair and the propriety of the way in which the Sampson inquiry was set up.

At this stage little was made of these events, although if they had occurred as the story suggested it would have meant that the normal proprieties for setting up an inquiry into the behaviour of a police officer of chief constable rank had not been observed, since it would be for the GMPA to make the decisions about suspension and the appointment of the investigating officer. If what Johnson claimed was an accurate account of events it seemed that the chief constables of West Yorkshire and Greater Manchester had already made the arrangements before Briggs was told. This issue was taken up the following day in the *Manchester Evening News* when Paul Horrocks reported that the Scarborough meeting about the allegations of misconduct by Stalker had taken place a fortnight before his removal from duty and had been attended by Her Majesty's Inspector for Constabulary for the whole country, Sir Laurence Byford, the North West Inspector, Sir Philip Myers, Colin Sampson, James Anderton and an unnamed 'Home Office official'.[13]

A further issue which could have cast more doubt on the propriety of the circumstances under which the inquiry was set up was not taken up by the mainland press. This was a story which appeared in the *Belfast Telegraph* on 9 June, in which Seamus Mallon claimed that Sampson had been in Northern Ireland 'some two or three weeks ago', that is before the allegations against Stalker were made public.

An RUC spokesman was quoted as confirming that Sampson, Myers and Hermon did have consultations 'concerning this development'.[14] This would have suggested that Anderton, Myers, Hermon and Sampson had all met one another some time before the allegations against Stalker were made public, and that the common factor was Sampson. The meetings also took place at a time when a crucial development in the Stalker inquiry into the shoot-to-kill inquiry was about to take place – namely his return to Northern Ireland to examine the hayshed bug transcripts.

At the time the main focus of journalistic inquiry was on other issues: the nature of charges against Stalker; his being kept in the dark and the shoot-to-kill revelations. The *Belfast Telegraph*, which took a different line from the mainland UK press, only ran the story as a short two-column news story with the meeting between Hermon and Sampson as a secondary line to the main issue that Mallon was to meet the Prime Minister. It was thus a piece of information which was lost in the mountain of information and to which no significance was ever attached subsequently in the search for the Northern Ireland connection. I am not arguing that objectively this was significant, simply that in the search for the establishment of a connection between the province and the allegations against Stalker it would have further suggested such a link. The fact that it was never taken up simply indicates the ad hoc nature of news: each story is produced under pressure of time and employs whatever information the journalist is attending to at the time, or to which his or her attention is being drawn, perhaps by interested parties at the time.

This book is concerned solely with the way in which the press made sense of the Stalker affair. I chose not to include the broadcast media because I did not have the means to survey their output. But the press do not work in isolation from radio and television. Perhaps the single news item in the coverage of the affair which caused more forward movement than any other, however, was a *Panorama* programme on the night of 16 June, the same date as Murtagh and Johnson did their exposé in *The Guardian*. The report was by Peter Taylor, who had been at work in Northern Ireland for a year already on the Stalker inquiry into the shoot-to-kill allegations. The programme examined the shoot-to-kill inquiry and the inquiry into Stalker. Kevin Taylor gave his side of the story in a long interview with a vivid description of a raid on his home when papers and photographs were taken away by police; Charles Horan, a former head of Manchester CID, spoke of John Stalker as a first-class detective.

But the programme broke new ground in revealing for the first time the presence of the bug in the hayshed when Tighe was shot. It also included an interview with Hermon and with former Northern Ireland Secretary James Prior. The new information, the interview with Hermon and Prior made the programme news in itself. The research for the programme also formed the basis of Taylor's subsequent book, *Stalker: The Search for the Truth*,[15] which contains the most thorough account of the shootings available aside from Stalker's own account of his inquiries in *Stalker*.[16]

The press generally carried reports of the *Panorama* film as news items the following day, and the stories focused on the presence of the bug in the hayshed and Hermon's interview in which he denied that Stalker's removal from duties had anything to do with the RUC. The crucial element was seen as the fact that Stalker was on the verge of discovering new evidence exactly at the point that he was removed from duty. In *The Star*, Frank Curran wrote: 'Last night, BBC's Panorama programme claimed Mr. Stalker was on his way to interview senior RUC men when he was taken off the case because of disciplinary action.'[17] Murtagh, in *The Guardian*, also angled his story on the new evidence which Stalker was seeking at the point when he was removed from the inquiry and in a summary of the programme referred in some detail to the statement made by Hermon.[18]

Murtagh quoted Hermon's rejection of the allegation that Stalker's removal from the inquiry had anything to do with the RUC, and his attack on the programme as a source of disillusionment for his force. But the report also tried to attribute meaning to what Hermon said, in particular in relation to the bug which recorded the shooting of Tighe and as to whether he had refused to suspend the two officers as recommended by Stalker:

> Asked if the shooting of Tighe had been recorded by the MI5 device, Sir John side-stepped the question . . . Sir John was asked why two officers had not been suspended as requested by Mr. Stalker in April last year. He replied that, without confirming the incident took place, he had to have solid evidence which would justify any action.[19]

In both of these cases the reporter was drawing attention to the fact that Hermon was not denying what the programme and *The Guardian* had claimed – that there was a bug in the hayshed and that a request for the suspension of two senior officers had been rejected.

The revelations about Northern Ireland continued. The report and exposé in *The Star*, referred to earlier[20] pressed further the idea that there was a plot to cover up illegal activities by the security services. By 20 June *The Guardian* was reporting

'Stalker planned to quiz Hermon for his Ulster Police Report', the headline for a story in which Murtagh and Johnson revealed that Stalker had planned to question Hermon and his deputy, Michael McAtamney, about the shootings and the subsequent cover-ups. The report alleged that Stalker had been told by Sir Philip Myers, the HMI for Constabulary, that Sir John did not wish to be questioned: 'According to sources Sir Philip told Mr. Stalker: "John would prefer you didn't."'[21]

The *Irish Times* of the same day carried a very similar story. Under the headline 'Stalker planned to ask Hermon about "cover-up"' the paper's London reporter, Conor O'Clery, wrote that the paper had 'learned' that Hermon and McAtamney were to be asked 'some very searching questions' by Stalker when he was taken off the inquiry.[22] An inside news feature by O'Clery in the same issue dealt in great detail with the shooting of the six Roman Catholics and Stalker's inquiry into them. The article was illustrated with photographs of the writer, Anderton, McAtamney and Northern Ireland's DPP, Sir Barry Shaw. A map showed Lurgan, Portadown and Lisburn with crosses marking the sites of killings by the RUC near Lurgan on 11 and 24 November 1982 and near Lurgan on 12 December. It also showed the spot at Kinnego embankment where a group of RUC men were killed on 27 October 1982 in a bombing by the INLA. This atrocity was referred to in Peter Taylor's *Panorama* film as related to the subsequent chain of killings by the HQMSUs. There was also a photograph of the hayshed where Tighe met his death. The long article followed the same line as the *Panorama* programme and the reports by Murtagh and Johnson in *The Guardian*.

O'Clery recounted how three months before the shooting in the hayshed the RUC had discovered one and a half tons of explosives hidden in a hay lorry, to which their attention was drawn because its front and rear number plates did not match. The police learned that the explosives were to be taken to the hayshed at Ballyneery near Lurgan. MI5 were brought in and a bug was placed in the shed, and a recording unit set up in a nearby caravan manned by a soldier and police officer. But 'according to information available to Stalker's team' an IRA unit picked up the explosives without being spotted either because of human error or a bug malfunction. On 27 October

1982 police were called to investigate a theft at Kinnego and three officers on the way to the scene of the alleged crime were killed by a landmine made with explosives from the hayshed.

O'Clery acknowledged the role of the *Panorama* programme in revealing this chain of events: 'Until BBC's "Panorama" programme revealed details of this incident earlier this week, fewer than a dozen people are believed to have known about the movement of the explosives. Certainly the families of the policemen had until this week no inkling of what had happened.' Having recounted in some detail the nature of the shoot-to-kill inquiry and presented a résumé of the charges against Stalker, along with his denials and the effect this was having on his family, O'Clery concluded: 'Since the affair began his mother has been admitted to hospital and he believes that it is partly responsible. If indeed, as his friends in the Manchester police and a growing number of people in Britain suspect, the whole thing is a conspiracy, she is one of its most innocent casualties.'[23]

While the contents, binding and title lettering of the Stalker report into the Armagh killings had now become public property, a dispute arose between the British and Irish governments as to whether the report itself was final or interim. On 18 June Peter Barry, the then Foreign Secretary of the Republic, said that Tom King, the Northern Ireland Secretary, had given him assurances that the report was final and the result of a completed inquiry. These were important assurances for the government in Eire since clearly, if this were the case, the removal of Stalker could not be seen as a means of preventing further questions being asked. The headlines claimed that 'Stalker planned to quiz Hermon for his Ulster police report'. This was supported by the revelation that the report was clearly marked in gold lettering with the word 'interim' as was revealed by Murtagh.

The junior minister at the Northern Ireland Office, Nicholas Scott duly appeared before the House of Commons the following day and acknowledged that the report was indeed an interim one. The normally discreet Irish Prime Minister, Dr Garret Fitzgerald, said on Irish radio on 22 June that he was taken aback by King's error, and added that it was important to get Stalker's outstanding questions answered so that Sir Barry Shaw, the DPP, could decide on what action should be taken. But it was widely believed and reported in the press that Scott's retraction of King's error had been the result of fierce protests from the Irish side.

At the time journalists in the mainland press did not pay attention to how the notion that the Stalker report was full and not interim had first arisen. The first public avowal that the report was complete appeared in the *Belfast Telegraph* on 6 June, a fortnight before the diplomatic row. In a story headlined 'MP to quiz King on Stalker issue', David Watson reported: 'According to the RUC the full Stalker report – not an interim one – went to the DPP. He subsequently decided that some matters required further explanation and referred the matter to the Chief Constable, Sir John Hermon.'[24]

It is difficult not to believe that this statement was a piece of conscious economy with the truth by the RUC, since Stalker had submitted three copies of the report to the RUC – one for Hermon and two for Shaw – and if all three were marked 'interim', and since this was a point at issue, it is hard to believe that such a wrong statement could be made publicly in error. What is more interesting, however, is how an inter-governmental dispute and a dispute between high-ranking police officials could have arisen about the use of one apparently innocuous word.

It was clear that the status of the document as an interim report would have shown that the removal of Stalker from the inquiry was more likely to have been to stop him before he got to the nub of the issue, while if it was complete this explanation is less feasible, but only slightly so, since as the Rev. Ian Paisley's sage intervention indicated, there were voices ready to rubbish the report complete or not purely on the grounds that an allegation, however trivial or groundless, had been made against its author.

Such a state of affairs exemplifies the sensitivity of the relationships between the UK and Ireland over issues to do with the civil rights of Northern Ireland Roman Catholics and police practices in the province. This is one of the factors which meant that the formulation of versions of reality by the mass media was always a central issue in the Stalker affair, and that journalists played a major part in the political process rather than simply being cast in the role of observers.

These lines of inquiry by journalists, along with the information they received from 'sources', produced from early on an agenda in which the official view of reality – that propagated by the Sampson inquiry and the official announcements about its set-up – was open to critical inspection. They showed that there was a motive for the removal of Stalker from the Northern Ireland inquiry in the shape of the suppression of the details of the outcome of that inquiry. The range of people sharing that motive covered the RUC officers directly involved, their sympathetic colleagues, Sir John Hermon, who wanted to protect his force, the MI5 and the government.

The issue about the way in which Colin Sampson was chosen at all, and, even more, to do both jobs, and James Anderton's role in this process was also raised. This meant that from the outset the press were engaged in inquiries which raised questions about the legitimacy of the system they were reporting. And in doing this they were always at pains to produce evidence that this challenge was based on good information: the names of the officers to be charged, the initials and names of the police units involved, what was said to Stalker by RUC officers, *The Star's* details about the Whitehall meeting of security chiefs, the lettering on the interim report.

Having established the conditions under which the charges against Stalker arose, journalists set about unearthing the proximate cause of these charges being made. *The People* and the *News of the World* both identified the Freemasons as the originators of the plot to undermine Stalker. The story originated from a source in the GMP.

Over the years previous to the Stalker affair, allegations that named senior officers were masons were made frequently in the alternative press, The *New Manchester Review*, which folded at the end of the 1970s, and subsequently *City Life*. It was this magazine which made the first passing reference to the masonic influence in relation to the Stalker affair when on 6 June Ed Glinert, in a biographical sketch of Stalker, commented, 'he does not seem to have taken up the most important and influential of police activities – that of freemasonry. It could count against him in the long run.'[25]

The police source rumour was that Stalker's Northern Ireland team had included known masons, among them Detective Superintentent John Simons, who subsequently began legal proceedings against the *Manchester Evening News* for alleging that he was involved in a masonic conspiracy against Stalker. This eventually led to a retraction by the paper and out-of-court settlement. Alan Hart, a Manchester-based journalist with years of experience reporting criminal and police affairs in the city, wrote in the *News of the World* on 29 June that claims that a 'Masonic Mafia' of senior colleagues set out to destroy suspended Stalker were being investigated by his boss. Hart wrote that Anderton was studying secret information naming eight key officers, all members of the same masonic lodge. Hart alleged:

> Friends of Roman Catholic Mr. Stalker believe the eight were asked by their mason colleagues in the Royal Ulster Constabulary to 'dish the dirt' on him . . .
> A friend involved in the investigation told me the RUC officers were not happy with the way the probe was going.
> He added: 'So the word went out to get Stalker off it.'[26]

The People of the same day carried a report by two other Manchester journalists, Andrew Leatham and Peter Reece, that 'top cop' Stalker was 'the victim of a plot by Freemasons that stretches all the way from Ulster to Whitehall according to his friends and colleagues' who were 'convinced that a "get Stalker" order originated in Ulster where he made enemies with his inquiries into an alleged "shoot-on-sight" policy.'[27]

This was as nothing compared with the assault on the masons launched by the *Manchester Evening News* on 25 July,[28] when James Cusick, in a 1,500-word centre page spread feature, attempted to identify the exact nature of the masonic conspiracy against Stalker. The article was preceded by a 'standfirst' which declared:

> The Stalker affair has revealed the extent of police membership of Britain's largest secret society – the Freemasons. Although police chiefs have criticised the secret structures and practices of the Brotherhoood as being incompatible with holding rank in the police service, most Masons regard their membership as nothing more than belonging to a secret club. The extent of the network cannot however be denied.

The article, headlined 'The Masonic connection' alongside a WOB (white on black) panel with the words 'The Stalker affair', was illustrated with four photographs, a single column of John Stalker over the standfirst and two-column blocks of Councillor Norman Briggs, Chief Superintendent Peter Topping and Sir John Hermon. All were named as masons or alleged masons in the text.

The article began as an attempt to analyse how the allegations against Stalker had been made and how the Sampson inquiry had come to be set up. Cusick pointed out that the exact chain of command in the decision-making process for this inquiry and Stalker's own Northern Ireland inquiry had never been clear, but pointed to the network of organizations and authorities from MI5 to the Inspectorate of Constabulary which had been involved in taking decisions. Behind this network, however, Cusick claimed, there lay another one 'of closed doors' with the 'potential to intervene in the decisions of all the organizations involved in the Stalker affair'. This other network was 'the brotherhood of Freemasonry'.

'Through investigation, interviews and checks in the secret *Masonic Year Book*', the article claimed, it had been confirmed that 'certain men taking crucial decisions throughout the Stalker affair' were members of the brotherhood who were sworn to help fellow masons in distress. This was important to the line the article pursued since it explained why masons in positions of influence anywhere in the police or security services help their colleagues in the RUC if they are in trouble.

Cusick argued that Stalker had been positively vetted before being appointed to head the Northern Ireland inquiry and that Hermon would have had access to various vetting reports. Cusick argued further that the vetting procedure would have made known Stalker's friendship with Taylor (who, the article revealed, was himself an ex-mason who had allowed his membership to lapse) and would have declared the Miami boating holiday 'clean'. There is then some confusion in his argument as to how Hermon would have known, but Cusick argues that the RUC chief already knew why Stalker was to be removed from duty before it happened. In the hypothesis which underlies the article the prior knowledge appears to have come either from Hermon's knowledge of the Stalker/Taylor friendship or from

Detective Superintendent John Simons, who was a member of the Stalker team in Northern Ireland. Cusick correctly identified Simons's role as head of the CID Fraud Squad at the Chester House HQ of the GMP at the time when the Taylor investigation seriously began (see pages 74–85 for an account of the relevant section of the Sampson report). 'As head of an operational Support Group co-ordinating specialist drugs, fraud and serious crimes investigations, he ordered a raid on Kevin Taylor's Summerseat home, near Bury', and at that time Simons's immediate superior, Cusick wrote, was Chief Superintendent Topping, whom he identified as Simons's brother-in-law.

Cusick then interwove an account of the nature of the Freemasons generally and their national involvement in the police and police inspectorate with an account of the way in which the allegations against Stalker had been put together. This correctly identified the senior officers who were engaged in the inquiry as Simons, Topping and the Assistant Chief Constable Ralph Lees, mentioned in the Sampson report. Into this account he inserted information from the masonic year-book among which was the revelation that there were 388 lodges for East Lancashire and 130 lodges in Manchester alone. These included lodge 7441, the 'Manchester Ulster Lodge', which, the writer claimed, was one of several police lodges, in the district where the 'predominant' occupation of members was 'Her Majesty's Police'.

Cusick claimed that both Topping and Lees were masons, along with Detective Superintendent James Grant who was head of the Operational Support Group and a former member of the internal discipline and complaints sections, the 'Y' Department. Hermon was also listed as a mason. Other police officers and officials of Her Majesty's Inspectorate of Constabulary were also identified as masons, by the use of such phrases as 'are widely regarded as masons'. In the case of Ralph Lees, one of those 'regarded as' masons, Cusick even appended the fact that Lees himself denied the claim.

The article contained, however, one provable error. This related to an entry in the *Masonic Year Book*. 'Norman Briggs JP receives a prominent listing in the *Masonic Year Book*. He is a Royal Arch companion of the Grand Chapter of Freemasonry, a close inner circle of fervent freemasons. His listed current office in the Royal Arch is the elevation of Past Grand Sojourner.'

Briggs was identified as the Chairman of the GMPA who had been told by Anderton that Stalker had to be taken off the Northern Ireland inquiry.

Photocopies of the relevant entries in the year-book were in the possession of a number of individuals at the time including researchers for Manchester City Council's Police Monitoring Group and Ed Glinert the news editor of *City Life*. The actual entry was Norman D. Briggs and Glinert was at first inclined to use the information as the basis of a story identifying Briggs as a mason as he had previously done on the basis of information from police sources about named police officers. But the middle initial worried him and he checked the name by the simple process of going through telephone directories and checking who the various Briggses were. He eventually traced Norman D. Briggs as a Blackburn businessman and consequently did not proceed with the story. This established that the Norman D. Briggs referred to in the year-book was not the Chairman of the GMPA, although it did not necessarily follow that the Chairman himself was not a mason. The difficulty for journalists in dealing with the masons is that the secrecy makes accusations of individual membership hard to substantiate and virtually impossible to disprove.

The GMPA Norman Briggs was suddenly removed from the dispute, however. He died during the weekend following the article, which appeared in the Friday editions of the paper. The Briggs family lawyers, Herwald Seddon & Co., held a press conference and issued a statement denying that Briggs had ever been a mason, and held a press conference to condemn what solicitor Basil Herwald described as a 'scandalous article' by the *Manchester Evening News*.

The East Lancashire Province of the Freemasons were also stung into action by the *Manchester Evening News* article and they held a press conference of their own for the first time in the Manchester Masonic Temple in Bridge Street, only a hundred yards from the offices of *The Guardian* and the *Manchester Evening News*. It was a deeply farcical occasion, at which the provincial grand secretary Mr Colin Gregory issued a statement denying that there was a plot by masons to smear Stalker, but refused to answer any questions of substance about the masonic order. There was no meeting of minds between the journalists packed into the room and the two masonic officials. Colin Gregory was repeatedly asked how many Manchester police officers were in the Freemasons, and how many masons were police officers. He denied that Briggs had been a mason but would not answer when asked if Lees, Topping, or Grant were members of the order.

Gregory and Ken Helps, the assistant to the Grand Secretary of the United Grand Lodge of England, were subjected to a barrage of questions about the Manchester police and about the nature of the oaths sworn by masons at the various stages in their *rites de passage* into the higher degrees of the order, some of which involved references to cutting out the tongue of those betraying the secrets of the brotherhood (a part of the ceremony the masons have now abandoned).

Gregory and Helps generally declined to divulge any secrets and frequently asked the journalists questions about why they had raised a particular issue. One reporter pointed out, to general laughter, that this was the first press conference he had come to where the journalists were expected to answer the questions. Under the influence of the oath-laden atmosphere of the temple some of the hacks eventually began their own ceremony of uttering the oaths of their own brotherhood, although these were generally of an informal nature and widely known among the general public. This was a prelude to a journalistic ritual which involved the participant uttering the ceremonial words, 'I've had enough of this. I'm fucking going', and stomping noisily to the door. By this means the room gradually at first and then with a sudden rush emptied. In the street outside the *News at Ten* reporter was recording his 'more questions asked than answered' on-the-spot summing up of the press conference into camera, while the brotherhood of the pen and bottle ceremonially made their way back to nearby newsrooms with a ritualistic display of laughter, jokes and contemptuous assertions that no one who had made such a cock-up of a simple matter of a press conference could possibly have organized a successful conspiracy against a senior police officer.

The overt antagonism of the press conference was reflected in the reports of it which appeared in the popular national dailies the following day. The *Manchester Evening News* of that day produced a summary of the conference based on the masonic statement and some of the few answers elicited to the questions asked. This focused on the denial of masonic influence in the

Stalker affair and in particular the statement that the paper's own article had been so factually incorrect that the masons had decided to call the conference. The report included Gregory's claim that the Manchester Ulster lodge only had one police member and that Superintendent Grant was not a member of that lodge as the original article had stated, while the Longsight lodge erroneously described in the media as the divisional HQ lodge had thirty-three members none of whom was a policeman. The article also included a report of Briggs's solicitors' statement that their late client had not been a mason.

At the end of the article, however there was an editor's note which said:

The article in the *The Manchester Evening News* of July 25 did not, as Mr. Gregory has suggested, make any allegation that there was a Masonic 'network' active in blocking Mr. Stalker's inquiry in Northern Ireland or in having him taken off the inquiry. No such allegation was made. Notwithstanding that we refute Mr. Gregory's interpretation of the article, we are publishing the details of today's Press Conference so that the views of Mr. Gregory and those Masons he represents be made known.[29]

The quality dailies followed the same line as the *Manchester Evnening News* except that their factual summary of the press conference was not qualified by an editorial comment. The popular dailies, however, were unrestrained in the fun they had at the expense of the unfortunate Gregory and the covert fraternity for whom he spoke or rather did not speak. For example the press conference gave the *Daily Mirror* the opportunity to rehearse with great prominence the rumours which Gregory was at pains to dispel, and in doing so used words which sustained the idea of the Freemasons as a secretive and malign brotherhood. 'For the first time in its 296 year history, the shadowy secret society of Freemasons has been forced to come out into the open', the story began, and went on: 'The society, which is fiercely anti-Roman Catholic by tradition, has been accused of "setting-up" Greater Manchester Deputy Chief Constable John Stalker, who has been suspended. John Stalker is a Roman Catholic.'[30]

Thus the use of the words 'shadowy' and 'forced to come into the open' dramatically convey the idea of a conspiratorial and furtive organization. And the specific reference to the anti-Catholic tradition of the masons, along with the fact that John Stalker was himself a Catholic, provided a clear indication of one of the reasons why the masons might have been willing to discredit him. The article went on to relate that he had been suspended following allegations that his Northern Ireland report included claims of 'cold blooded killing by RUC men'. His suspension had been put down to 'a link between Freemasons in Northern Ireland, Manchester and Yorkshire'.

The article by Roger Todd, entitled 'Brotherhood on trial' also related the press conference to 'a series of fierce attacks on the brotherhood over its alleged infiltration of the police force', in particular an attack by the then Metropolitan Police Commissioner, Kenneth Newman, and an allegation by Chief Inspector Brian Wollard that he had been 'stitched up' by masons in order to hinder a corruption investigation he had been engaged on in Hackney. The article was illustrated with a photograph of Stalker identified as 'police Chief "victim"', the logo of the masons – a divider and a set-square – and a panel with drawings illustrating three masonic handshakes, one for new members, one for a full member and one for a master.[31]

The Star went in more directly for fun at Gregory's expense. The headline, 'Secrets of the Masons. They open their doors but not their mouths', set the jovial tone of the article, focused on the lack of information provided by the press conference. Their reporter Robert Wilson began his story in a vein which indicated a less than awestruck attitude to the brothers: 'It was hard to imagine the Provincial Grand Master with his left trouser leg rolled up and one breast bared.' He went on to describe the press conference with the fifty photographers and journalists at the Masonic lodge and highlighted the unwillingness of the representatives of the masons to answer such questions as how many members they had in the police. Referring to the fact that the masons had dropped the part of the oath about cutting out the tongue of those revealing the society's secrets Wilson commented: 'Mr. Gregory's [tongue] would have been safe anyway.'[32]

The outcome of the encounter between the masons and the press was that although a number of people were named as masons, and most of them did not deny membership, the press were never able publicly to produce the evidence on which the original allegations of masonic influence were based. Shortly after the press conference Sir Philip Myers the North West HMI of Constabulary attended a meeting with the GMPA. According to a report in *The Guardian* by Peter Murtagh, when he was asked if he was a mason he said he had been sent a questionnaire asking the same thing and he had thrown it in the wastepaper basket, and he proposed to deal with the question in the same way. He was also alleged not to have answered when asked if he intended to investigate the allegations of masonic links between the RUC and the GMP. This story epitomised the state of this aspect of the Stalker affair. The press had raised the issue, but in the absence of movement from officialdom and without any damning evidence made public, the issue came to rest as a suspicion that had been raised but not proved, but which had been given some new vigour by the press conference called by the masons themselves to quash it.

Thus by early August of 1986 the press had established in some detail what Stalker's Northern Ireland inquiry was about and that that inquiry into the RUC shootings had arrived at a crucial point in late May in that Stalker was pressing Hermon for the transcripts of the tape-recordings in the Lurgan hayshed where Michael Tighe met his death, and that he was about to charge senior officers with criminal offences. This provided a motive on the part of numerous people from MI5 to the masons, but no newspaper was able to provide the sort of evidential link which would establish who made the connection between Manchester and Ulster and how it was made. In the next chapter we will examine how other theories to explain Stalker's downfall were floated and how the leaking of the Sampson report provided new lines of inquiry for journalists to follow.

CHAPTER EIGHT
Sampson, the aftermath

By the time that the Sampson report was issued to Greater Manchester Police Authority (GMPA) the general nature of the inquiry which informed it was already known. Due in particular to the investigative coups of the *Manchester Evening News*, the central importance of Kevin Taylor to the matter and the role of Stephen Hayes were established from early on. Tory party infighting, which was covered in some detail by Sampson had also been well turned over by *The Observer* and *City Life* (pages 191–3). But not only had the press established roughly what the report was about, they had established that Chief Superintendent Peter Topping, Superintendent John Simons, and Assistant Chief Constable Ralph Lees were the prime movers in the GMPA in starting the inquiry into Stalker's conduct and his relationship with Taylor.

Their examination of the Northern Ireland inquiry conducted by Stalker and his conflicts with the RUC over the bug in the hayshed, the transcript from the bug and his desire to charge RUC officers also meant that the whole Sampson inquiry was placed in a context in which there was an established public perception that there had been a plot. To account for this there was a selection of believable motives: to silence Stalker to protect the RUC; to save the Anglo-Irish agreement by maintaining the unity of the RUC during the Orange marching season; to save the government from embarrassment. There were equally a number of suspects for whom compelling prima facie cases could be assembled: the MI5; the RUC; the Freemasons; the government.

And, according to the logic now established by the press, the means also could in part be established. Identifying the suspects identified some of the available means: the security services operated a dirty tricks department; the Freemasons were a fraternity of mutual support for members in time of trouble. Some of the means by which the inquiry had been set up could be seen to be part of a generalized conspiracy. The meeting between James Anderton, Colin Sampson, the HMIs of Constabulary and the Home Office officials at the Police Federation Conference in Scarborough a fortnight before Stalker's removal from duty was clearly when the scheme was set up and a plan hatched to pre-empt any decision to be taken by the GMPA. But its precise function in the context of a more general conspiracy was never identified by a newspaper. Was it, for instance, a way of conveying the government's instructions to the two chief constables? Or a means of the police service deciding to cover up the wrongdoings or errors of its own members?

This established view of what was happening meant that the Sampson report would not be accorded the normal routine acceptance that an official government document would enjoy, as would, say, the road accident statistics as a source of information routinely regarded as factually reliable and communally significant. Only the latter quality was automatically accepted: it was regarded as communally significant. The validity of the document as a source of information was challenged from before it appeared in the sense that the motives for the inquiry were identified as suspect both by the press and by politicians. As the inquiry into Stalker's conduct proceeded, it was labelled as 'jack booted policemen searching for any little hint of improper behaviour by John Stalker over the last 30 years'.[1]

When the report was actually produced and leaked to the press the process of critical examination began in two ways. First, journalists themselves sought to discover the basis in truth of the allegations about Stalker's behaviour. This involved speaking to witnesses who had been interviewed by the Sampson team, to Stalker himself and to other informants in the police who had heard internal gossip about the quality of the information in the report. The picture that was presented was of a report which was trivial in its import and shot through with inaccuracies.

Examination of the contents of the report began where other revelations in this affair began, with the crime reporter and the editor of the *Manchester Evening News*. On 15 August 1986 the paper carried the first accurate report of the contents of the report and the recommendations for action against Stalker, with the exclusively tagged front page lead that the report strongly criticized Stalker for giving lifts in police cars.[2] *The Sunday Times* had already carried a report that the inquiry would exonerate the deputy chief constable, but given that this story was not accurate it cannot be regarded as revelation.

The *Manchester Evening News* story detailed a number of occasions when Stalker had allegedly given lifts to friends, including Kevin Taylor, on one occasion for the staggering distance of 3 miles. It also revealed that the 1,500-page report which had been delivered to the Police Complaints Authority (PCA) in London included a claim by Stalker that he had been given permission to use police cars at any time because he was being followed as a consequence of his Northern Ireland inquiries. The informant for this information was 'one top-level source in London'.

Paul Horrocks put this revelation in the context of the fact that the report summary mentioned Taylor many times and centred on the relationship between him and Stalker. The outcome of the 'more serious charges' of associating with known criminals was not known. A statement from the solicitor Roger Pannone refrained from specifics but stated that Stalker believed he had performed all his duties and 'conducted himself in a manner consistent with the wishes of his Chief Constable', and had used his discretion about the use of police vehicles on the five occasions to which the leaks referred, 'and on each occasion he believes he was totally justified not only because it accorded with the above, but also for security'.

The statement which ended the story finished by establishing some distance between Taylor and Stalker. It said:

> It has been suggested that much of it [the report] relates to Mr. Taylor. Mr. Stalker must be judged by his knowledge of Mr. Taylor on those limited occasions when he met with him socially and, certainly not with the benefit of hindsight, after a very detailed and far-reaching enquiry conducted by Mr. Sampson and his men.[3]

Two days later *The Observer* reporters Jonathan Foster and Paul Lashmar reported that Anderton was ready to defend

Stalker's use of police cars. This was based on information from a source in the GMP, and was given greater credibility by rehearsal of each of the five journeys in all their boring detail such as that a passenger was picked up on the way to a football match at an address 'which did not divert him' and the revelation that they were spread over a year and 'clocked up a total of less than 100 miles'.

The suggestion in the story was that the criticism by Sampson of Stalker's use of cars was due to a policy difference between the two forces and would therefore be rebutted by Anderton as chief constable:

> Mr. Sampson's criticism of Mr. Stalker over the use of police cars seems to be rooted in a difference of policies between the two forces. We attempted to ask Mr. Anderton about his use of the car and driver for domestic arrangements, however, he has refused to answer any questions raised by *The Observer*.[4]

This was a reference to a number of allegations from anonymous sources about Anderton's alleged use of his police car and driver, which we will examine in the next chapter.

The following day, 18 August, the *Manchester Evening News* once again led with another revelatory coup with the dramatic headline 'A new blow for Stalker' over the news that the 145–page Sampson report for the GMPA finished with a recommendation that an investigation of the case should take place before an independent tribunal where eleven disciplinary charges would be heard.[5] These related to the alleged misuse of police vehicles and unwise association with known criminals. Stalker's career was 'hanging in the balance' as the GMPA waited to meet to decide on what action to take over the report, which included a claim that he had disobeyed warnings about unwise friendships. In a small second lead headlined 'Denial on warnings' Steve Panter reported the denial by solicitor Pannone of his client Stalker ever having received such warnings. Pannone said he did not know of any mention of such warnings and declared that Stalker had a complete answer to the allegations against him.[6]

This story was clearly based on information from someone who knew what was in the Sampson report but not perfectly, probably a member of the GMPA or a police officer who had either only glanced at the document or who had been told about its contents and had remembered them wrongly. In principle it was correct: Sampson was recommending that Stalker should go before a full tribunal, but the case was about ten disciplinary charges not eleven and the report did not refer to any warning given to Stalker by Anderton about the company he was keeping. Far from it, it was clear, according to the report, that Anderton, Topping and Lees had sedulously avoided any mention of Taylor while in Stalker's presence. They had made a point of not speaking at all to him about the case.

None the less the local knowledge and experience of the Manchester paper's staff were keeping them ahead of the field in discovering what was happening. In this respect the story contained one particular nugget of information in two paragraphs at the end. It was known from the report, Paul Horrocks wrote, that the Stalker inquiry began in the CID. It was also known that Stalker had opposed the appointment of two senior members of the CID but had been overruled by Anderton. The implication was clear: there was a motive for scuppering the career of John Stalker in the injured professional *amour propre* of his fellow detectives.

This lead was followed up by the *Daily Mail* two days later with a story by Kevin Dowling and Edward Scallan who claimed that Stalker had opposed the promotion of 'two top policemen whose inquiries later led to his suspension from duty'. The story named Ralph Lees and Peter Topping as the two men both of whom were regarded by Stalker as too inexperienced for the promotions they had been given. The reporters alleged that Lees had been at the Scarborough meeting with Anderton, Sampson, the Chief HMI of Constabulary, Sir Laurence Byford, and his regional HMI, Sir Philip Myers. They referred to Topping's role in investigating the connection between Taylor and Stalker and to the role of Simons, allegedly Topping's brother-in-law, who, according to a nameless source, was 'the Greater Manchester force's eyes and ears in Ulster'. Stalker declined to comment on the story.[7]

Clearly, in however an imperfect form, the contents of the secret summary of the even more secret report were starting to ooze out. But if there were any doubts left that the report had been leaked to the press, a news feature by Peter Murtagh on page 17 of *The Guardian* of Thursday, 21 August, the day before the GMPA met, must have eliminated them. The article 'on the document that summarises the case of the deputy chief constable' identified the dead informer David Burton as the starting point of the police inquiry into Stalker's alleged relationship with the Quality Street Gang (QSG). By the second paragraph of the article, Murtagh was quoting directly from the summary of the report to be considered by the police authority the following day.

The article summarized the police inquiry into Stalker's social life and the criminal associates of Taylor, beginning with the revelation that

> Dead men don't tell lies. Colin Sampson, the Chief Constable of West Yorkshire, came across one recently whom he was inclined to believe. 'The person who could be said to be principally responsible for the allegations against Deputy Chief Constable Stalker is now dead,' he says in paragraph 396 of the summary of his nine week investigation into Mr. Stalker. 'David Burton was a professional criminal who was also a regular informant to the police and other bodies . . .'[8]

In this article Murtagh made no further examination of the reliability or otherwise of Burton's evidence, other than to say that 'glancing through' the summary it seemed that Sampson did not reveal what information Burton gave to the police but that it was backed up. And he did not at this time pick up the phrase 'to the police and other bodies' and question whom else Burton was sourcing with his 'backed-up' information. For the first time however there was a clear public statement of how Wareing the businessman had allegedly told Detective Superintendent McGourlay, the policeman, of the allegations that Taylor associated with the QSG and that a senior officer in the Manchester police attended parties at Taylor's house.

Murtagh told the story, recounted in Sampson's report of McGourlay's reporting the matter to Topping, Topping's telling Lees and, in turn, his telling Anderton, and how this resulted in the formation of the Drugs Intelligence Unit with information passed up directly from Topping to Lees to Anderton without

Stalker being informed – pre-empting any suggestion that he could have interfered on behalf of his friend. Murtagh also made the point that the information supplied to Anderton was passed on to Sir Philip Myers, who was also responsible for Northern Ireland and therefore liaised with Stalker during the course of his RUC inquiry.

The article summarized the investigation of the QSG and Taylor, and the latter's relationship with Stalker. It did not rely entirely on the Sampson report for information. Murtagh referred to the fact Stalker's private life had been positively vetted three times in 1973, 1978 and 1983, and had been cleared, and that his friendship with Taylor had been an open one. He also related the findings of the Sampson report to the inquiries John Stalker was carrying out in Northern Ireland.

He picked out the incident referred to by Sampson which concerned Chief Superintendent Arthur Roberts who is reported by Topping in the report as having said he had a meeting with Ian Burton, Taylor's solicitor, who was supposed to have told him:

(a)   Taylor is saying that he has been to the USA and to parties with Mr. Stalker at Taylor's expense.

(b)   If nothing is done to squash inquiries, that Taylor will blow out John Stalker and his associates.

(c)   Taylor talks continually of his friendship with Stalker.

Murtagh quoted the denial by Chief Superintendent Roberts of almost the entire substance of Topping's claims.[9]

In his reference to the misuse of police vehicles charges Murtagh offered the scathing comment: 'The summary makes the extraordinary comment that had Stalker not disputed the issue of the cars and simply accepted that he had been wrong, a mere rebuke would have been recommended.'

The *Manchester Evening News* of the same day appeared in two versions. The early editions carried a page one lead entitled 'Send police chief back', which was based on a survey of the members of the GMPA, and which indicated that at their meeting the following day they would probably send him back to work.[10] A page two news story by Paul Horrocks headed 'Stalker's mistake' was a detailed write-up of some

parts of the Sampson report, in particular those which dealt
with the inadvisability of Stalker's association with Taylor.
Quotes from specific paragraphs clearly indicated that the paper,
like *The Guardian*, had its own copy. The paragraphs quoted
were different from those which appeared verbatim in Peter
Murtagh's articles, which demonstrated that Horrocks had not
simply digested and reworked the earlier Guardian story.[11]

The *Manchester Evening News* 'late city' edition of the same
day, 21 August, beefed up the force of the page one story so
that it became a stronger prediction that Stalker would be
given his job back. The strapline was a quotation, 'He has
suffered enough', and the headline declared 'Move to send
Stalker back'. The story by Paul Horrocks, Steve Panter and
Michael Duffy said that 'strong moves' would be made at the
following day's meeting of the GMPA to send Stalker back to
work, and that councillors and magistrates looked set to reject
the Sampson report's recommendation that the matter should go
before an independent tribunal. The story was then substantiated
by quotations from councillors on the GMPA, including Tony
McCardell the Chairman of the GMPA's 'powerful policy committee'. This was followed by a statement from Roger Pannone
and an analysis of the political make-up of the authority.[12]

The page two story by Paul Horrocks on the Sampson report
changed its focus completely. Where its earlier headline had
referred to 'Stalker's mistake' it now focused on James Anderton,
and took the form of a question, 'Stalker: why no warning?'
and although it was still concerned with the section of the
report it stressed one paragraph for the introduction rather than
another. The story now began: 'Chief Constable Jim Anderton
should have given a direction to his deputy John Stalker about
the wisdom of attending political fundraising events. This is
one of the findings of the controversial Stalker Report which
has been compiled by West Yorkshire Chief Constable Colin
Sampson.'[13]

The criticism of Stalker was then referred to: 'And the report
says Mr. Stalker, Greater Manchester's Deputy Chief Constable,
should have checked more thoroughly on the associates of his
friend Kevin Taylor.' The paragraphs in the Samspson report
summary were from 426 to 434. The basis for the angle of
the story was paragraph 434 which includes the statement in

reference to Stalker having attended a Tory party fund raising function: 'It may well have been that Mr. Anderton should have given a direction to him, but he chose not to, and therefore Deputy Chief Constable Stalker attended'. Paragraph 426 was quoted further down the story on the subject of Stalker's relationship with Taylor:

> Here we have a police officer who has achieved the rank of Deputy Chief Constable on his ability as a shrewd, perceptive detective and police manager yet he failed even to suspect that Mr. Taylor, who he knows frequents gaming casinos and clubs and has owned yachts in Miami and subsequently Spain, might have attracted some police attention. Had he done some checking he would have found information concerning Taylor's associates.[14]

Whereas in the earlier edition the focus of the story was on the Stalker paragraph, in the later one it shifted to that referring to Anderton. This is in line with our examination of the structure of the news story in Chapter 2 where it was seen how a story about Taylor's ruin would equally have been focused on the fact that he had been the victim of a campaign of phone tapping. Clearly, the editor had decided that the angle that Anderton had been the target of some of Sampson's criticism was more newsworthy than that he had commented adversely on Stalker's behaviour. This is a judgement which it is easy to comprehend given that there was a wide expectation that the report would be critical of Stalker, who was after all the target of the inquiry, while Anderton, who helped to set in motion the whole process, was seen as behind the guns, not in the line of fire.

The newspaper references to the Sampson report at first were concerned to know what was in it, but as is indicated by Murtagh's *Guardian* article they quickly began to take an interest in its quality, which led them to focus on two aspects: the triviality of the charges against Stalker and the flimsiness of much of the evidence.

The momentum of criticism of the report was helped by Stalker himself who appeared on Granada TV's local news magazine programme *Granada Reports* on Thursday, 21 August, the night before the GMPA meeting where his future was to be decided.

He said he had only met Taylor four or five times and for about twenty-four hours in all each year. There had been more than 150 people at the functions they had attended, and at one of them there had been 500. He challenged people to judge him by the things that he knew at the time, and to ask themselves how much they knew about their friends.

> How on earth am I, anyone – a high court judge, a journalist, a bishop – how on earth are any of us in a position to know who is going to be there before we go, and when we do arrive, how are we to know that they have criminal convictions?

In *The Guardian* of the day of the meeting Murtagh revealed the names of 'nine behind Stalker charges'.[15] This referred to nine men who were at functions attended by Stalker who had previous convictions. The summary to the GMPA from which the members would have formed their impression of the seriousness of the charges against Stalker did not include details of the offences for which they had been convicted nor the dates of their convictions. Seven of the nine men referred to, associated by Sampson in his report with the QSG, had convictions between them dating from 1944 through to the most recent – 1979 – for offences ranging from wounding with intent to receiving and dishonesty. Of the other two, Stephen Hayes had two convictions for attempting to bribe a police officer in 1980 and demanding money with menaces in 1981, while Colin Peter Brown had fourteen convictions for offences ranging from theft to robbery with violence.

Again the article located these convicted men in terms of their significance at the functions attended by Stalker by reference to the total numbers of people. Hayes was identified as one of thirteen convicted people out of at least seventy-four at a January 1984 affair, and one of seven with convictions out of a party of at least fifty-one in August 1985. This is a concentration of one convicted person in six, which is a considerably greater leavening than that suggested in the statement by Stalker of two days before where he was claiming that the functions were attended by at least 150 guests and in one case over 500.

None the less the impression in the article was of a mountain having been made out of a molehill, and Murtagh included

Stalker's response that he had not known of the convictions of the men he knew and that his discovery of the record of Colin Peter Brown, which had caused him to have misgivings which he had expressed to Anderton was one of his reasons for breaking his relationship with Taylor.

The triviality and injustice of the misuse of cars charges were illuminated by the revelation that one of the allegations of private use of a police vehicle related to attendance at the Masonic Hall, Dunkinfield (Murtagh forbore to labour the obvious irony here), for a farewell celebration for an inspector with thirty years' service, combined with a town twinning ceremony attended by the mayor. Stalker had presented mementoes to representatives of the French town and bade public farewell to the retiring inspector. In a news story of the same day the Trojan Peter Murtagh reported that a Labour member had referred to Sampson as 'Mickey Mouse'.[16]

If the subtext of the Murtagh output of that day was that the Sampson report on Stalker was a document essentially to do with trivia the leader article in the same issue made this message clear. The charges of associating with known criminals, the leader argued, appeared to mean attending the same functions, while the car allegations were dismissed by Sampson's own report as relatively unimportant, and would, if admitted, only warrant a rebuke. In referring to the charge of associating with criminals it continued:

> It needs to be said, and said very loudly because Mr. Taylor has been paraded as a certain kind of person, that he has no criminal record and has been charged with no crime. As the Manchester Police Authority meets today, Mr. Stalker is charged with associating with an innocent man. And if that is regarded as in any way dubious, what about the Conservative Party, which chose Mr. Taylor as its local chairman? And those Government ministers who sat down to dine with him?'[17]

On the same day the *Manchester Evening News* ran two stories and a leader about the Stalker affair. On the presses before the meeting even began, the paper seemed to be possessed of an extraordinary prescience. The front page lead was based on the reported statement of Stalker, who said that he did not bear grudges and would be able to work with Anderton. The headline 'I can work with Mr. Anderton' seemed to be predicated on the assumption that he would be returned to work.[18] In a leader entitled 'End of the agony' Michael Unger, the editor, argued that the GMPA should return Stalker to work with a rebuke for his lack of judgement in some of the company he had kept. They should reject the Sampson report's main finding that the case should go to an independent tribunal. Stalker had suffered enough. This was exactly what the authority did decide.[19]

But the third offering in the *Manchester Evening News* that day could be seen as the most significant contribution to developing a generally accepted view of the quality of the report. It was a story by Steve Panter which appeared on page three under the headline 'Stalker and a Mitty liar' and went to the heart of the Sampson inquiry and found what seemed to be a false core to the whole issue. The intro made no bones about the nature of the story or how the reporter and editor assessed the value of the evidence in the Sampson report. The thirty-year career of 'one of Britain's most accomplished' police chiefs hung in the balance largely because of the false revelations of a 'lifelong liar'. The contrast between the two, entirely to the advantage of the one man and the detriment of the other, was carried on into the next paragraph, which declared that as Manchester's deputy chief constable waited anxiously 'the man responsible lay in a Manchester cemetery'.

But this story was no soft option attack on a dead man who could not sue for libel. The paper had in any case established a willingness to attack living targets where the editor and reporters thought they were establishing the truth about the Stalker affair. And for the same reason they had also run stories as the affair unfolded which seemed to be damaging to the case of Stalker himself. The purpose of the story was to look at the evidential basis of the case against Stalker as the police had made it and as it appeared in the report by Sampson.

The story revealed that the man behind the allegations, a petty crook with 'Walter Mitty fantasies', had offered to·do a deal with police when he had been arrested in 1983 along with two others in connection with a £500,000 fraud conspiracy. Quoting 'friends of David Bertlestein and police sources', Steve

Panter revealed that the informant himself had suggested the deal, which was for leniency in return for information. At the trial in 1984 Detective Superintendent McGourlay had told the judge that Bertlestein was helping police with information about other matters. While Mark Klapish, a co-defendant charged with identical offences, was sentenced to four years Bertlestein was sent down for two and a half.

He told police that the QSG was involved in gun running and had IRA connections, and accused Stalker of being involved with the gang, Panter's story revealed. As a result the 'highly secret' Drugs Intelligence Unit was set up and undertook the Taylor investigation. In addition to quotations from Sampson's report on Bertlestein's unreliability as a source of evidence Panter had obtained a statement from a ticket dealer, Mickey Martin, who said he had liked David Bertlestein for a long time but he had always been 'a pathological liar', always in trouble for cheating and fraud. Nine-tenths of his information could have been thrown away, and it had landed a lot of people, including Stalker, in trouble. He was 'a Walter Mitty character who always wanted to be Mr. Big'. In a nice touch of characterization, Martin revealed that Bertlestein, his 'so-called friend', had as a guest at the Martin home stolen a lighter and a pendant. A senior detective, unnamed, described Bertlestein as a regular informant who undoubtedly 'made things up' but the allegations were so grave that they had to be investigated.[20]

As we have seen, the previous coverage had called into question the terms under which the investigation had been set up and the motives which might have lain behind the denunciation of Stalker. This story began the process of examining critically the quality of the evidence in the report itself.

The Observer, two days after John Stalker's reinstatement, in its leader column took up the use of the term 'Mickey Mouse' and opined that this description 'may seem a little harsh' but pointed out that the Sampson inquiry had not addressed itself except by assertion to any of the issues to do with Northern Ireland and other matters that had 'so disturbed public opinion'. Instead, the paper argued, Sampson semed to have 'concentrated on the essentially trivial pursuit of turning over the engagements in Mr. Stalker's social diary and examining in the minutest detail the log-books of various police drivers'.

This was proof – if any were needed – of the 'profound unwisdom' of the initial decision to appoint the same man to undertake both the inquiry into Stalker, 'mainly founded on local rumour and innuendo', and simultaneously to continue Stalker's own inquiry into the RUC. The only way that any good could come out of the 'totally botched and unjust affair' was that Sampson should lose no further time in pursuing his main investigation into the RUC and MI5 and 'that it should be publicly shown to have been conducted without fear or favour'.[21]

The critique being developed through the *Manchester Evening News*, *The Guardian* and *The Observer* was to cast doubt on the wisdom of the way the Sampson inquiry had been set up, to question the appropriateness of one man inquiring both into Stalker's conduct and the RUC, to cast doubt on the seriousness of the charges against Stalker and to point out the nit-picking quality of the investigation into the use of police vehicles. Some doubt was also cast on the quality of the logic in the report and the reliability of the claims, given the denial of Chief Superintendent Topping's account of their meeting by Chief Superintendent Roberts, and the fact referred to by Panter in the *Manchester Evening News* that the story about Stalker's dubious social behaviour came from the Walter Mitty character, Bertlestein, alias Burton. Peter Murtagh also indicated the dubious nature of Burton's evidence.

On 9 September the papers carried stories that lawyers working for Stalker were considering whether to take legal action against Sampson over his report. The action contemplated was for libel, and the papers pointed out that such an action would have to prove that Sampson had not acted in good faith. Stalker was quoted as claiming that the report contained 'material inaccuracies' about the events which led to his three-month suspension.[22]

Most of the stories on the Sampson report were either the result of journalistic investigation based on a combination of critical examination of the Sampson report and inquiries among strictly anonymous police sources, or were reportage of comments by named public figures, involved directly or indirectly in the affair, who were commenting openly on the report. In this context the story about Stalker's possible libel action was simply the press reporting what a man who had become perforce a directly involved public figure was saying in an apparently public context.

But on 17 September *The Guardian* ran a story by Peter Murtagh, 'Officer claims Stalker report distortion', which appeared to breach the normal boundary between the public speaker whose views were openly available for reporting and the hidden and anonymous social world of police officers. It was the result of investigation by Murtagh into the origin of the charges against Stalker, and concerned Chief Superintendent Arthur Roberts, who, according to evidence from Topping in the Sampson report, said that Taylor's solicitor Ian Burton had said during a game of squash that Taylor, who was then the object of close CID scrutiny, would 'blow out' John Stalker if the police did not stop investigating him.

As we saw earlier (page 82) Roberts was quoted in the Sampson report as denying this. Murtagh's story now recounted Roberts's reaction to this part of the Sampson report. The story began: 'A senior Manchester police officer has threatened to confront his chief constable, Mr. James Anderton, over what he has claimed is a gross distortion of comments the officer made to a colleague about John Stalker.'

Murtagh wrote that the Sampson report referred to what Roberts allegedly told Topping, and then contrasted Roberts's version with what 'the report claimed'. According to Murtagh, Roberts and Ian Burton, the solicitor, had known one another for years and regularly played squash together. On one such occasion Burton had said he thought his client Taylor was the businessman under investigation over his relationship with a senior police officer, and in view of this asked whether the relationship with him (Burton) might be an embarrassment to Roberts. Roberts thought not. Later, according to Murtagh, Roberts had met Topping about a separate matter and 'casually mentioned' the issue of his conversation with Burton. From this innocent comment, according to the story, arose Topping's report to Anderton that, according to Ian Burton, via Chief Superintendent Roberts, Taylor was threatening to 'blow out' Stalker.

The evidential basis of the story about Roberts's state of mind was only referred to in one paragraph: 'Mr. Roberts

refused to comment yesterday but has made his feelings known
to colleagues. He is said to have been incensed that Mr. Topping
reported the conversation without informing him and that the
report was totally at odds with his recollection of what had
been said'.[23] But Peter Murtagh's informant was a police officer
sufficiently well known to Roberts for the paper to be willing to
use the story on this basis. And no public denial was ever made
by Roberts.

The story also contained a second plank in the structure of
doubt about the Sampson report which Murtagh built. This
was a reference to the evidence of the businessman Gerald
Wareing. While playing golf with Chief Superintendent Bernard
McGourlay in 1984 he had allegedly said that Stalker was at
parties in Taylor's house when 'known criminals' were present.
Murtagh revealed that 'Mr. Wareing said yesterday that he did
not know any criminals and had only seen Mr. Stalker once
at Mr. Taylor's house.' The inference drawn from this is made
clear in the final paragraph of the story:

> Despite this, the report seeks to use Mr. Wareing's conver-
> sation with Mr. McGourlay as lending weight to a string of
> other allegations made by a Manchester criminal, Mr. David
> Bertlestein, about Mr. Taylor and Mr. Stalker, five of which
> directly concerned Mr. Stalker. When these were investigated
> by Mr. Sampson, none was substantial.[24]

Thus the denial by Wareing, like the reported protest of
Roberts, is used to demonstrate the evidential weakness of the
Samspon report. Unreliable evidence, by implication, was used
to damn Stalker. The inference then is that a report dependent
on such evidence is unreliable. The question raised by such a
conclusion is why were people in authority willing to place
reliance on such inadequate and tainted testimony. The answer,
as we have seen repeatedly, came back to the idea that the pursuit
of Stalker was some sort of plot to cover up the truth about
Northern Ireland.

In a report on the remarks of the Conservative MP for Barrow,
Cecil Franks, Paul Horrocks produced a story which cast further
doubt directly on the reliability of the report. His story in the
Manchester Evening News of 27 September, 'Stalker report

rapped by MP', was angled on the claim in a statement by Franks, a former leader of Manchester City Council Conservative group, that the police had completely 'distorted' a statement he had made to the Sampson team during their investigation of Stalker. Franks was quoted in the Sampson report as being rather surprised at the presence of such a senior policeman at the fiftieth birthday party thrown by Taylor. Sampson referred to the reaction of Franks and five other guests at the party as evidence of the disrepute being brought on the police by Stalker's presence there.

Horrocks wrote that since the rejection of the Sampson inquiry findings by the GMPA 'it is known that at least three people, including a senior police officer' had complained that their views were misrepresented in the report. He then quoted the MP's statement that he could not see how comments he had made could possibly be used to support the view that Stalker was bringing discredit on the force. He further quoted Franks's view that because of inaccuracies and distortions in the report on Stalker doubt might be cast on the Sampson report on the RUC. He had lodged a protest with Home Secretary Douglas Hurd and was demanding a judicial review of the whole affair.[25]

The following day, under the white on black strapline 'The Irish Connection' the *Observer* team of David Leigh, Paul Lashmar and Jonathan Foster produced a detailed critique of the report which challenged its whole basis in fact and suggested as the strapline indicated a connection between the RUC end of the drama and the man who laid the allegations against Stalker in the first place – the copper's nark and convicted criminal David Burton alias Bertlestein. The headline 'Lying pest behind the Stalker probe' identified the nub of the article, that it *explained* the Sampson report, in the sense that it showed how it had arisen, by revealing what had gone on beforehand and unseen. The by-line was extended into a stand-first which made clear the connection the writers were attempting to establish: 'David Leigh, Paul Lashmar and Jonathan Foster detail the life and death of David Bertlestein, the criminal who peddled falsehoods and provides a link between Ulster and the suspension of Manchester's deputy Chief Constable.'

The story returned to the topic already broached by Murtagh in *The Guardian* and examined in some detail in Panter's story in the *Manchester Evening News*. They looked in more detail at the £500,000 fraud case referred to by Panter and raised the issue of who else than the GMP had the witness Bertlestein been sourcing with information. The earlier stories referring to this character in the drama had referred to the centrality of his evidence in the case against Stalker along with the implication that his compulsive lying must cast doubt on his evidence. *The Observer* took up the issue of Bertlestein's provision of information about the IRA to the police in Northern Ireland, and in this way provided an hypothesis which related the connection between the police and security services in Northern Ireland and the information laid against Stalker in Manchester.

In addition to the contacts they had already made in the Manchester police they also dealt with a solicitor who had other documentary information about Bertlestein's long criminal career in which lying and fantasy had always played a major part. In particular he had been a 'professional fraudster and confidence trickster'. The handle 'pest' was a quotation from a particular police officer, who remained anonymous, who reported that Bertlestein would sell people stolen goods and then inform on them, pick up scraps of information from one policeman and then sell them to another: 'He was notorious for claiming particular policemen were bent. He was a pest, always on the phone to different people.'[26]

The article was essentially based on two contrasted themes: first, the establishment of the fact that Bertlestein had been a liar, and had in particular lied to the police, and, second, that the police investigating Taylor and Stalker had believed his stories. The first gave a particular significance to the second. The narrative sense now involved a certain ironic appreciation of policemen pursuing a chief police officer on the basis of information provided by a man who had been convicted precisely because he told lies for his own profit. And what is more he had been prosecuted by the same police force for offences of fraud and deception: he was a professional criminal liar with a prison record to prove it.

Leigh, Lashmar and Foster went back to the Klapish trial featured in the *Manchester Evening News* of five weeks before and examined exactly what had happened there, and using contacts within the GMP they pursued the role of Bertlestein as an informant. They produced a chronological account of his career as it related to Northern Ireland and the Stalker affair, which involved an interweaving of his own activities as a scallywag with the development of the case against Stalker to which his own contribution was so fundamental.

The fraud case involving Klapish had taken place in 1983. It was what is known as a 'long firm fraud', that is to say the firm is set up from the outset with the object of obtaining goods on credit from its suppliers without any intention of ever paying them. Klapish had set up a company, Cut-Price (Wholesale Fancy Goods) Limited (CPWFG) in August 1979 in Manchester. The object of the firm was to wholesale jewellery and fancy goods, in fact by acquiring them by fraud and selling them quickly and cheaply at below the purchase price. Bertlestein, who already had a prison record for his activities as a fraudsman, was employed by Klapish as a con-man who would act as a buyer.

When suppliers put pressure on for payment for goods some would be paid from overdrawn bank accounts, some would be put off by issuing dud cheques, and others would be kept at bay by excuses about cheques being in the post, the firm was changing banks or the director who signs the cheques was away at the time. Eventually, however, Klapish knew this would no longer work and a simple ruse was to be employed to dig the firm out of its consequent difficulties. A warehouse was leased in Kent Street, Belfast, in a pro-IRA area and was to accommodate some small proportion of the stock on which payment was owed. This was then to be blown up by the IRA, and Klapish would claim that goods to the full value of the outstanding amount had been destroyed. An application for compensation was to be submitted to the Northern Ireland Office, who pay out to those who suffer loss from terrorist action in the province. The goods in the warehouse were worth £52,000, and because he needed nearly £600,000 to pay off the creditors a claim of £540,000 over the odds would be required.

The plan ran into a difficulty. In October 1983 Bertlestein was wanted for his part in the CPWFG long firm fraud, and, according to the *Observer* story, in order to avoid arrest, he told Sergeant Derek Burgess of the Manchester Fraud Squad that the Kent Street warehouse was to be blown up. On 6 January 1981 he again warned the Manchester police of the proposed attack on the CPWFG warehouse and on the morning of 26 January the attack took place. The tip-off by Bertlestein led to the failure of Klapish's scheme, a fact not referred to by *The Observer* because they were concerned primarily with those aspects of the case relating to the Stalker affair.

The security forces were ready for the attack, arrived quickly and prevented more than minimal damage. Northern Ireland fire loss assessors were also at the ready and were able to put a figure of £52,000 on the value of the stock in the building at the time of the attack. In order to rectify the failed bombing of nine o'clock in the morning the contractors, with a nice sense both of symmetry and dramatic irony, returned at nine o'clock in the evening and fired the building, gutting it. Forewarned by Bertlestein the police now had further evidence of the fraud that Klapish was set on committing.

According to the *Observer* team the information about the Kent Street warehouse bombing 'appears to have been one of Bertlestein's few genuine tips'. Accordingly 'his stock rose' and he supplied further dramatic information to the RUC and the Regional Crime Squad about the IRA. 'On one occasion' there was an unsuccessful high speed motor-cycle chase near Preston, after RUC intelligence identified two senior IRA brigade commanders travelling via Stranraer for meetings in Manchester.[27]

The article revealed that when in January 1983 Bertlestein was arrested for cheque frauds in Bolton he was held in custody and only obtained bail by claiming he had evidence of police corruption. The Regional Crime Squad had found its investigation of the QSG hampered by apparent leaks, and as a consqeuence the GMP internal investigation and complaints section, the 'Y' Department in the person of Chief Superintendent Derek Ankers, obtained bail for Bertlestein when at a special hearing in chambers he handed a request for it in a sealed letter to Judge Prestt.

But the *Observer* team were at pains to point out that the senior police officer whom Bertlestein identified as the source of leaks to the QSG was not Stalker:

But he originally [in 1983] named an entirely different senior police officer as corrupt. This officer, who we have traced, was under internal suspicion, his colleagues confirm. At around this time, he retired from the force. Yet the officer was never charged. Instead, Stalker's name began to figure in Bertlestein's corruption allegations.[28]

In order both to substantiate the line of the narrative now determined by this claim and to demonstrate that their inquiries were well grounded the writers then produced an impressive list of Manchester police officers who used Bertlestein as an informant. This also indicated that their informant was also a well-placed serving or recently retired Manchester police officer:

Bertlestein had apparently no evidence to give against Stalker in January 1983. Nor did he in his lengthy statements about the IRA connections to Sgt. Burgess the following February. Nor did he make any in his approaches to Det. Chief Inspector Douglas Savage of the special branch whom he asked to intercede on his behalf. Nor did he make any to Ch. Supt. Bernard McGourlay, of the regional crime squad, whom he asked to tell the court about his help as a paid informant.[29]

The first mention of John Stalker's name came eighteen months later in another context, the article claimed, in the golf course conversation between Wareing and McGourlay. The construction they put on this conversation was, however, different from that put forward by Topping in his evidence to the Sampson inquiry. According to Leigh, Lashmar and Foster Wareing had only mentioned to McGourlay that Taylor was a friend of Stalker and his name was 'constantly cropping up' as being associated with the QSG. 'McGourlay thought Stalker should be warned that the innocent link could be compromising. He mentioned it to Y Department headed by Ch. Supt. Peter Topping.'

The way in which this piece of information was treated was then presented by *The Observer* to show that at least it was doubtful and seemed to show both an enthusiasm to put Stalker in the worst possible light combined with an unwillingness to warn him of the dangers arising from his friendship with Taylor:

Stalker was never warned. Instead Topping demanded a written report on Taylor and his links to the Quality Street Gang.

The Drugs Squad confirmed to Topping that they were also watching Taylor's BMW car. Almost simultaneously with this incident, *Topping later maintained* [my emphasis], Bertlestein made a startling new allegation: that Stalker himself was also corrupt.

After Topping had written a confidential report about these allegations which was passed on to James Anderton, even though, as he told Sampson, 'he was doubtful about the quality of some of the information', Anderton had taken no action and 'Again, Stalker was never warned.'[30]

The *Observer* team then returned to the fraud trial in 1984, which was a devastating illustration of the unreliability of Bertlestein as a witness. It was also when 'Bertlestein got his reward for all this activity'. Klapish had pleaded guilty, which meant that the IRA charges never emerged in court. (Evidence of culpability in criminal cases is only produced in court where there is a not guilty plea.) They reported that at a later bankruptcy hearing Klapish had denied having made deals with the IRA. The court had then been cleared, and McGourlay had revealed that Bertlestein was a paid informant. Chief Superintendent Ankers of the 'Y' Department then told the judge about Bertlestein's allegations against corrupt policemen. Bertlestein's sentence 'was cut to two-and-a-half years'.

Bertlestein's unreliability as an informant was illustrated by the progress of the CPWFG trial. There was a third defendant, Joe 'Swords' Monaghan, who had a later trial. 'Bertlestein retracted his statements, and never testified: Monaghan was acquitted.' Bertlestein had won lenient treatment by his information and 'there the . . . matter might have rested', the origin of the 'vague claim about Stalker' being 'to say the least obscure' but in 1985 Topping was in command of the newly formed Drugs Intelligence Unit, and 'his men returned to Bertlestein in prison and obtained lengthy and lurid new details about "Stalker's corruption"'. The value of the new revelations was measured against Sampson's own assessment: 'there is remarkably little corroboration for Bertlestein's allegations'.[31]

The significance of this article is that it not only showed that Berlestein was a liar, and that he had been central to the inquiry – that had been shown already by the *Manchester Evening News* and *The Guardian*. It showed how Bertlestein's evidence about Stalker was tainted in that it had originated as part of a campaign on Bertlestein's part to obtain lenient treatment from the courts. It also showed, by reference to his failure to give evidence against his co-defendant Joe 'Swords' Monaghan and the lack of action by Anderton at the outset, that the matter appeared to have died a natural death until Topping revived the issue later. Finally, it related the relatively minor disciplinary charges which Sampson eventually laid against Stalker to the original line which had been pursued by the internal corruption inquiry. The impression left by the article was that what had begun as an investigation of a probable corrupt relationship between another officer and the QSG had proceeded through the fanciful denunciations by the liar Bertlestein to a dredging operation for anything, however minor, with which to discredit Stalker.

The following day, in *The Guardian*, Peter Murtagh was able to put a name to the connection between the Manchester police, the RUC, Stalker and Taylor. This was Chief Superintendent Bill Mooney, who was in command of a special team of RUC detectives set up in 1982 to investigate IRA involvement in extortion. Murtagh also referred to the Bertlestein–Northern Ireland connection. Bertlestein was related in a stand-first to the extortion issue, but the body of the story did not actually demonstrate that Mooney and Bertlestein ever met. The whole thrust of the story was to establish the link between the Stalker affair and the province. The headline read: 'RUC officer in Stalker link to province', and the stand-first declared 'an informer who alleged extortion in Ulster made false claims against John Stalker, writes Peter Murtagh'.

The two parts of the case were linked in the intro thus: 'An RUC officer who knew of the friendship between Mr. John Stalker and Mr. Kevin Taylor headed a team which investigated extortion in Northern Ireland. Allegations about bogus compensation claims were made by the Manchester-based criminal who also made unsubstantiated claims against Mr. Stalker.'[32]

In the body of the story Murtagh explained that the RUC officer in charge of the extortion investigation, Bill Mooney, had featured in the Sampson report: 'Mr. Sampson describes how in 1976 Mr. Mooney and RUC colleague, Chief Superintendent Willie Hylands, came to Manchester and met Mr.

Taylor through Mr. Stalker during an evening of work. The two RUC officers were in the city to find a safe house for an IRA informer.'

In relation to the connection between the Stalker inquiry and the RUC in relation to Bertlestein, Murtagh wrote: 'Government ministers and spokesmen have consistently denied any link between Mr. Stalker's work in Northern Ireland and the allegations which led to his removal from duty. However it has now been disclosed that Bertlestein, the source of the allegation against Stalker, was also working for the RUC.' There was no evidence in his report to suggest that Sampson investigated Bertlestein to the point where he learned of his relationship with the RUC, Murtagh added.[33]

Thus for the six weeks following the leaking of the report of the summary of the Sampson inquiry there was a concentrated examination of its contents by the *Manchester Evening News*, *The Guardian* and *The Observer* which had both reported the views of those involved and had investigated the report itself. This had enabled them to show who had been behind the original allegations and which senior police officers in the GMP pursued the case against the deputy chief constable. They had also shown that much of the evidence had been unreliable and that police officers and 'respectable' citizens quoted in the report subsequently denied words or meanings directly or indirectly attributed to them; that the original allegations against Stalker made by Bertlestein involved the serious charge of corruption; that when this failed to materialize the issue had been pursued by Sampson first into the less serious charge of associating with known criminals and then into trivial hair-splitting over the use of police vehicles, and finally that there had been a connection between the Stalker–Taylor relationship and the RUC in the shape of both Chief Superintendent Mooney and David Bertlestein, a connection of which, in the words of Murtagh, Sampson had not learned.

CHAPTER NINE

James Anderton's silent suffering

The Stalker troubles did not occur in a vacuum in relations between GMP and the press. James Anderton's penchant for publicity had made him probably the best known chief constable in the country. His battles with the Labour controlled Greater Manchester Police Committee and its precursor, the police committee over public order policing and the acquisition of riot control equipment and firearms meant that police issues were reported in the regional and national press as ideologically charged controversies. Anderton's views on religion were also widely canvassed. There had been since the early 1970s an alternative press in the city which had often criticized Anderton as a policeman and lampooned him as a person, and the current alternative magazine, *City Life*, had carried numerous stories about disciplinary action taken against senior officers, about their embarrassing friendships with members of the opposite sex, their suspensions from duty and their membership of the Freemasons.

Allegations that Stalker had been treated to free meals in a Chinese restaurant (referred to by Colin Sampson who found it groundless) was one of the stories that was current among many others about senior police officers which were never published because they were never supported by evidence. Numerous stories abounded also about Anderton. Taylor, who was Chairman of the Manchester Conservative Association, was also the focus of numerous stories. When the Stalker affair put these often essentially petty anecdotes into a context of uncontested national significance they all came to take on an importance for journalists they did not previously possess.

For about a year and a half before Stalker's enforced extended leave was announced *City Life* had been receiving anonymous letters about the Manchester Conservative Association, alleging that some prominent members had been members of the National Front, had criminal records, had been rapists. The news editor, Ed Glinert, had generally found that these stories could not be stood up, but filed them away for information.

In their inquiries into the Stalker affair the *Observer* team, Jonathan Foster, Paul Lashmar and David Leigh approached the local press, including *City Life*, as is normal when national newspapers come to a locality. In the small social world of journalists there are numerous connections in the network and the *Observer* reporters knew a former Manchester alternative magazine editor, now a broadcaster, who was already in contact with *City Life* and also put them in touch with a police 'mole'. This led them to make inquiries about the Conservative anonymous letter campaign and about allegations which were current about the social life of James Anderton.

These inquiries centred around two issues in relation to the Stalker affair: the first was again the legitimacy of the way in which the inquiry into Stalker's behaviour had arisen; the second was whether Stalker's patterns of social life and friendships were materially any different from other senior police officers', in particular Anderton's. Both themes were combined in an article entitled 'Tory infighting led to Stalker probe', by Leigh and Lashmar in *The Observer* of 29 June 1986.[1]

This article argued that the campaign against Taylor in Manchester led to a complaint against him to the then Conservative Party Chairman John Gummer which in turn resulted in a police dossier being compiled on him. 'The dossier was then activated – not to charge Mr. Taylor with offences but to remove deputy chief constable John Stalker, a personal friend, from his politically controversial Ulster Constabulary inquiry on vague "disciplinary" grounds.'

In tandem the writers raised the question of whether the behaviour of Stalker was in any way unusual among similarly placed policemen: 'Criticism of the way in which Manchester chief constable James Anderton removed Mr. Stalker from his duties is likely to increase following disclosures that other senior officers, including the chief constable himself, have socialised with rich Manchester businessmen.' This was followed by claims that Anderton had had dinner at the house of scrap metal dealer Freddie Pye and had accepted a 'personal gift' from him; that he had 'accepted a kind invitation' to take a holiday in the apartment in Portugal of a businessman, Luis Anton, at whose house he had also attended parties where police officers directed traffic and that he had presided at mess dinners at police headquarters where Taylor was present as Stalker's guest.[2]

The article claimed that after Taylor became Chairman of the Conservative Association he became deeply unpopular among members who thought that as a heavy gambler he was 'inappropriate' and then the poison pen letters from 'some local Tories' accused him of malpractices and criticized his 'then aide' Jerry Carey and his associate, the ex-policeman Stephen Hayes. When he tried to move the association headquarters to his own offices matters came to a head because of what his critics regarded as his dominance in fund raising. This resulted 'according to senior Manchester Conservatives' in a request from an association member for a police inquiry to check Taylor's activities. The same member also approached Gummer who 'took steps to assist in having Mr. Taylor ousted and the association reorganised'.

Leigh and Lashmar then formulated the connection between this chain of events among the Manchester Conservatives and the removal of Stalker from the Northern Ireland inquiry:

No 1 Regional Crime Squad's investigations into Mr. Taylor's activities proved inconclusive despite the tapping of his phone. It was when Mr. Stalker insisted on returning to Northern Ireland to obtain a vital MI5 surveillance tape which had been withheld from him that Mr. Taylor's house was raided on 9 May.

Photographs of Mr. Taylor and Mr. Stalker together led Mr. Anderton to remove him from duty, and Sir John Hermon, the RUC Chief Constable to remove him from the Ulster inquiry with the knowledge of two members of the Government, the Home Secretary and the Attorney-General.[3]

The writers turned their attention to Anderton to substantiate their claims about his social life. He had confirmed, they said, that he had accepted a holiday invitation from businessman Luis Anton, who was honorary Portuguese consul. They quoted his own statement that he had stayed at the consul's flat in Portugal with his family 'only once', in August 1982; that he had paid his own air fares and took more than £1,000 from his bank to cover his holiday expenses. They quoted Pye's acknowledgement that he mingled socially with senior police officers and had been at the 'top table in the senior officer's mess'. Neither Pye or Anton, it was acknowledged, had a criminal record or any criminal associates.[4]

This article marked a total schism in relations between *The Observer* in particular and the press in general and James Anderton, over what he regarded as private matters. The concluding part of the article reported the attempts of the writers to gain information from Anderton about his relations with the two men. He refused to answer the thirteen questions submitted and said he would make a complaint to the appropriate authorities about their approaches. His final words, quoted by the paper, were, 'The chief constable considers himself under no obligation to account to an inquisitive and inquiring Press about his personal or professional conduct or behaviour.'[5]

The 'Citizen' column in *City Life* took the attack on Anderton further, lampooning him for his public avowals of his special relationship with the Almighty. Ed Glinert, who wrote the column, revealed that the gift from Freddie Pye to Anderton was a miner's lamp and then went on to recount the collapse of the Manchester branch of the Irish Trust Bank in 1976. Pye, said the article, was a director of the bank, which had advanced a sum 'believed to be more than £200,000' to Pye Metals, and when the sum was called in Pye Metals failed to pay and the receiver was called in. Glinert wrote that the GMP said they had never investigated the bank's collapse, nor had any members of the public complained about their temporary loss of funds.

The article also pursued the issue of the party at the home of Luis Anton, and revealed that at the eighth annual party thrown by Anton as Portuguese consul in the city the 150 guests enjoyed the services of at least one policeman to help ease the traffic. 'One guest' was quoted as saying there were at least two police officers present, but the GMP said that only one was there. The article pointed out that Anderton had recently been complaining that the force was understaffed by nearly 2,000 officers, and despite the assurance from the GMP that anyone could ask for a similar facility, cast doubt on the idea that police would be deployed for a party in Moss Side or Cheetham Hill (two predominantly poor areas with black and Asian communities in the inner city).[6]

The original information about Anderton's relationship with Anton came from sources in the police and predated by some years the Stalker affair. However, its publication in *The Observer* led to a series of other leaks in the form of unsigned letters to *City Life*. These letters alleged that *The Observer* had 'got it right' and then went on to make other allegations about Anderton. They were all of a trivial nature and related to what might have amounted to misuse of police vehicles, associating with men with suspect pasts or using police officers to carry out private work for him. The letters appeared to be from a police source because they revealed some detailed knowledge of procedure and apparently were based on an intimate knowledge of Anderton's use of his staff car. The first one ended with the rhetorical imprecation 'let's see what you do with this' and the promise 'we will write again'. It was an invitation for journalists to dig up evidence to substantiate the allegations in the tip-off letters. In the event none of the claims was ever substantiated.

Journalists searched for the source of the letters among former police officers who had been drivers of Anderton's staff car who might also bear a grudge against him. Police contacts told them of two. One was an elderly man who had retired, and had moved on to work for a security firm. He had reputedly been forced to retire and bore an animus against his old boss as a result. He was traced and when found denied this and expressed nothing but admiration for his former chief. He would not confirm any of the claims in the letters. The second was a younger man who had allegedly been sacked as a driver because he had had an affair with a senior officer's wife. Having been sent back on the beat he was now pounding the mean streets of the inner city with his heart full of vengeance. Despite the endeavours of the press's finest hacks he was never found, and the story was not disproved, or confirmed. My own inquiries indicate that this driver had in fact never been transferred for such an amorous adventure, but had moved to the CID and had married a woman who had previously been married to another officer of similarly low rank.

The BBC Radio Four programme *File on Four* researched a programme on the Stalker affair and Anderton's role in it, but this was never broadcast. Researchers had made inquiries in affluent, leafy Broad Lane, Hale, in stockbroker Cheshire where Anton lived. The BBC researchers and newspaper journalists also looked into claims in letters about a fishing holiday in Scotland and Anderton's contacts with the boxing community in Manchester.

Another letter referred to an allegation about free meals by senior police officers at a Greek restaurant and told the recipients to 'ask Mrs. Cox', a reference to Mrs Gabrielle Cox, Chairwoman of the Greater Manchester Police Committee, the precursor of the GMPA. This was a reference to an inquiry into the allegation that Anderton had received free meals from the Acropolis restaurant near the city centre. When a member of the legal department of the then county council asked Anderton for a copy of the file on the restaurant he was refused, and it was agreed that the inquiry should be carried out by the HMI of Constabulary for the North West. When no evidence of favouritism to the restaurant was discovered the inquiry was closed.

A further source within the police informed *City Life* that an emergency meeting of assistant chief constables and chief superintendents had been called early in July by Anderton to discuss the crisis of force morale caused by the Stalker affair. The meeting took place, according to the police source, only two days after the regular two-monthly meeting of the thirty-six top GMP officers, and was their first emergency meeting in the twelve-year history of the force.

The mid-July issue of *City Life* launched into another attack on Anderton. Glinert reported the meeting with the senior officers claiming that during this meeting Anderton had 'desperately attempted to rally his troops' and had demanded to know from each whether the Stalker affair had had any effect on morale. 'No one dared place their career on the line, but there were suggestions from brave quarters, denied by Anderton, that there had been a conspiracy against John Stalker', the article claimed.[7]

It also pressed the issue of the use of policemen as car park attendants at the parties given by Luis Anton, and reported that neighbours of the Antons reported that several police officers had been in attendance at two or three parties a year since the turn of the decade, with traffic police turning up in the morning to place cones along the street in preparation. Referring to questions about the Acropolis restaurant and fifty-eight others submitted to Anderton, Glinert quoted Anderton's refusal to answer questions from the media and his expressed willingness to answer to the 'appropriate authority'.

The article concluded with a series of questions on which it suggested members of the GMPA should focus attention. These were the holiday which the chief constable had spent in Portugal; his trip to Portugal, on another occasion, to inaugurate direct flights between Manchester and Lisbon; the alleged use of policemen as car park attendants and of the police band at a 'lavish firework display' at Anton's house on 5 November 1981; a similar allegation about another party at Anton's at Christmas 1983; an allegation that the police band dance combo had played at a twenty-first birthday party for Anderton's daughter in July 1983; the gift of the miner's lamp from Freddie Pye, and the issue of why no inquiries were carried out into the collapse of the Irish Trust Bank in 1976.

The questions were a combination of allegations contained in some of the anonymous letters, information from contacts within the police force and inquiries by *City Life* in Manchester and Dublin. The allegations on which they were based were a combination of some which were new and some which had been current in Manchester for a number of years. Glinert's use of them at that time was in their relationship to the Stalker affair. None of them could be regarded as serious issues in themselves, but they were seen by Glinert as being in the same category of triviality as those against Stalker. The *Observer* team saw them in the same light. On the other hand, journalists such as Peter Murtagh of *The Guardian* felt that the allegations made against James Anderton related to his private life, and you could not object to the hounding of Stalker but do the same sort of thing to Anderton. Mike Unger of the *Manchester Evening News* was not prepared to entertain what he regarded as allegations unsubstantiated by evidence. He had previously not used the same sort of unsubstantiated material about Stalker.

What began in the small alternative magazine in July took off in the national press nearly two months later, when the issue had been taken up by members of the police authority. Whereas *City Life*, after its own investigations into allegations in some of the anonymous letters, had gone out on a limb in raising these allegations as issues, the established press, apart from *The Guardian* and *The Observer*, generally merely reported on the proceedings of the GMPA or leaks about what was to happen there. On 31 August 1986 *Today* reported that Anderton was facing questions from members of the GMPA about 'holidays with a criminal' and unauthorized trips in a helicopter.[8] The following day *The Star* carried a report, 'Now Anderton faces inquiry' stating, 'Now his [Stalker's] £40,000 a year boss faces similar accusations from the left wing of the Labour dominated authority. Mr. Anderton will be asked to answer allegations concerning a holiday with a man with a minor criminal conviction and the use of a police helicopter.'[9]

These allegations arose out of two of the anonymous letters. It is a reflection on the poor efficiency of Anderton's critics that they did not even get the accusations right. The first allegation was that he had spent a salmon fishing holiday in Scotland with an ex-bookmaker and a former Conservative Chairman of the GMP Committee, Archie Thornhill, and a third man, allegedly with a criminal record. The second allegation to do with the helicopter did not even relate to Anderton or to the GMP. It was that a former Manchester officer, who had become a chief constable of another force, had given a businessman friend of Anderton a free ride in a helicopter belonging to the other force. Anderton's only connection with the allegation was that he knew both men!

Anderton rebutted the charges against him in a statement issued on 2 September 1986 and challenged anyone with evidence of alleged misconduct to pass it on to the chairman and clerk of the GMPA.[10] But the matter did not rest there. On 3 September *The Guardian* reported that the Labour group on the GMPA might call an inquiry into the allegations against Anderton. Peter Murtagh and Michael Morris said that Tony McCardell, leader of the 24-strong Labour group, had said the group would have to decide what they would be doing at the next meeting of the GMPA about approximately twenty questions they wished to put to Anderton.[11]

Behind a relatively small amount of coverage there lay a lot of journalistic activity. Apart from the attempts to track down his former drivers, journalists turned up in large numbers wherever Anderton made a public appearance. When he went to an innocent routine meeting to present medals to long-serving inspectors the journalists who had been invited as part of the normal public relations procedures were suddenly seen as a threat and were excluded from the meeting. Granada TV news cameras were barred from the presentation. The unfortunate GMP PR man Superintendent John Harrington, an ex-Special Branch officer with a soft Irish brogue, was obliged to do the job of keeping out the cameras. When they then attempted to film through a glass door he placed himself between the prying eyes of the millions and his chief silently, for the viewer, speechifying in a room full of consenting adults.

Anderton was also pursued by a posse of journalists and cameramen from the August meeting of the GMPA back to his home in The Avenue, Sale, where he was filmed retreating across his lawn to his front door, in a scene reminiscent of the Watergate-dogged Nixon fleeing indoors across the Pennsylvania Avenue lawn. But the cause of his becoming the quarry in a form of blood sport was not simply questions about his own social life. His role in the Stalker affair itself was also the subject of journalistic inquiries: both the terms under which the inquiry had been set up and the way in which Anderton had behaved towards his deputy, particularly on his return to work after having been cleared of any serious misconduct by the GMPA.

Although Anderton reportedly regarded *The Observer* reporters as the worst offenders in a campaign of harassment none of the journalists from any of the serious national newspapers pursued a series of personal attacks on him made in other anonymous letters and related entirely to his family life. The letters about his alleged relationships with rich individuals and allegations about his use of his staff car and the deployment of his own staff officers were written in block capitals and concerned matters which, if true, could only have resulted from direct knowledge of what happened within the GMP. One of the letters, for instance referred to two constables, Smith and Patience, who were both members of his personal staff who worked on the eleventh floor of the GMP headquarters, Chester House.

The letters which concerned Anderton's family were written in a cursive hand and showed no familiarity with general police practice or with the particulars of the GMP. None of them was ever substantiated. One made an allegation about Anderton's relationship with his son – Anderton does not have a son. It was a version of a rumour which circulated widely in the city – that there was a son who had been thrown out of the family home because he was either a homosexual or a drug addict and had subsequently taken up residence either above a public house in North Manchester or in Canada. The purpose of the story was to show what a cruel man the Chief Constable was. The only reason for recounting this untruth here is that it did have a consequence in terms of publication in the press.

Shortly before Christmas 1986 Anderton spoke at a conference at the GMP's Sedgely Park Training College on the police handling of Aids and hepatitis. During this speech he said: 'Everywhere I go I see increasing evidence of people swirling about in a human cesspit of their own making', and,

> Speaking as a man, Christian, husband, police officer, father, lover of the human race, believer in God's creation and, above all, someone who wants to see a future for children born today, we must ask why homosexuals freely engage in sodomy – let's be blunt about it – and other obnoxious practices, knowing the dangers involved. We must ask it head-on, challenging them to answer it.

He also said we should ask 'why so many happily married men seek prostitutes, instead of publicising the wearing of condoms'. And he further warned his audience to 'avoid feelings of intolerance and rejection to others'.

The press reported the speech as an attack on gays and prostitutes, stressing this rather than the attack on adulterous married men, or the plea for tolerance of others. The furore generated by this speech was further compounded by remarks made by Anderton after the month's GMPA meeting which had voted by twenty-one votes to twenty to investigate whether to take disciplinary action against him. This was also the meeting that heard of Stalker's decision to ask for retirement. Anderton told journalists that he had not written the speech beforehand and had been 'moved by the spirit of God' to way what he did while being driven to the conference.

He expressed himself in no mood to retract. He said:'I have never felt such peace of mind in my life before. I was completely calm. I was completely contented. I have got no regrets at all.' The press linked the Chief Constable to God. The *Daily Mail* in a composite of three stories on the Aids speech, Stalker's retirement and the search for the bodies of the moors murders referred to 'an astonishing claim' by Stalker's boss. The headline declared 'Aids speech was inspired by God, says Anderton' and the intro said, 'A police chief who blamed the spread of AIDS on homosexuals and prostitutes claimed yesterday that he was inspired by a message from God.'[12] The *Daily Express* reported in similar vein: 'Anderton: I was moved by God's spirit.'[13]

Journalists from the national and regional newspapers began to search for the missing son, and after a time discovered that the story referred to a daughter. Eventually, Paul Horrocks of the *Manchester Evening News* found her in London. He discovered where she worked and left a message for her to ring him at his hotel. His only contact with her was a refusal to give an interview. He received a call from Anderton's staff officer, saying that she did not wish to speak to him. After consulting his editor Horrocks returned to Manchester. The *Manchester Evening News* decided to respect the request, realizing that the call from Chester House meant that she had called her father and asked for the call to be made to Horrocks, who wrote the story without any further attempt to pry into her private life.

The story simply related that Gillian Anderton worked among the London homeless. It was flagged 'Anderton's girl quits college to help the homeless. A quiet Samaritan among drop-outs' and portrayed Gillian Anderton in an entirely admirable light, as a person who was both altruistic and retiring.[14] The matter did not end there however.

In March 1988, the *News of the World* ran a series of articles on Anderton. In the third week of this series, their front page lead declared 'GOD'S COP GIRL IS A GAY!' It claimed that 'anti-gay' police chief Anderton was 'bravely facing up to the fact that his only daughter is a lesbian'. The story by Tim Carroll had her living in a 'love nest' with a 'blonde girlfriend'.[15] There was a classic *News of the World* crosshead, 'Pervert', which related to something Gillian allegedly said she feared her father would say when told of it, whereas in fact he reportedly said that it was 'okay' and 'all right' and had asked why she had not told him earlier.[16]

The story included a reference to the cesspit speech in the fourth paragraph: 'And Greater Manchester's Chief Constable, who once accused gays of "swirling around in a cesspit of their own making" has accepted Gill's lover . . . into the family.' The *News of the World* found Gillian Anderton by taking over where the *Manchester Evening News* had left off. They knew that she worked in Croydon for a housing trust and found the pub where she spent some of her evenings and waited there for her to obtain an interview.

Thus, aspects of the Anderton family life originally became part of the public domain as a consequence of Stalker's private life being made a public issue through the actions of agencies of social control, of which Anderton was an important part, and through a series of actions in which he was a major player. The publicity related to two quite separate areas:

(a) Anderton's relationships with rich businessmen and questions about the use of police vehicles where a case could have been made out as weak as the one brought against Stalker, provided the allegations in the anonymous letters were true;

(b) matters to do with his family which only seemed to be newsworthy because of his own outspoken religious and social views, but which only bore coincidentally on the Stalker affair in that they gave a high public profile to matters associated with the GMP, and in particular James Anderton.

The relationship between Anderton and the GMPA was both an object of public scrutiny in the form of news coverage and a consequence of that news coverage. The Aids speech earned Anderton a further increment to his already considerable national notoriety. By 22 January 1987 representatives of the GMPA and Anderton were holding separate meetings in London with Sir Laurence Byford, the Chief Inspector of Constabulary, and the head of the Home Office Police Department. The subject of these meetings was the issue of whether Anderton was free to express his views in the media on controversial matters. The GMPA wanted him to refrain or resign, and Anderton was, in public at least, defending his right to express his views.

In particular some members of the committee were concerned about remarks made by the chief constable on the BBC's Radio Four programme *Sunday* on 18 January in which he had said that he had to accept that he might well be used as a prophet by God. As could have been predicted, this was widely reported by the press, and was used in unforeseen ways. Typically, in *The Independent*, Malcolm Pithers reported the case under the headline 'Row over Anderton prophet claim' with quotations from two members of the Manchester City Council's Police Monitoring Committee. The then chairman, Councillor Tony McCardell, who was also Chairman of the GMPA Finance and Policy Committee, said, amongst other comments, that 'if he were the chief executive of a council or a firm we would be advising him to seek medical help'. A pocket cartoon next to the front page story showed a constable with the words 'and God said' coming out of his walkie-talkie.[17]

The *Daily Mirror* referred to the 'AIDS outburst police chief's amazing claim' and, alongside a photograph of the bearded Anderton, ran a massive block capital headline, 'I MAY BE GOD'S PROPHET'.[18] That evening the *Manchester Evening News* ran a story under the strapline 'He needs medical help', which referred to a statement by Tony McCardell.[19] Anderton himself answered this suggestion from McCardell the next day in a statement which described the suggestion that he needed treatment as defamatory, and attacking the notion that he should be treated in such a way for simply expressing his beliefs.[20] The following morning the *Daily Mirror* returned to the theme with a full page news feature with the subtle strapline '"Prophet" Anderton is given a down-to-earth message: Resign' which topped the even more subtle white-on-black block capital headline 'HOW DO YOU TELL A CHIEF CONSTABLE HE'S OFF HIS ROCKER?' And should any reader be in any doubt as to who was the subject of the article there was a photograph of Anderton at the top right of the page with the caption

'ANDERTON: needs medical help' and a block of the previous day's page one headline and photograph.[21]

There was a novel use of the issue by News UK, the owners of *Today*, as part of a poster sales campaign for the paper. A series of massive billboard posters was issued, based on a strong visual joke. They lampooned prominent figures in the news, and in the top centre of the poster the paper's name *Today* was displayed. One of the series was a giant portrait photograph of the smiling Anderton fifteen feet high against a cloudy sky with the sunlight bursting through – clearly signifying God speaking. Across the bottom of the picture were the words 'Halo, Halo, Halo, have our police ideas above their station?'

This poster reportedly angered Anderton, as the *Manchester Evening News* reported under the headline 'Jim upset as ad knocks his halo'. The ribald story appeared alongside a picture of the poster and made clear to readers what the subtext of the advertisement was: 'Controversial top cop Jim Anderton is seeing his lawyer over a cheeky advert which splashes his picture over street hoardings. Huge portraits of the Greater Manchester Chief Constable attacked for his "Prophet of God" speech are appearing all over the country.' The *Manchester Evening News* reported that Anderton said he had not given permission for *Today* to use his picture in the advertising campaign.[22]

This reflected the increasingly tense and rancorous relations between the chief constable and the media. The meeting at the Home Office on 22 January was the scene of another confrontation between the assembled pack of hacks and Anderton. Instead of arriving at the Home Office by car Anderton, in full-braided uniform, arrived from St James's Park across the road without an escort, and in the words of Gareth Parry of *The Guardian* 'was pinned on the walls of the Home Office by the pressure of around 50 reporters and several television and radio crews'.[23]

Papers such as *The Guardian* and *The Observer* might have been expected to have criticized Anderton: the abyss between the social and political attitudes exemplified by these papers and those of the chief constable would seem to make antagonism inevitable. But criticism came from all sides. *The Independent* accepted that it might be seen as a sign of the times that a chief constable expressing his religious views left himself open to attack by a 'politically motivated' monitoring committee and a 'rather more moderate' police authority.[24] This exemplified the normal Conservative ideological construction of 'politically motivated = left-wing' and 'moderate = right-wing', exposed by the Glasgow Media Group and others. But the leader went on to argue that if Anderton did not realize the impact of phrases like 'cesspits' and 'degenerate conduct' or his call for homosexuals to abandon their 'obnoxious practices' then common sense indicated 'he should consider restraining his impulse to air his religious beliefs'.[25]

The Daily Telegraph editorialized the same day that it would be wrong to call for Anderton's resignation because of a foolish public pronouncement, but there were already 'doubts about his professional performance'. The Stalker affair, the moors murders investigation and his relationship with Manchester's 'ultra-Left police committee' had all served to damage the image of Anderton's force. 'For his own sake and the sake of his colleagues, the Chief Constable should now observe a Trappist silence for a decent period', the leader declared, and added, 'It is all very well for Mr. Anderton to be ever-conscious of his Great Taskmaster's eye upon him. But it would help were he a little less in the public's.'[26]

The Manchester Evening News at the this point took a similar line to these national establishment voices. In a leader entitled 'Time for quiet' it laid blame on both Anderton and the Labour GMPA Chairman Steve Murphy for telling Anderton to shut up or get out and on his more left-wing colleagues, Tony McCardell and Ken Strath, the former for suggesting that the police chief needed medical help and the latter for comparing him with Hitler. The paper wanted Anderton to leave moral issues to the church and concentrate on halting the soaring crime figures in Greater Manchester.[27]

But this was untypically mild for the treatment of Anderton by the Manchester Evening News. From very early in the Stalker affair the leader column questioned his actions and offered forceful criticism. A leader which complained about his attitude to the reinstated Stalker referred to Anderton's 'strange behaviour' and raised the issue of whether he was fit to take his turn as president of ACPO (the Association of Chief Police Officers): 'members of this prestigious body might well question he has behaved in a manner which deserves such a high honour'.[28]

At the end of his year's office with ACPO he was again embattled with the media and the *Manchester Evening News* was once more on the attack, as the best form of defence. In a speech at Bolton Anderton had attacked the media as arrogant and guilty of 'blatant nosiness' in prying into domestic and private matters. He also objected to media comments on 'anything at all affecting the role and duties of the police'. The paper used the 'prophet of God' reference to lampoon him. 'Prophet Jim hath spoken again', the leading article began. And in reference to his call for controls on the press it commented: 'It is not clear whether this is one of the Almighty's ideas or whether Mr. Anderton thought it up for himself, but it sounds remarkably like censorship to us.' The final sentence maintained the same combative and satirical pitch: 'Prophet Jim, who is not renowned for being averse to a spot of personal publicity, should practise what he preaches.'[29]

The antagonism towards Anderton emerged then from journalistic investigation of the Stalker affair and his role in it, from the follow-up to the poison pen letters and from his public disputes with the GMPA in particular, and the godless left in general. It took a variety of forms, from public disputes of principle through leader columns, angry exchanges at press conferences and the revelation of family matters which could only be seen as publicly significant by the exercise of extreme ingenuity by the *News of the World*. But there was a further source of journalistic activity which publicly called into question Anderton's actions.

This was litigation brought by Taylor against Anderton to force the revelation of the nature of the material the police acquired through their search of Taylor's house on a warrant alleging a £240,000 fraud on the Co-operative Bank. The first stories appeared in late September 1986. On 24 September *The Guardian* ran a story by Peter Murtagh headed 'Taylor launching legal action against Anderton'.[30] Anderton and the GMPA received such a summons that day. The date of the hearing was 2 October when an adjournment was granted until 15 October.

When the case began the *Manchester Evening News* led with a news story headed 'Anderton accused of conspiracy'. The intro focused on the allegation that 'Jim Anderton has been accused of conspiracy to pervert the course of justice, a high court heard today.' This referred to a revelation by Taylor's barrister, Robin de Wilde, in the case to force the police to justify the search of his house. De Wilde revealed that a summons had been issued the previous day by magistrates at Bury alleging that Anderton had conspired with others to 'procure and cause to lay false information on oath' when police had applied for the search warrant against Taylor on 7 May 1986. Peter Topping and Detective Inspector Tony Stephenson were also named on the summons.[31]

The application to the court to make the police disclose the information failed, as did the conspiracy charge. But for the time that they were current they provided one more focus for a press coverage of Anderton which metamorphosed him from the people's friend and the spokesman for the common man to a figure of fun with a proneness for getting things wrong where a level of savoir-faire was required.

The stories referred to in this chapter are a small sample of those centred on Anderton which appeared in the press around the time of the Stalker affair. This coverage, as we have indicated, became increasingly antagonistic, and the activities of journalists at press conferences and on public occasions became increasingly combative in questioning the Manchester police chief, especially in the light of the Aids/cesspit speech. He stepped down from a formal duty to receive the Queen on a vist to the city, and his place was taken by his deputy, John Stalker, who was then already working out his notice. The view was widely accepted that Anderton had done so to avoid embarrassing the monarch, because he had actually managed to make himself more controversially high profile than Stalker, whose fame as the victim of a state plot to suppress murder and pervert the course of duty had spread around the world.[32]

Conclusion

The Stalker affair blew up in a political context of conflict between the GMPA and Anderton, and, even more so, between the Manchester City Council Police Monitoring Committee and Anderton. There was a more general ideological conflict between the left and the police which surfaced in the press in issues such as the 'Battle of Brittan', the Jacqie Berkeley allegations of rape against the Moss Side police and has continued more recently with the Viraj Mendis deportation.

In the right-wing national press Anderton had enjoyed a good deal of support, locked as he was in battle with groups of people who were easily characterized as members of extremist left-wing groups, troublesome students, sexual deviants, black extremists and, worst of all, members of a self-evidently 'loony left' local authority. The perception conveyed by the *Daily Mirror, The Guardian* and *The Observer* had been quite different. Anderton was portrayed as a policeman with extreme religious views who was prone to authoritarianism.

As the Stalker affair ran its course Anderton became the focus of much journalistic scrutiny because of his role in setting up the inquiry in the first place and because of his subsequent behaviour towards Stalker, his deputy. This gradually spread to an examination of his private life, at first as this constituted a comparison with that of Stalker and thus a basis for judging the legitimacy of the moves against him. Later this developed into a prurient search for anything which might provide an entertaining sidelight on a man who had become a national metaphor for religiosity and a sort of rigid puritanism, even though a closer examination of what he actually said would usually reveal that his puritanism was not devoid of compassion. In this, his genius for the one-liner which had made the name 'Jim' instantly recognizable in Manchester as the 'controversial top cop' became something of a curse. The word 'outburst' came to be used increasingly to describe what the chief constable had said, with the clear implication that those who give vent to outbursts are less stable than those whose utterances are normal and measured.

Finally, even the right-wing nationals became critical of him. It seemed that espousing the values of the moral majority was acceptable so long as it could be seen as a support for the established order, but Anderton's interpretation of his personal relationship to the Almighty was over the top. The populist press was increasingly willing to cast Anderton in the role of the villain in the Stalker affair and openly to raise issues of his health, even by recourse to terms such as 'off his rocker' which, when used to refer to left-wing bogeymen such as Arthur Scargill and Tony Benn, are regarded as evidence of the anti-left bias which is systematically built into the British press.

It is important to make the point, however, that the view taken of Anderton by the press was not monolithic, and nor were the motives which lay behind the treatment he received. Sources in the GMP reported that he was particularly angry about the reference by *The Observer* to members of the Northern Ireland team as sources in a revelatory piece about the shoot-to-kill inquiry, while his own public pronouncements seemed increasingly to depict the whole press as a pack motivated by a common blood lust. Given the prurience of some of the stories which appeared about him and his family this is easy to understand.

None the less it is important to differentiate between papers such as *The Observer*, *The Guardian* and the *Manchester Evening News*, which were primarily concerned in the inquiries with either GMPA politics or issues raised by the Stalker affair, and papers such as the *News of the World*, which were primarily interested in following the scandal sheet version of the human interest story. For a time, however, from mid-1986 to the end of 1987, on a number of occasions, the press presented the appearance of a commonly motivated collectivity in their pursuit of the prophet motive.

CHAPTER TEN

That was then

As time passed the nature of journalistic work changed. When the announcement of Stalker's departure from duties was first announced reporters and editors adopted the task of discovering, first, what had happened and, second, explaining why and how it had happened. We have seen how this involved a process of using information, testing hypotheses and constructing scenarios which seemed empirically reasonable and made narrative sense. In that much of their activity as investigators was based on the absence of information from normal, established news sources they had to rely on contacts who often could not be quoted, and who in the final analysis had to be assessed for their reliability on the basis of professional judgement. Sometimes this brought the press into conflict with people in the news and in particular with James Anderton. Others, such as the Northern Ireland inquiry team, took action against *The Observer*, some of the senior officers mentioned in the *Manchester Evening News* masonic stories were compensated and received an apology in May 1989.

The main outline of the generally accepted theory was established early on in the progress of the affair: that Stalker was an honest policeman who had approached too closely to the truth about the killings in Northern Ireland and was the victim of a trumped-up inquiry into charges which were probably not true, and even if true would always have been trivial, but especially so in the context of a man about to make a break-through in a major investigation of homicide by squads of police officers. Within the first weeks of the progress of the affair the main outline of the charges against Stalker had been established by journalists, in particular those working for the *Manchester Evening News*, and any inquiry based on the notion that Stalker was guilty of any serious misconduct was dropped.

The sources of information for journalists were individuals whose interests or occupation gave them access to what official sources were denying them. Most important among these was Stalker himself. He generally avoided giving operational and similarly sensitive information to reporters: no one for instance had apparently been leaked a copy of the interim report on the Northern Ireland inquiry, although revealing this would almost certainly have strengthened his case enormously. But he did talk to individual journalists at his home and he did speak at public press conferences usually organized by his solicitors.

These sorts of contacts gave the Stalker camp an opportunity to do two things in the conflict over the establishment of a generally accepted 'true' version of events. The first was to convince reporters of his own innocence and the second was to answer their questions about issues as they arose. And when not willing to answer questions himself he could suggest lines of inquiry they might follow, and thus influence the final outcome in terms of the version of reality produced.

The first of these processes involved what for the journalists and Stalker himself must have been an extraordinary departure from the normal restraint in the relationship between a senior police officer and members of the press. He submitted himself to question and answer sessions between himself and journalists at his home at times with his family present, in order to remove any doubts on their part about his honesty and innocence. They were able to put to him whatever allegations they had heard about him and he was able to provide answers. These were emotional meetings at times since they involved the repetition of claims about the behaviour not only of Stalker but also about his family. His openness in being prepared to submit himself to this form of catechism and in the fullness of the answers he provided convinced the journalists he was not guilty of any significant wrongdoing. It also convinced them of his integrity as a person.

In achieving the second objective Stalker had to tread a delicate line of telling journalists facts which would benefit his own case. He needed to demonstrate why his actions might precipitate a plot to discredit him while at the same time he had to avoid revealing operational information or information which might interfere with potential legal action or endanger life. In public he avoided committing himself when, for instance, he was asked questions about the possibility that he might have been the victim of a conspiracy. He would reply at press conferences with a response of the sort: 'Well, those are your words, it's not up to me to say.' This meant that he did not confirm such suggestions but answered in such a way that did not dismiss them as wildly improbable.

But journalists wanted to know what had happened in Northern Ireland in order to discover whether there was any basis for the theory that he had been stopped because he was getting too close to the truth for the comfort of the government. Journalists will not reveal what they have been told in private, nor the source of particular information. But the stories they ran about rows between Stalker and Hermon, and about the investigation of the tape of the hayshed shootings were borne out by Stalker's own account of events in his book eighteen months later.[1]

Indeed, by early 1988, no longer a policeman but with a book to publicize, Stalker was ready to endorse publicly precisely the theory that he had been silenced by the government. He said on the Channel Four television programme *Dispatches* on 7 February 1988 that he believed he was removed from the inquiry because he had been on the threshold of causing a major police scandal and a political row, and that the decision to remove him must have been taken at Cabinet level. In 1986 *The Observer* ran a story by Paul Lashmar and David Leigh alleging that Stalker had been frozen out of the GMP by James Anderton.[2] In early February 1988 a Daily Express extract from his book was preceded by a stand-first which took an identical line: 'The very man who spoke of being moved by the finger of God deliberately isolated me and forced me into bitter resignation.'[3]

But the normal curtain of reticence which hides the passing of confidential information between journalist and well-placed informants had already been lifted the week before by the editor of the *Manchester Evening News*, Michael Unger, who wrote two articles for *The Guardian* in which he revealed that Stalker had made contact with him a little over a year to the day before

Anderton's notorious Scarborough meeting, and at about the same time as the disputed meeting between Chief Superintendent Topping and Chief Superintendent Roberts.

On 13 May 1985, he recorded, Stalker whom he hardly knew at that time, telephoned him early at his office to tell him that he was seeking some papers from Sir John Hermon which could show that RUC officers murdered members of the IRA, and that if he didn't get the papers he would resign from the inquiry. Unger wrote: 'I ask Stalker why he is telling me this, because I hardly know him and the information if published would be extremely damaging . . . He also says that it is an insurance policy if anything happens to him.'[4]

The first long article revealed that Stalker was the source of much of the original material on which subsequent investigations were based: the existence of the bug; the nature of the shooting of Michael Tighe; the involvement of MI5, the disputes with Hermon, that some senior GMP officers had been promoted against Stalker's opposition; Stalker's relationship with Taylor; the fact that when Taylor rang to inquire about an Inspector Stephenson who was investigating him Stalker terminated their relationship and put down the telephone. The article also revealed that Unger had been a visitor to the Stalkers' home and had been a lunch guest of Stalker's at police headquarters. These articles demonstrate what one could infer from much of the coverage by journalists from the outset: that it was based on information either from Stalker or from people who were equally familiar with the progress of the Northern Ireland inquiry.

Such inferential logic is however only a way of judging the source who, perhaps unintentionally, originates the flow of information which eventually reaches the journalist. The journalist's informant may be someone quite distant from such a source. For instance, information about the meeting of chief superintendents and assistant chief constables at which Anderton asked if anyone knew of any lowering of force morale only came into the hands of *City Life* because someone at the meeting had divulged what had happened afterwards. But the *City Life* informant was not this person. The information was at least fourth hand when the news editor Ed Glinert heard it. In referring to the sources of his information which he knew to be reliable he would describe them as 'sources close to James

Anderton' or 'sources in Chester House'. This protects the real source, gives a convincing gloss to the story and in the final analysis it is true – the *original* source was a person who had attended the meeting and who told other employees of the GMP, but who never knew or intended that the information should end up in print.

The Unger article, however, whose accuracy has not been contested, provides empirical confirmation of the inference that John Stalker was the source for some of the information at least which underlay the revelations about parts of the Northern Ireland story. It is important to stress that Unger himself, like other journalists, has pointed out to me that his paper had numerous other sources in putting together their investigation of the Stalker affair. It is also important to understand that in writing this article Unger had not breached the normal etiquette of complete confidentiality between journalist and informant. He maintained an absolute silence about the contacts until late January 1988 – nearly three years after the first telephone call – and then only made the revelations because Stalker himself was publishing his own account of events which covered the ground investigated by the press. This then put the matter into the public domain. It is also worth pointing out that his original reason for keeping the diary was not primarily eventual publication. His understanding of Stalker's use of the words that the call was 'an insurance policy' in case anything happened was that Stalker thought that in the final analysis there was a chance he might be killed, and under those extreme circumstances Michael Unger would have had to make public the matter of the telephone conversation.

Stalker approached the press and was in turn approached by them. He undertook his original contacts with journalists on his own account but shortly after the commencement of the affair as a public issue he engaged the services of the solicitor Roger Pannone, who developed a systematic press campaign. Stalker's relationship with Pannone began in the same way as his relationship with journalists: a long and intensive cross-examination. Pannone was not prepared to take on the police chief as a client without being absolutely convinced of his innocence, and after administering a grilling he was satisfied that he had a spotless client.

The publicity campaign to demonstrate the truth of this assessment began with a press conference that John Stalker has likened to being thrown to the lions. He was unrehearsed and Pannone was relying on the honesty of his client to see them through. Stalker has said that if he had failed both he and Pannone would have been publicly completely undone.

They continued their campaign, issuing statements, organizing further press conferences and providing interviews with specific, trusted reporters. As the story developed the press was faced with an account given by the Stalker camp which was coherent, convincing and professionally disseminated with a due understanding of the work practices of the press, while established authority were in some disarray with no common or coherent account of events to offer. In fact some parts of the fabric of public authority, the left-wing members of the GMPA and a number of MPs for instance, strongly subscribed to a version of events which more readily entertained the notion of a government conspiracy as an explanation of events than did Stalker or Pannone. This was after all a mode of analysis which they had been employing as a routine device for making sense of the world for many years already.

The Police Complaints Authority issued public statements limited to a bald statement at the time of Stalker's removal from duties when they simply acknowledged that this had happened, but added no comment. Subsequently, and equally formally, they issued a statement at the end of the initial period of the Sampson inquiry to the effect that the inquiry showed that there was a prima-facie case of a disciplinary offence to be investigated.

James Anderton as chief constable refused to comment on the case, a situation which was made complicated by his own involvement in it and by issues to do with his private and public conduct, some related to the Stalker affair, some related to his own public role as police chief and some purely domestic matters of his own family which some sections of the press decided to make into a form of public entertainment.

No attributable statements came from the Home Office, from HM Inspectorate of Constabulary or from any parts of the security service named by journalists as they made their way through the maze of theories and evidence. The only official police source which was forthcoming was the press office of the RUC, and these statements tended not to find their way into the mainland press, although they were reported by the *Belfast Telegraph*, the Northern Ireland newspaper associated with and primarily read by the province's majority Protestant, or Loyalist, community. The newspaper reading habits of the province are divided, as are other aspects of life, on religious communal lines, with the Roman Catholic or Nationalist community reading the *Irish News*.

The GMPA did not present a unified front in their relations with the press. Roger Rees, the clerk to the authority, had been involved as an official with Anderton and Councillor Norman Briggs in making the arrangements to carry out the decision to send Stalker on extended leave and to appoint Colin Sampson to undertake the investigation. In this sense he was privy to some of what had happened without having been a principal actor. He kept a discreet silence.

Members of the GMPA varied in their responses. In general, the Stalker affair could be described as a public relations war by other means between the Labour left members of the authority and Anderton. In particular, Tony McCardell and Ken Srath, who were each chairman of the Manchester City Council's Police Monitoring Committee, were both vocal supporters of the view that Stalker had been the victim of a conspiracy to discredit him and were willing to say so in public and to the press.

Thus, in the early stages of the development of the Stalker affair as a public issue, the agencies of established authority did not have a unified view of events to articulate publicly. The press on the other hand needed to produce news about events which threatened to become a story of historic dimensions. A number of theories were being canvassed which involved the decision to discredit Stalker having been taken by the Cabinet. If proved true this theory would have had serious political repercussions, even given the somewhat generously indulgent interpretation of the doctrine of Cabinet responsibility and ministerial resignation which has characterized the Thatcher administrations.

Hence, from early on in the affair, as we have seen, although the main thrust of the investigation came from the *Manchester Evening News*, *The Guardian*, and *The Observer*, the

national newspapers of the right carried stories which entertained seriously the ideas of conspiracy as an explanation of
Stalker's removal from duty. In particular, the *Daily Express*
covered the story in this light, as did *The Star*, while the *News
of the World* produced a masonic influence account of events
before even the entry of the *Manchester Evening News* into this
particular part of the field.

Thus, by the time the Sampson report was delivered in its
summary form to the GMPA and became the best-read secret
document in the history of official secrets, there was an accepted
view of events purveyed in the press. This interpretation had
become as solidly established as the paradigm of the industrial
unrest as the fault of trades unions with the concentration on
effects rather than causes referred to in their analysis of industrial
unrest by the Glasgow Media Group, or of the notions of news
impartiality analysed by Philip Schlesinger in his analysis of
the BBC.[5]

When the newspapers began to deal with the contents of the
Sampson report, journalists, editors and readers were all ready
to see it as the outcome of a tainted process and the force of
the overall narrative logic was that it would be flawed, it would
contain significant contradictions and that it might be based on
lies. The central role played in the origination of the charges
against Stalker by the informant Bertlestein fitted the scenario
perfectly, as did the information added by *The Observer*, the
Manchester Evening News, and *The Guardian* which showed
that he was both unreliably prone to Walter Mitty fantasies
and had connections in Northern Ireland. The fact he was
dead and therefore not capable of being libelled also gave the
journalists then and me now licence to exercise greater freedom
than is usually the case in describing him and his activities. Even
had he been alive, however, his criminal convictions for fraud
would have made it much easier than is the case with respectable
citizens, or at least citizens who have not yet been caught, to refer
to him as a liar.

The summary of the report by Sampson was not only the
object of critical examination by journalists, it was also the
source of information about who originated the complaints
against Stalker, about how the police pursued the case and about
other aspects of police conduct, which appeared to indicate

that Stalker was being investigated for having associated with criminals while other policemen were doing the same thing without any action being taken. David Leigh, Jonathan Foster and Paul Lashmar, for instance, in *The Observer*[6] of 5 October 1986 revealed that the former Deputy Co-ordinator of the Manchester No. 1 Regional Crime Squad, Detective Superintendent Donald McIntyre, had been friendly with Brian Buckley, who was convicted on 12 January 1982 for his part in a fraud on William & Glyn's Bank. The *Observer* team quoted the Sampson report which referred to evidence from McIntyre: 'Mr. McIntyre has no recollection of meeting Mr. Taylor. However, he does recall taking Brian Buckley to functions at the Manchester senior officers' mess prior to Mr. Buckley's conviction for fraud.'[7]

As the case developed with Stalker's reinstatement and as the Sampson report became more widely read the focus of journalistic inquiry continued to be into the suspect nature of the evidence against Stalker and the means by which the case against him was ever mounted. At the same time the press continued to worry at the six killings in Northern Ireland, the circumstances under which they were undertaken and the crisis in the Stalker investigation at the point when he was removed. Anderton became involved first as a main participant in the decision to remove Stalker from his duties and second through his own conduct.

But then, towards the end of 1986, the press were faced with a new set of circumstances which needed to be explained. Apparently without warning, shortly before Christmas, Stalker decided to retire. After apparently triumphing over his detractors he had now decided to throw in the towel. Although there were rumours that this was about to happen for some weeks before only the alternative magazine *City Life* predicted that it was about to happen.[8] In order to understand how the press made sense of this episode it is necessary briefly to outline a number of apparently unrelated events.

As we saw earlier, Stalker's plight as the man in the dark and the plight of the Stalker family had been a theme the press had pursued from the early stages of the development of the affair. In examining the way this process evolved we saw how these themes were used by newspapers and by the Stalkers to explain why Stalker had opted for an early end to his career. He was portrayed as a man who was giving up for the sake of his family or who had been broken or exhausted by the tribulations he had suffered.

At the same time as this was happening, Chief Superintendent Peter Topping, the senior police officer who began the Stalker investigation, was digging up parts of Saddleworth Moors in a search for the undiscovered bodies of two teenagers who had been missing since the time of the moors murders in the mid-1960s. The digging began in November as the weather began to deteriorate. Soon, members of the Tactical Aid Group, detectives and specialist sniffer dog handlers were working in snow and freezing conditions. Well-equipped and victualled national newspaper reporters were also on the moor keeping a gruesome vigil, waiting for the discovery of a body or the visit of Ian Brady or Myra Hindley, the Moors Murderers, to help the police locate the bodies in the wilderness of bleak featureless peat hags between Oldham and Huddersfield.

Relatives of the victims of these horrific killings were sought and found by journalists to produce an eerie re-run of their threats to kill Brady or Hindley, or recount their unassuaged agony at the loss of their children, which could not even be resolved by the discovery of their bodies and a proper funeral. Local television news included street interviews with Mancunians giving their opinions about whether the children should be left in peace or be found if possible to end their families' misery.

This took place a month before the announcement of Stalker's retirement. When he did retire, the press used it to help explain why he had taken the decision to go. The *Daily Express* made the moors search and the way in which decisions were taken to undertake it the central theme of their explanation of his retirement. A page one story by Derek Hornby under a picture of Stalker with his wife Stella and daughter Francine was headlined 'Stalker quits over Moors snub' claimed:

The final straw for Mr. Stalker, after a summer of anguish and pressure, was the Myra Hindley affair. For it emerged last night that he was not told about the timing of Hindley's return to Saddleworth Moor, near Manchester, to help the search for more bodies. 'The first he knew about Hindley

going to Saddleworth was through the media. It is a disgrace
for a deputy chief constable to be treated like that,' said Mr.
Stalker's daughter Francine.[9]

The story made the connection between the 1986 search and
the fact that Stalker worked on the actual moors murders investigation in 1966 as a detective sergeant: 'In the mid-sixties Mr.
Stalker was a detective involved in the original Moors Murders
inquiry.' The story also obliquely made the connection with the
fact that Topping, who had set in motion the inquiry into the
relationship between Stalker and Taylor, was in charge of the
new moors search: 'And he is known to have had an uneasy
relationship with the man leading the new hunt, Manchester
CID chief Peter Topping. Last night Mr. Topping said of the
resignation: "I'm sad. I'm very sorry to hear it."'[10]

The *Daily Mirror* headline declared 'Stalker: I quit over Myra's
trip to moors. It was the last straw, says daughter.' The story was
angled on the same quotation from Francine Stalker: 'It was the
last straw for dad. The first he knew about Hindley going to
Saddleworth was through the media. It is a disgrace for a deputy
chief constable to be treated like that.'[11]

In *Today* the same day David Wooding and Ian Fletcher
reported: 'The final straw came this week when he was not
consulted about Myra Hindley's involvement in the search for
bodies on Saddleworth Moor.'[12] Malcolm Pithers, in *The Independent*, also referred to sources in Manchester who said that
the final straw for Stalker was that he was not briefed on the
operation to return Myra Hindley to Saddleworth Moor.[13] Peter
Murtagh, in *The Guardian*, made the same connection.[14] On the
following day Jonathan Foster, in the *The Observer*, invoked the
Myra Hindley visit, Stalker's doubts about Topping's handling
of the search and Topping's role in collecting allegations against
Stalker as reasons for his retirement.[15]

In *The Sunday Telegraph*, Christopher Elliott wrote:

It is ironic that he should be leaving at the height of the search
for more children's bodies on Saddleworth Moor. It was the
Moors murder investigation which made his reputation as an
outstanding detective sergeant in the early 1960s, and it was
the renewed search for bodies and the lack of consultation

over the return of Myra Hindley to the Moor which finally tipped his hand to resign.'[16]

The *Sunday Mirror*[17] and the Sunday edition of *Today* both referred to the moors search and Hindley's involvement in it but both actually quoted Stalker himself who wanted to avoid saying anything which might distress the parents of the victims. The *Today* story, 'Hunt had part in big decision' again referred to Stalker's part in the original case: 'He was a young detective on the Moors Murders case 20 years ago, and recently there have been rumours of unease between Detective Superintendent Peter Topping, the man leading the new hunt, and Mr. Stalker.'[18]

Stalker's own account of his departure makes it clear that the moors search played a major part in his final decision to resign, but that what rankled most was the fact that the decision to bring Hindley to the moors, an operation involving 400 police officers, was taken without his knowledge. The reasons for this are easy to comprehend: at the time she was brought north, Anderton was away, leaving Stalker formally in sole operational command; he was also one of the few serving officers who had also been involved in the case when the murders took place and the perpetrators were caught. From either point of view he needed to know what was happening, at least in order to be able to answer questions from the numerous reporters who flocked to the scene. The anger which Stalker expresses in his book is directed on this occasion not at Topping but at Anderton.[19]

A further element in the explanation which the press offered for Stalker's departure related to the legal bill he had incurred in retaining Pannone and Lakin to represent him. The amount was £21,000, and on 17 October 1986 the GMPA refused to give him any help. He was criticized by Chairman Steve Murphy for going to a solicitor too soon. He also said that if Stalker were paid it would open a floodgate for other claims.[20]

Leigh, Foster and Lashmar reported in *The Observer* that Stalker was 'said to be bitterly upset' at the decision and that his solicitors were considering suing the GMPA.[21] Donations from members of the public began to flow in, but these presented a problem. Police discipline regulations make it an offence for a serving officer to accept a gift or place himself under a 'pecuniary obligation' in such a manner that might affect the execution of his duties – unless he first obtains the permission of his chief constable or police authority. In early November this became an issue in the press with reports of statements by Anderton that he was looking into the matter. The issue went before the GMPA in November and they decided that Stalker could accept the gifts, provided that the fund, which had been organized by the *Manchester Evening News*, was supervised by ACPO. This left ACPO to decide whether it would supervise the fund. The then President of ACPO was James Anderton.

A month later ACPO decided not to administer the fund. The role of Anderton in this decision was not entirely lost on the newspapers. The *Daily Mail* reported: 'The move comes after the Association, whose president is Stalker's superior Mr. James Anderton, refused yesterday to administer an appeal fund.'[22] The potential for an Anderton against Stalker confrontation of the 'Anderton stops Stalker cash' sort never materialized. Nor did a story that relations between the two men were deteriorating. Some papers reported that Stalker was off work ill, with nervous exhaustion. But none, except *City Life*, ran a story floating the rumour that Stalker was then about to retire.

In the issue 5 December 1986 the alternative magazine *City Life* ran a story raising the probability that Stalker was about to resign. Larded with characteristic vulgar but harmless abuse the nub of the story by Ed Glinert centred on Stalker's absence from work and claimed that Chester House was 'awash with rumours that Stalker may never return to his desk' and that 'Anderton is easing him out of Dock Green and into early retirement' with 'a £15,000 a year pension and a £70,000 odd gratuity'.[23]

The story related the departure to a scheme by show business personalities in the North West to organize a concert to raise money to pay the now-famous Stalker legal bill. It was based on offers of free stage performances by characters from the Manchester-based Granada TV soap opera *Coronation Street* and had been trailed in a number of stories in the *Manchester Evening News*. The man organizing the concert was Frank Pearson, a wealthy drag artist, who sported the Runyanesque soubriquet Frank Foo Foo Lamarr and owned a locally famous night-spot Foo Foo's Palace. Pearson was interviewed by the Sampson inquiry team as one who had attended one of Kevin Taylor's functions.

City Life could 'reveal that the top unbearded cop is back in the doghouse following a recent *News of the World* exposé on local drag queen Frank Foo Foo Lamarr Pearson who was convicted for keeping a disorderly house'.[24] This was a reference to a story in the 24 November *News of the World* headlined 'My top cop pal, by drag star Foo Foo. Ex-vice boss plans a concert for Stalker.'[25] It was written with all the usual *News of the World* genteel restraint by a Manchester-based reporter, Alan Hart, who had covered the original court case in 1979.

The intro declared that the 'top drag queen', who was was organizing a fund raising concert to help Stalker, had a 'murky past'. It went on: 'For Frank Foo Foo Lamarr has a conviction for running a gay vice den at a massage parlour he owned with an ex-policeman.' Lamarr was quoted as describing Stalker as a 'friend in need'. The brief summary of the events associated with his removal from duty concentrated on the warning Stalker received from the police authority on his reinstatement: 'He was sent home because of alleged associations with criminals at social functions. On his reinstatement he was warned to be more circumspect about his friendships.'

A paragraph stating that in 1979 Foo Foo and his partner were fined £2,000 each for running a disorderly house was followed by two quoting him. The first implied that he had known Stalker over a period of time and the second that they had met since the reinstatement: 'Foo Foo added: "I've met John and his wife Stella at a variety of social functions. We met again earlier this month and I told Stella my plan."'[26]

There was no other reference to the trial in the press until the *City Life* story, and this did not reveal that a solicitor, Charles Buckley, had attempted on the Saturday to persuade the Sunday paper to abandon publication.

The *City Life* story also referred to stories in the *Daily Mirror* and the *Daily Mail* [27] in which the possibility was raised that Stalker might be called by Taylor's lawyers to give evidence against Anderton in the case alleging conspiracy to pervert the course of justice. The *Daily Mirror* story, headlined 'Stalker versus his boss! *He faces courtroom clash*', claimed that Stalker

might be called as a witness and that he had already been interviewed by Taylor's solicitors.[28] These speculations and diverse
versions of events, called on to explain a situation which was
unclear, did not find their way into the mainstream of press
theorizing about the Stalker affair. They remained marginalized
either by being restricted to the alternative press or they simply
appeared in national newspapers as isolated stories which were
never taken up as part of the general explanatory framework.

In 1988 the Stalker affair was again raised with the government's decision on the Stalker–Sampson inquiry into the
shoot-to-kill allegations and publication of Stalker's own book.
Doubt about Stalker's private life or his reasons for resigning
were now no longer relevant. The issues were whether or not
the RUC officers involved were to be prosecuted and what effect
government decisions on the matter would have on Anglo-Irish
relations, in the light of the Gibraltar shootings and the failure
of the defendants in the Birmingham bombing trial to win their
appeals. The Stalker affair had now become focused in the press
in this country and abroad on issues of national and international
politics.

The Manchester ticket touts, tenth rate fraudsters, receivers
of stolen property, brothel keepers, grasses, back street Baron
Munchhausens, boxing promoters, getaway drivers, bearers of
false witness, their victims, Freemasons, self-seekers and pathological exhibitionists who had so entertainingly peopled the news
pages now exited stage left, right and centre and then were heard
no more. They had only fretted their hour upon the stage in order
to clarify the central character in the drama – John Stalker. That
was now done, and he was now portrayed almost universally
as a detective who had formulated the questions to which the
government and other police chiefs had to provide answers.

On 21 January 1988 the Attorney General, Sir Patrick Mayhew, announced in the House of Commons that no criminal
charges would be brought against the RUC officers who were
named in the file submitted as a result of the inquiry started
by John Stalker and completed by Colin Sampson. According
to press reports the file recommended bringing criminal charges
against the officers including two Special Branch superintendents. The Attorney General based his explanation of the failure
to prosecute on reasons of 'national security'. In the House of

Commons he was accused himself of being an accomplice to murder. The Irish government expressed its great dismay and cancelled a meeting between the Garda commissioner and the RUC chief constable as a protest.

The Stalker affair had now achieved a new lease of life in the press, and during this period Stalker's book appeared, with its revelations of his own version of events, including his treatment by Anderton and Hermon, as well as his account of the six shootings, the missing tapes from the hayshed and the repeated attempts to thwart his inquiries. The book in itself became a news item. The former Labour Home Secretary Merlyn Rees raised the question of whether Stalker should be proceeded against for revealing information covered under the official secrets legislation. Superintendent John Simons complained in a letter over the revelations in Michael Unger's articles on his Stalker Diaries that Stalker had been revealing operational information while still a serving officer. Anderton complained of his portrayal in the book. So did Hermon. So did Topping.

But very little new was added to the public knowledge of events portrayed in the book by its publication. For this we must credit the journalists who had so assiduously followed every lead they were presented with and the newspapers who gave them space to do so when the matter first arose in the summer of 1986.

The *Daily Express* serialized the book in extracts for a week at the beginning of February. Newspapers ran stories on the book and reactions to it in Parliament and by public figures named in it. The interesting issue from the point of view of understanding the role of the press is how a more or less unanimous view, an orthodoxy entirely as potent as the normal anti-union or anti-CND orthodoxy of the British press, had been established.

The standpoint of the news now adopted was the telling of the story of how the 'shoot-to-kill' plot was covered up. Headlines implicitly accepted the reliability of the Stalker book. The *Daily Express*, for instance, in all its treatment of the book, whose serialization rights it had bought, naturally used headlines which assumed the truth of Stalker's version of events. On the Monday of their week of serialization this was exemplified by their first lead which took up the whole of page one in which headline and story were based on the portrayal of events in the book.

Without enclosing the words in quotation marks the headline declared 'Why they had to silence me' and the report on the book by Peter Grosvenor and John Burns began

The Stalker inquiry into the Ulster police's alleged shoot-to-kill policy was sabotaged from the start.

Today the Daily Express can reveal the full extent of the attempts to stop former Manchester Deputy Chief Constable John Stalker getting at the truth about the deaths of six unarmed men.

Stalker has broken his silence to tell how Sir John Hermon, Chief Constable of the RUC, thwarted his efforts to see vital evidence.

He also discloses the MI5 involvement in the province and how a tape recording made by MI5 of a killing by RUC officers eventually led to his sacking from the inquiry.

His revelations come at a time of growing controversy over Attorney General Sir Patrick Mayhew's decision not to prosecute RUC officers even though he admitted there was evidence of a police conspiracy to pervert the course of justice in Ulster.[29]

In this story, presented as fact, the *Daily Express* was using the Stalker book as a source of information so reliable that it had adopted its versions of events and its agenda as factually accurate and well judged in its interpretation of events – in short as the truth. When referring to information provided by a source a newspaper may simply quote the source and itself stand away from commitment. It then reports the claims by using phrases such as 'according to a book published today' or 'a senior police officer claims', or it may simply put quotation marks around the words in a headline. These devices mean that the newspaper is reporting what is said, and that the fact of its being said is the fact reported. When, however, the paper simply reports the information without quotation marks, without using phrases such as 'according to', or 'claims' it is then adopting as its own the source's account of the facts.

An interesting distinction here lies in the difference between the verb to claim and the verb to reveal or to disclose. News-papers use 'claim' as a way of placing the responsibility for what is being said on a source. Two different sources can be quoted offering different versions of the same events, which might then be characterized as 'rival claims'. When a journalist uses the word 'claims' the implication is that it is the claim that is being reported. Revelation or disclosure clearly implies something quite different – that the information is the truth. In using the word 'reveals' the paper is adopting the substance of a source's information as its own. When newspapers conduct their own investigation the product is frequently presented as revelation, and the formula for the presentation of the outcome of such investigation is 'we can reveal'. The act of revelation or disclosure is to make known what was previously being kept secret, and in the *Daily Express* story we see both the paper and Stalker revealing and disclosing. For the story to mean anything it is necessary for these disclosures to be true, for them to be important and for them to uncover what was previously hidden or unknown.

A Peter Murtagh story in *The Guardian* two days previously similarly implied a cover-up over the shoot-to-kill policy and did so by making claims on its own account without naming its source. The story stated that the Stalker–Sampson report was 'shelved' to protect top RUC officers who would have been forced to resign if prosecutions of officers had taken place as a result of the inquiry.[30]

The use of quotes and attributions could still allow the message of the book to be conveyed in news columns. *The Independent*, for instance, carried the headline 'Unarmed men "deliberately shot"' and the story by Mark Rosselli began: 'The main thrust of John Stalker's allegations revealed to date are that, despite constant obstruction by the Royal Ulster Constabulary, he uncovered evidence which convinced him that its officers had either murdered or unlawfully killed six men in 1982.'[31]

The recrudescence of the shoot-to-kill scandal in the press was also the outcome of the routine reportage of events in Parliament. On 2 February the Labour MP Dale Campbell Savers asked the Attorney General to

specify the precise considerations which led him to inform the DPP for Northern Ireland about the nature of the public interest in relation to the possible prosecutions of Superintendent

Thomas George Anderson, Superintendent Samuel George Flannagan and Chief Superintendent Desmond Browne for seeking to pervert the course of justice in respect of the alleged suppression of information of an unlawful killing.

The Independent reported 'MP names "men in Stalker inquiry"'.[32] Similarly inter-governmental meetings between Irish and British ministers and meetings of the Cabinets in London and Dublin were all subjects of news reports on the Stalker affair. On 4 February *The Guardian* reported that Charles Haughey had told a meeting of his parliamentary party in Dublin that the Stalker affair had serious implications for Anglo-Irish relations.[33] The following day *The Independent* reported statements by Irish politicians under the headline 'Decision not to prosecute was a bombshell to Dublin government.'[34]

Further instances of the news coverage which attended the publication of John Stalker's book and the government's decision not to prosecute the RUC officers would simply be repetitious. It was characterized throughout the press by the same agenda as that already indicated. The decision not to prosecute was a central issue. So were John Stalker's revelations about the attempts to silence his inquiry into the shoot-to-kill allegations. The question of his own behaviour, which had been an important element at the beginning of the affair, had now become settled almost as a matter of established history: his reputation was unblemished.

CHAPTER ELEVEN
The trial of Kevin Taylor

Throughout the period during which the press and the broad-casting bodies investigated the Stalker affair and collectively formed a version of reality to explain the data available to them, Kevin Taylor was depicted in the media as a secondary character in the narrative. At first his role was to explain John Stalker's removal from duty, then to be the innocent victim of a plot to silence the Stalker inquiry and finally, after he had been charged with conspiracy to defraud the Co-operative Bank, to be ignored, hidden beneath the blanket of sub judice, while his trial ponderously took shape beyond the public gaze in the offices of the GMP, the Crown Prosecution Service and the Director of Public Prosecutions.

As we have already seen, he was depicted in the *News of the World* early in the affair as the host of a party which the Stalkers had attended along with 'gangland' guests. There were also innuendoes elsewhere in the press that Stalker had received 'lavish hospitality' from 'known criminals' and Taylor, who realized that he was the target of these descriptions, publicly rebutted such press stories. Subsequently, when it became clear that he had never been charged with any crime, his own account of himself as a businessman wrongly accused of criminal activities became the dominant version of events appearing in the news columns of the press. Stories which peddled an association between Taylor and drugs still occasionally appeared. In early 1987 the *Daily Mail* ran a news story reporting that the yacht *Diogenes* (which he had by then sold to another owner) had been seized in a drugs case by Spanish police, who had also found an automatic pistol on board. The story, with a picture of the boat prominently displayed at the top of page two, was angled around the fact that Taylor had previously owned the boat.[1]

The papers reported in greater or lesser detail Taylor's legal battle with the GMP over the seizure of his papers during their investigation of his business affairs. As we saw earlier the *Manchester Evening News* reported one such court battle under a headline stating that James Anderton had been accused of conspiracy.

But from early 1987 Kevin Taylor's role as a significant actor in the press presentation of the Stalker drama was dormant until the sudden and dramatic end of his trial at the close of January 1990. The full trial at Manchester Crown Court began in October 1989 and lasted for sixteen weeks. At an earlier committal Taylor had been charged with three other men, a bank official Terence Bowley, a chartered accountant Derek Britton and a quantity surveyor Vincent McCann with conspiracy to obtain overdrafts from the Co-operative Bank by falsely overvaluing plots of land which Kevin Taylor intended to purchase, develop and sell. By the time the full trial began the charges against the four had ceased to be conspiracy and had become those of actually obtaining overdraft facilities and attempting to obtain overdraft facilities by deception. The charges were that Taylor, Britton and Bowley dishonestly obtained an overdraft of £771,500 for Rangelark, one of Taylor's companies, in 1985; that they had earlier attempted to obtain an overdraft of £996,000 for Rangelark by making false statements about the land offered as collateral and that all four had attempted to obtain an overdraft of £160,000 between November and December 1984. Other charges of fraudulent trading were brought against Taylor and Britton and charges relating to banking law were brought against McCann and Bowley.

Clearly, the trial would bear crucially on the narrative of John Stalker, since, as we saw earlier, by common consent among the police, press and broadcast media, his relationship with Kevin Taylor was at the centre of the campaign mounted against him and this campaign was the proximate cause of his removal from the Northern Ireland 'shoot-to-kill' inquiry. If Taylor were found guilty those who denied that there was a conspiracy against the former deputy chief constable and those who were behind the original complaints would be able to point to the verdict as justification for the actions. If he were acquitted the case against John Stalker would then be shown publicly to be bereft of any basis, since the claim against him would be that he had associated with an innocent man.

Given the vital explanatory role which this trial was to play in the Stalker saga it may seem surprising that the national press ignored the case completely in its early stages. Only the *Manchester Evening News* carried reports of the first week of the prosecution case. This coverage was, as always, entirely unfavourable to the defendant, simply by virtue of the fact that the journalist can only report what is said in court. This means that at the beginning of a trial he or she summarizes and quotes the nub of the prosecution case for the day and angles the story on what appears to be the most attention-grabbing aspect of what has been said. The stories from the first week of the trial illustrate this process.

Page four stories by the paper's staff reporter Alan Slater in two editions of the Manchester paper for 4 October 1989 were headlined '"Bank fiddle by a tycoon"' and '"United link" in fraud trial'. They were both slightly variant versions of the same story which referred to an allegation by the prosecuting counsel Michael Corkery QC that Taylor had recruited the corporate business manager of the Co-operative Bank in Manchester, Terence Bowley, into a dishonest scheme to arrange an overdraft of £250,000 part of which was to buy a warehouse in Trafford Park in Manchester. According to the allegation, Taylor had claimed that this building was to be developed as a sports complex and that the Manchester United Football Club chairman had been interested in buying it, a claim which Corkery said was untrue.[2]

As the week proceeded the prosecution's opening address provided the narrative basis for the accounts in the evening papers. 'Taylor's "money go-round"'[3] retailed the prosecution claim that the Manchester property developer had switched money between his companies to put one in the black when asking for overdrafts from the bank. '"Bank man's cover-up"'[4] summarized the case against Terence Bowley by stating that, although unauthorized to do so, he had arranged an overdraft of £240,000 for Taylor who 'wanted cash desperately'. For the prosecution Corkery claimed that Bowley had tried to cover up what he had done by making an application to the advances department (the proper authority for such an overdraft) only after the loan had been granted.

At this point all coverage of the trial in the press ceased for ten days. This was because the *Manchester Evening News* withdrew their staff coverage on the basis that the trial had become too technical and detailed to justify the daily commitment of a reporter's time. The absence of coverage by the national daily press can be understood in the context of major organizational changes which had taken place in their news production during the 1980s. The *Daily Express, Daily Mail, Daily Mirror, Daily Telegraph, Daily Star,* and *Sun,* had all made reporters redundant or reduced staff through natural wastage to levels which were a fraction of those of the heyday of the national press in Manchester. The same departure from the city centre to industrial suburbs for printing took place in Manchester as had happened in the movement away from Fleet Street in London.

Two major centres of news production and newspaper printing and distribution, Maxwell House in Withy Grove and the nearby *Daily Express* building in Ancoats Street, a copy of the 'Black Lubyanka' in Fleet Street, were abandoned. Maxwell House, previously known as Kemsley House, had housed the newsrooms of several national newspapers whose owners had rented office space and printing capacity. The *Daily Mirror* moved to a factory site in Oldham, the *Daily Telegraph* to a similar site in Trafford Park. The *Manchester Evening News* printing presses in Deansgate became the only major central site for newspaper production in the city, while Manchester ceased to exist as a regional centre of journalistic activity for the national press. National newspaper reporters had become the local representatives of their London offices. There were simply no longer the personnel in Manchester to watch over the court case for the nationals in case a 'new angle' might manifest itself in the Taylor trial.

A further change was effective cessation of the local alternative magazine *City Life* as a source of news. When the Stalker affair first became a public issue the magazine received information from its own sources in the police and the police authority and through anonymous letters. The news editor Ed Glinert published stories in the magazine and passed on information to the national press, particularly to *The Observer*. Glinert himself ceased to write for the magazine, which then went into receivership, before being taken over by the *Manchester Evening News*. It now operates independently as part of the *Evening News* and *Guardian* group, but with a much reduced staff and news coverage. The balance of its content has moved more completely towards the coverage of rock music, the arts and events.

Furthermore, changes in personnel reflect the degree to which investigative coverage in the British press, and that relating to the Stalker affair in particular, depends on the activities of particular individuals. The two national newspapers which gave most coverage to the affair were *The Guardian* and *The Observer*. In each case the relationship between the teams of reporters at work on the story with John Stalker and the trust which was established between him and them, as we saw earlier, was crucial to the form that the coverage and the journalistic inquiries took. Peter Murtagh, the *Guardian* reporter whose own Irish background gave him an understanding of the context of the affair, was convinced of Stalker's innocence and integrity as a result of a meeting with him at the outset. Between the three months of drama in the summer of 1986 and the Taylor trial in the autumn of 1989 Murtagh was promoted to the editorship of the paper's foreign desk. Paul Johnson, who wrote much of the material on the Northern Irish aspect of the affair and co-authored a number of investigative features with Murtagh, became the paper's news editor. At *The Observer* the team of Paul Lashmar, David Leigh and Jonathan Foster had ceased to exist. Foster, who had undertaken much of the early interviewing of Stalker, left the paper first. Then Leigh resigned during a period of disagreement between the editor Donald Trelford and some members of the reporting staff over his request for them to investigate an alleged corrupt relationship between British Aerospace and the Saudi Arabian government over the sale of Tornadoes. The reporters felt that rather than acting as disinterested investigators they were being used to fire bullets for Lonhro, which had an interest in the French competitors of British Aerospace. Lashmar's resignation soon followed.

The absence of coverage also needs to be related to the development of the Stalker affair as a campaign by Stalker himself to establish his own innocence and the integrity of his inquiry in

Northern Ireland. During the first three months of the affair an inquiry was being undertaken by Colin Sampson and the police authority had to act on its outcome. It was necessary for Stalker to survive as a police chief to lay facts before the public which would tend to vindicate him, and would incidentally call into question the good faith of others. This generated a constant level of journalistic activity, as journalists sought the solution to the mystery of the affair and tried to make sense of events and Stalker trod the delicate path of telling them enough and pointing them in the right direction without divulging official secrets or operational matters.

During the Taylor trial this did not happen. Stalker's own occupational survival had ceased to be at issue with his resignation from the police and his adoption of a new career as a successful writer. Taylor's own future depended on what went on in court and any press activity had to be restricted to reports of what happened in court. There was then a combination of factors which reduced the probability of intense levels of press activity over the trial, and in the case of the *Manchester Evening News* Paul Horrocks, now the news editor, made the judgement that what was happening in court was too legally technical to make interesting reading. But he retained the services of the city's specialist court freelance news agency, Stewart & Hartley, to keep a watching brief. And ten days later they produced a report of the first cracks which began to appear in the prosecution case as witnesses were subjected to cross-examination by Taylor's barrister.

The story was headlined 'Police were getting at Stalker QC'.[5] The story was angled on the claim by Taylor's QC Richard Ferguson that the sole reason for the prosecution of Taylor by the police was to mount an attack on Stalker. This claim was made during the cross-examination of a prosecution witness David Davenport, the deputy to the Co-operative Bank Corporate Business Manager Terence Bowley, one of Taylor's co-defendants. But the extraordinary aspect of the cross-examination was that Davenport, a crown witness, agreed with this proposition. The news story revealed that Ferguson asked: 'Did you get the impression that Mr Taylor was being investigated as a means of getting at Mr Stalker?' and that Davenport replied 'Yes, to discredit him.'[6]

The cross-examination produced an admission which was perhaps even more astonishing, given that the whole basis of the case against Kevin Taylor was that he had falsely overvalued that property on which he had borrowed money from the bank. Davenport agreed that 'if Mr Taylor had been able to sell one of his sites in Trafford Park, the Co-operative Bank would have received all the money it had loaned him'.[7]

Of the national press, only *The Guardian* seemed interested in the story at this stage. They ran the same story from the same news agency, including the revelation that the bank had sold the Trafford Park site and made a profit of £360,000. This meant that Taylor's counsel had now established that a major prosecution witness had agreed that Taylor could have repaid the money he had borrowed by the sale of one of the properties he had bought in Trafford Park and that the police seemed concerned to make a case against Taylor in order to get at Stalker. If this were not damaging enough he had also shown that the bank had made a profit of £360,000 on the deal. It would surely now be hard to convince a jury that Taylor had falsely overstated the value of land which had been sold with the complete recovery of the money lent plus a profit.

But this did not produce any further coverage in the national press. Only the *Manchester Evening News* gave any coverage at this stage. They reported a further part of Davenport's long cross-examination, this time by Peter Birkett QC, counsel for Terence Bowley the accused bank official. In this story the witness said that while Bowley had broken the bank's rules he had simply been cutting corners because the advances department of the bank was 'over cautious'. Others, the prosecution witness said, did the same thing. 'I know rules were broken. Ultimately it was always done in the best interests of the bank.'[8] This, combined with the earlier acknowledgement by the prosecution counsel that Bowley had not obtained any personal benefit from any of the transactions, must have made the jury ponder what major criminal deed he was supposed to have committed.

Certainly, to an outside observer the trial was beginning to show signs of a major prosecution failure to make any of their charges stick. And given the direction in which the defence were directing their questions it was clear that the Stalker affair was going to be made once again a public issue. For the next eleven weeks, however, there was no further coverage of the case, until in the last week it became clear that the prosecution was falling apart in a spectacular and public way.

In this interim period, however, the defence case drew out a number of issues which supported the proposition canvassed widely in the press in the summer of 1986 that there was a plot to discredit Stalker. Davenport and other bank witnesses, it was revealed, had been questioned repeatedly by police officers and in the process their statements had been changed to strengthen their evidence of alleged false applications for overdrafts. The defence used the access they had to evidence from police notebooks in order to probe the process of the inquiries into Kevin Taylor and their relationship to the Stalker investigation.

David Hood, who took over as Taylor's counsel, pressed Detective Sergeant Keith Ware over a number of matters relating to the way in which the police had obtained information about Taylor's business affairs and about the relationship between these inquiries and Northern Ireland and the inquiry by West Yorkshire Police into John Stalker's social life. He was concerned to show that the police had lied to a judge in order to obtain orders of access to Taylor's bank accounts and that this had been a means of obtaining evidence about Taylor's trip with Stalker. Detective Sergeant Ware acknowledged that on 25 September 1985 he had been ordered to make an urgent report to Chief Constable James Anderton about the progress of the inquiry into Kevin Taylor's business affairs. He also revealed that on 25 March 1986 a senior officer from the RUC had visited Manchester.

He said that on 16 June 1986 he and Detective Inspector Stephenson had visited Britannia Building Society to obtain information about accounts *for West Yorkshire Police*. When asked by Hood what inquiry this was for, DS Ware replied that it was for the 'current inquiry', (that is to say, the Taylor case). This meant that what had been inferred from the way the Sampson report into the Stalker affair had been written was now shown to be the case: that the West Yorkshire team had not been independent of the Greater Manchester force, but had relied on information from them to arrive at their conclusions. Under the pressure of persistent questioning about his role in the police inquiry, DS Ware said: 'I've been made use of.'

Although these exchanges went unreported as the press turned their attention to the end of the Ceaucescu regime and the invasion of Panama by America, the Taylor case emerged into the light of full public exposure in the third week of 1990 with the return of staff coverage by the *Manchester Evening News*. The paper took up the story as the defence began to press increasingly their main line that in order to get at Stalker the GMP had been involved in a fraudulent investigation of Kevin Taylor. In a story headlined 'Cop denies Ulster link to Taylor' *Manchester Evening News* reporter Ray King recounted an exchange between the defence barrister David Hood and Detective Inspector Anthony Stephenson.

During this exchange, Stephenson agreed that during the investigation in 1986 officers were working nights and weekends and that 'a pitch of quite frenetic activity was reached'.[9] Hood pointed to the fact that within days of a raid on Kevin Taylor's home when photograph albums were seized these were used to remove John Stalker from his Northern Ireland inquiry at a point when the MI5 tape recordings of a fatal shooting were due to be handed over to him. He said that on 9 May 1986 the album had been taken from Taylor's house and that five days later Stalker had been told to cancel an interview which had been arranged with the RUC Chief Constable Sir John Hermon. On 29 May, said Hood, a secret meeting at Scarborough between Anderton and various others decided to remove Stalker from the Northern Ireland inquiry and have him investigated for suspected disciplinary offences. DI Stephenson said: 'It is an unfortunate set of coincidences. There is absolutely no connection whatsoever between the events in Northern Ireland and my inquiries other than the name of John Stalker.'

The following day the first major intervention by the bench took place with an astonishing coup for the defence in the shape of a police admission of contempt of court. This contempt arose out of the fundamental difficulty in the police case: the provenance of the information which had been acquired about Kevin Taylor's business dealings. DI Stephenson, who was giving evidence over a period of days, had discussed the evidence he was giving to the court with the previous witness DS Ware, in an attempt to discover the origin of the information held by the Drugs Intelligence Unit on Taylor's land dealings. Discussion outside the witness box by a witness of evidence being given while that witness is still under oath is a basic contempt of court, familiar to all 'professionals' involved in court proceedings, including police officers and journalists.

The admission by DI Stephenson formed the introduction of a *Manchester Evening News* story by Ray King. The headline under a photograph of Taylor declared 'Taylor trial furore for top cop', and was nosed on Stephenson's admission of perjury: 'A senior detective at the heart of the drugs and fraud investigation into businessman Kevin Taylor admitted today he was in contempt of court.'[10]

King recounted the police officer's acknowledgement that he had discussed his evidence with 'fraud squad colleague Det Sgt Keith Ware', the previous night. The story continued with Judge Michael Sachs's comment, 'You knew perfectly well this was a contempt' and Stephenson's one word reply: 'Yes.' Having focused on this dramatic revelation the story then explained how it had occurred in the context of the day's proceedings. After an hour-long adjournment, Hood, the defence counsel, had told Stephenson that Ware had been brought back into court and questioned by the judge about 'certain matters'. Hood put it to the detective inspector that he was aware that there had been an inquiry as to whether a serious contempt of court had been committed. The witness had replied that he understood. Hood said that the circumstances arose because Stephenson broke one of the most fundamental rules in any court of law, that a witness may not discuss that evidence with anyone else. Stephenson had told the court that after the previous day's hearing he had sought the origin of the information held by the police Drugs Intelligence Unit on Taylor's land holdings. 'He told the court that the Det Sgt had recalled a relevant file and produced it and the two had "run through the mortgage register and directors' schedule".'[11]

The cross-examination then moved on to the nub of the defence attack on the prosecution case, the means by which the police had obtained access to Taylor's bank, and Hood began the repeated questioning of Stephenson on how this had occurred. As this happened the prosecution case collapsed. But still the only paper which was giving the case coverage was the *Manchester Evening News*, whose accounts of the court case changed with each edition through the day. Moved on by the impetus of events in court the press coverage now switched from its early focus on the substance of the prosecution case, which had emphasized the allegations against Taylor of wrongdoing, to a concentration by the defence counsel on the shortcomings of the prosecution case.

Early on 17 January the account of the case centred on a suggestion by Hood that 'undercover detectives may have burgled a company office of accused businessman Kevin Taylor'. Taylor had suggested that police who suspected he was laundering money may have paid a covert visit to one of his companies because their inquiries had reached a dead end. Ray King reported the barrister's statement that nothing had been stolen in the raid in February 1986 but files had been disturbed. Police could have been seeking information to substantiate a court application for access to Taylor's bank accounts. That was 'absolute rubbish', Stephenson had responded, but he was reported as acknowledging 'there was insufficient evidence to charge him with anything and I was under pressure to complete the inquiry'.

The story continued:

Inspector Stephenson revealed that the probe began because police suspected Mr. Taylor could be laundering drug money.

He added: 'The yacht Diogenes had landed half a ton of cannabis on the south coast on February 3, 1985. That load would represent over £1m.

'We did not know to what extent Mr. Taylor was involved if at all.'[12]

The story then arrived at one of the central problems in the prosecution case: the apparent contradiction between their portrait of Kevin Taylor as a major criminal money launderer and as a man so desperately short of money that he was on the cadge from the Co-operative Bank. Hood asked if anything could be farther from money laundering than debts of more than £1 million. and Stephenson replied: 'No, but there was a possibility.'[13]

Hood continued to press the prosecution witnesses about the way in which they had pursued their inquiries into Taylor's bank accounts. He asked about the court order which allowed the police to inquire into Taylor's American Express account by which he had purchased the two air tickets for himself and Stalker to travel to Miami. If the inquiry had had nothing to do with Stalker, why had they not also investigated Taylor's Visa card? Stephenson said he was not aware of the existence of the Visa card at the time.[14]

Later in the day this element in the cross-examination became subsumed under the news coverage by a further startling development. Continuing the line of questioning out of which the earlier contempt of court arose, Hood pressed Stephenson about the origin of the information about Kevin Taylor's business affairs until he obtained the admission that two filing cabinet drawers of files had gone missing. As a consequence Judge Sachs halted the trial for two hours and called three senior police officers to appear before him, to explain the absence of the files.

The *Manchester Evening News* headline now ran across five columns and read 'Taylor case snag', with a subsidiary triple-decker underlined headline: 'Judge calls top police to court.' The report said that under cross-examination Stephenson had revealed that the files were the source of information on which the trial had been based. He had told the court: 'I don't know who originated the information. I have been left holding the baby. I have asked everyone in the unit where the files are and nobody knows.'[15]

Stephenson said that a number of files were kept at the headquarters of the Drugs Intelligence Unit in an office shared by Detective Inspectors Murray and Waterworth, and that they had served under the then Detective Chief Inspector Norman Born. 'I think the three of them should attend this court', Judge Sachs told the prosecuting counsel Michael Corkery, who said he was proposing to have inquiries made by someone from the Director of Public Prosecutions. In case anyone should be in any doubt as to the seriousness or the esoteric quality of these Byzantine transactions, defence counsel and judge both underlined their own dissatisfaction and surprise at the situation. Hood commented that it was very unsatisfactory to cross-examine with only a certain degree of knowledge. The judge said he was very concerned and found it quite extraordinary. He inquired of Stephenson: 'Have you ever in your experience encountered a situation like this?' The inspector replied: 'No.'[16]

The next day the former Detective Chief Inspector Born of the Drugs Intelligence Unit, now promoted to the rank of superintendent and serving with the CID support group, was summoned before Judge Sachs but could provide no further light on the matter. But he was able to introduce a new meaning into the English language for the word 'missing', when he explained: 'I can't tell you where the documents are but I can't accept that they are missing.'

Events now began to speed up with the inevitability of a solid object accelerating through the air under the force of gravity. The defence counsel Hood now began to probe for the rotten core of the prosecution case against Taylor. He questioned Stephenson about the application he had made in February 1986 to gain access to Taylor's bank accounts. The application for orders of access was made before the Recorder of Manchester Judge Arthur Prestt, who was asked not to make notes during the hearing because of 'the sensitivity of the matter'. Stephenson acknowledged that the sworn police statement made to Judge Prestt had been placed in a sealed envelope and kept from Taylor's lawyers for two years. He admitted that at first the police had claimed that the defence were denied access to the statement because of an order made by the Recorder, but that when defence lawyers approached Judge Prestt he said there was no reason why they should not see the application.

Hood's cross-examination of Stephenson about the nature of the police statement to Judge Prestt made it clear why the police might not have wanted their statement to the judge to be seen by the defence. Police witnesses had said that their case would be dead and buried without access to these accounts. They had obtained this access by telling Judge Prestt that there was 'no likelihood of Mr. Taylor authorising scrutiny of his bank accounts'. On the last day of the trial Hood said this could not be true. When he asked Stephenson if he had ever asked Taylor for access to his accounts, the detective replied that he had not. Stephenson also admitted that over a long period Taylor's solicitor had written to the police offering Taylor for interview and his co-operation and assistance in any way. Stephenson admitted that the statement in the application to Judge Prestt for access to Taylor's bank accounts had been 'inaccurate'. The prosecution of Kevin Taylor was dead.

Appropriately, the paper which first announced the acquittal was the *Manchester Evening News*. Early editions carried a story on page two which focused on the secrecy of the submission to Judge Prestt for the orders of access: 'A blanket of secrecy cloaked attempts to build a case against businessman Kevin Taylor, a jury heard today.'[17] The front page lead story referred to a strike threat by ambulance men, but by the late edition the 'Mercy men call strike' story had move into the slot earlier occupied by the Taylor story, and with its flair for major headlines of few words the paper ran 'Taylor cleared' across the top of its front page under the strapline 'Judge throws out fraud case.' Now freed from the constraints of simply reporting as a record events which took place in court the reporter Ray King described the scenes outside the court after the case as well as the end of the case itself.

The story was angled on the collapse of the case, the scene outside the court and a summary of the sixteen-week trial. The intro declared: 'The million pound fraud trial of businessman Kevin Taylor dramatically collapsed this afternoon.'[18] In the second paragraph, Taylor, described as 'the 57-year-old friend of former Deputy Chief Constable John Stalker', and his three associates were said to have been discharged by Judge Michael Sachs after a trial lasting almost sixteen weeks. The circumstances in court which marked the end of the trial were then described: the statement by the prosecuting counsel that it would not be proper to seek adverse verdicts against any of the defendants and the direction of the jury by the judge to bring in not guilty verdicts on all twelve counts.

Events outside the court now became part of the coverage for the first time since the beginning of the trial. Taylor was described shaking hands with Stephenson and 'saying a few words to Mr. Stephenson before they left'. Mrs Taylor was quoted as saying justice had been done, and Taylor himself as commenting favourably on the behaviour of the judge and as paying tribute to his solicitor Charles Buckley who had worked long and hard, often without pay: 'I am also grateful to my barrister David Hood who really is a rising star of the bar.'[19] The story then summarized the case, beginning with the terminal acknowledgement by the police that 'inaccurate' information was put before Judge Prestt in February 1986 to obtain access to Taylor's bank accounts. The report went on:

> Throughout the trial Mr Taylor's lawyers had contended that his investigation and the prosecution had been 'little more than a smokescreen' to discredit Mr Stalker who at the time had been leading the 'shoot to kill' inquiry in Northern Ireland, from which he was later suspended.
>
> Police witnesses admitted under cross examination that a large part of their inquiry had been to establish links between Mr Stalker and Mr Taylor; and Mr Taylor with criminal elements.[20]

What is apparent from this story is the way in which the structure of events in the court imposes a narrative structure on the news story, with an ideological consequence. At thee outset of the case reports took the form of summaries of the prosecution case against Taylor. They were accounts of alleged financial manipulations such as the 'money go-round' and this required that these were explained in order that the story could make sense. As in all reporting of court cases, during the period of the prosecution case or the case by the plaintiff the structure of the story therefore becomes a demonstration of the deviance of the defendant and an attack on the idea of deviance itself.

Now in the Taylor case, as in the case of, say, the 'Guildford Four' appeal, a verdict in favour of the defence changes *ex post facto* the significance of events. And the authority for such change is the verdict of the court. In the context of a not guilty verdict, in order to contribute to the logic of the narrative any summary needs to *explain* that verdict. Ray King's report concentrates on the 'admission' that the claim to Judge Prestt was inaccurate, what Taylor's lawyers had contended and what 'police witnesses had admitted'.

The coverage of the Taylor trial had been almost exclusively undertaken by the *Manchester Evening News*. Now the verdict was covered by the entire national press. They had been alerted as to the likely outcome of the trial by a Manchester freelance journalist, Peter Reece (who in June 1986 had co-authored a story for *The People* on the role of police masons in the Stalker affair).[21]

The presentation of the story in the nationals on the day following the acquittal was entirely in terms of its significance for the Stalker affair. The word 'Taylor' scarcely appeared in the headlines. In the *Daily Express* there was 'Joy after Stalker's old friend is cleared', in the *Daily Mirror* the reference was to 'Freed Stalker tycoon', in the *Daily Star* it was to 'Free Stalker pal'.[22] The stories set the collapse of the trial in the context of the allegation that it had been an attempt to discredit Stalker and in relation to the probability of a case against the GMP by Taylor for compensation for the loss of business and his reduction to reliance on state benefit as a means of support. In *The Daily Telegraph* a back page article by Chris Ryder went over the history of the Stalker affair and, although the article was at pains to avoid commitment to a clear statement that there had been a conspiracy against Stalker, Ryder drew a conclusion which seemed to support such a view:

> Whatever the real truth, the verdict in the Taylor trial will fuel again the belief among those who subscribe to the conspiracy theory, that Taylor was removed to bring Stalker down, whether for reasons connected with Manchester or Northern Ireland or even both. The affair has had a profound effect on the lives of both men and no first hand account from any other major players has yet emerged to confirm or contradict what they have claimed.[23]

The Daily Telegraph gave a lengthier coverage of the story on the day following the verdict than any of the other nationals and like the other 'quality' papers its treatment of the trial was placed in the context of the political significance of a claim by Stalker that he had evidence which would show that the decision to remove him from the Northern Ireland inquiry was taken at Cabinet level. The Labour spokesman on Northern Ireland, Kevin McNamara, was quoted as saying that the Stalker affair 'stinks to high heaven'. The following sections from the report by Nigel Bunyan and David Millward typified this report and others in the quality press which focused on the embarrassment which the case posed for the government and on the Stalker allegation that the decision to remove him from the original inquiry in Northern Ireland had been initiated at a high level:

> Throughout his trial Mr Taylor maintained that he had been investigated by Greater Manchester police as a means of discrediting Mr Stalker. This latest embarrassment for the Government comes with the dust barely settled over the fresh 'shoot to kill allegations' which followed the shooting of a gang of raiders outside a Belfast bookmakers by undercover soldiers. Last night Whitehall moved quickly to lower the temperature, insisting the collapse of the Taylor case was a matter for the police and the Crown Prosecution Service. But the Government's hands off approach failed to convince MPs. Mr McNamara said: 'This has put a fresh complexion on the whole of the Stalker inquiry in Northern Ireland. The reason why he was taken off the case has now collapsed.'[24]
>
> Mr Stalker, now a writer after giving up a 28-year police career, said last night that the case's premature conclusion had saved 'embarrassment' at a high level in the Greater Manchester force. Asked whom he blamed, Mr Stalker replied firmly: 'It has to be those at senior political level. It was at senior Cabinet level, with the involvement of senior policemen.'[25]

The reference to what Stalker had said was to an interview he had given the previous evening to Channel Four television news. The allegation of involvement by individuals at Cabinet level now became the focus of the news coverage of the affair. Concentration on the trial of Kevin Taylor became once again the province of the local and regional press. The Cabinet involvement centred around a document which Stalker said he had which identified by initials senior officials in the decision to remove him from the shoot-to-kill inquiry. The police authority announced it was to hold an investigation into the Taylor prosecution and the Director of Public Prosecutions asked Anderton to hold an inquiry into the case. Even more than is usually true of the British system of law and order, these events were characterized by people being asked to investigate their own possible shortcomings. This is a system which combines the greatest possibility of achieving a full knowledge of events by the investigator with the minimum probability of its ever being made public. The Home Secretary David Waddington turned down the more adventurous option of holding a full independent inquiry into the affair.

While all of these issues were aired in the press, the document which Stalker held and which was said to implicate Cabinet level officials became the main hare which journalists chased. At the same time, the original shootings of the six unarmed Northern Ireland Catholics, Stalker's investigation and his removal from the inquiry in 1986 were all re-examined in feature articles.[26] The general consensus spanned views ranging from a strong sense of unease to qualified support for the conspiracy theory. Only the *Sunday Telegraph* stood outside the broad general view.

In an article entitled 'Stalker: no case for a conspiracy' Peter Taylor, the author of *Stalker – the Search for the Truth*[27] and one of the best-informed journalists on the shoot-to-kill incidents, argued that there were no grounds for believing that Stalker had been removed because he was getting too close to the truth. Referring to the proposal rejected by the Home Secretary for a public inquiry Peter Taylor concluded:

> The problem is that the emotion and prejudgement now surrounding the Stalker affair are so great that if such a public inquiry reached the conclusion that there had been no conspiracy, no-one would believe it. Cover-ups are more appealing than facts.[28]

Mary Holland, for many years a reporter of events in Northern Ireland, drew a different conclusion in the Observer: 'John Stalker was not only dispensable; his inquiry, which had serious implications for the RUC, was adding to their [senior civil servants] difficulties.'[29]

The standfirst with the Peter Taylor article in the *Sunday Telegraph* said 'Peter Taylor . . . reflects on the implications of the latest twists in the tale and maintains his long-held theory that a simple explanation is the best.' Simple and best in the case of the *Sunday Telegraph* meant not accepting that there might have been a government conspiracy or one by senior police officers to quash the Stalker inquiry. Peter Taylor's theory was that the removal of Stalker from the inquiry was to save the shoot-to-kill inquiry. While this theory might have been the best, if it was simple, reporters, feature writers and leaderwriters outside the *Sunday Telegraph* seemed unable to grasp its simple logic.

The mood of the leader in *The Independent* was reflected in its title, 'An abscess bursts'. Unless the government acted swiftly and frankly to explain 'what on the evidence available looks to be inexplicable' the Stalker affair, already a scandal, would become something worse, 'a centre of infection threatening public confidence in the integrity of government'.[30] The tone of the leader had now hardened by comparison with the paper's opinion two years earlier at the time of the publication of Stalker's book and the decision by the DPP not to prosecute any of the RUC officers who were the subjects of the original Stalker inquiry. In the interim a number of police scandals had become public, including the successful appeal of the 'Guildford Four' and the disbandment of the West Midlands Serious Crimes Squad by the then chief constable of that force Geoffrey Dear after allegations that prosecutions had been obtained by falsification of evidence against defendants. The leader declared:

> The Deputy Chief Constable of Greater Manchester, John Stalker, was called in to investigate killings by Royal Ulster Constabulary officers that looked unpleasantly like revenge for policemen believed to have been murdered by some of the men killed. When he pressed for evidence, he has said in his memoirs, he was first obstructed by the RUC, then taken off the case, and smeared with vague, false accusations. His friend Kevin Taylor was prosecuted for fraud.
>
> On Monday the abscess burst. The unconvincing case against Mr Taylor was finally dropped by the prosecution.[31]

The paper went on to refer to an extraordinary gloss by the former chief constable of the RUC on television the previous evening on the acquittal of Kevin Taylor. The reference was used to begin a general and damning critique of the police:

> Sir John Hermon, in the course of the same programme, said that just because the case against Mr. Taylor had been dropped, it did not mean he was innocent. The condition of the

police in Britain can best be described as one of institutional rot. Too often insensitive in their dealings with the public, sometimes aggressive in their stance towards ethnic minorities, trades unions, the media and anyone else who dares to criticise them, a significant minority of police officers convey the impression that they see themselves as a thin blue line defending, not the public against crime, but a besieged citadel, manned by themselves, against the public. In this almost paranoid mood, many officers seem to have taken to breaking the law more or less systematically: only yesterday brought another depressingly familiar tale of a window-cleaner 'fitted up' by the Metropolitan Police for armed robbery.[32]

The paper did not simply explain this condition by reference to the police as an institution but by reference to the obsessively secret world of government where the 'elementary principles of natural justice and common law too often take second place to a cynical *raison d'état*', and where 'the Government had no sooner dropped its case against the Guildford Four than great lawyers rushed to explain that just because they were not guilty, that did not mean they were innocent. Sir John Hermon says the same of Kevin Taylor.'[33]

The *Daily Express* on the same day also identified the government as involved in the affair and declared that a grave wrong had been done to Stalker but, unlike *The Independent*, left open the possibility that this was not necessarily as a consequence of a plot. The wrong had been done 'whether through blunder or design', the *Daily Express* leader declared. 'Ministers cannot wash their hands of this matter. Only the Government commands the means and the authority to get to the bottom of this disturbing business. And it should now do so.'[34]

In the instance of the *Daily Express* leader we see the classic role of the 'free press' at work within the confines of its role in a pluralist capitalist state or in any system in which the press is seen as the watchdog on the lookout for faults in a generally reliable system. The government is seen as the final authority and the means to 'get to the bottom of this disturbing business'. In *The Independent* the government is seen as being at the bottom of the disturbing business. The images of stench, bad taste and decay in earlier eruptions of the

Stalker story have now (pages 257–9) become an image of disease – an abscess which has burst – and the decay is seen as fundamental and institutional. The rectitude of the core of the system is called into question: the police, the courts, the lawyers, judges and the state are all seen as corruptible and corrupt. The paper's mood of cynicism, despair and rising paranoia is encapsulated in the following passage, the conservatism of whose rhetoric only emphasizes its poignancy: 'Quis custodiet ipsos custodes? At the moment, with half a dozen of our major forces investigating one another, the police are in danger of running out of investigators to investigate the investigators.'[35]

The aftermath of the Taylor trial was dominated by the allegation made by Stalker that he had a document that would prove Cabinet-level involvement. In their coverage of this the national press fell into the mould of behaviour already established at the height of the drama in 1986. Stalker's initiatives set the agenda for coverage. This had happened in the summer of 1986 as the outcome of a selection process from among a number of sources of information and authority. Now Stalker was the automatic man to be contacted in relation to the Taylor case. His role as a more general authority for news producers in relation to police and crime-related matters is illustrated by the fact that he was interviewed by television news reporters for his opinion about whether the Strangeways prisoners would be willing to speak frankly to the judicial inquiry into the prison disturbances in March and April of 1990. His name and the role he played in the shoot-to-kill inquiry have now become institutionalized as part of the system of attributing meaning to situations. Every incident in which a shoot-to-kill allegation is made involves a reference to the name Stalker in at least one national news outlet. His name has become a means of quickly identifying an issue – a metaphor for a certain depiction of state behaviour. In this sense the name has become part of a process of stereotypification by the media, not of deviant social groups but of the state itself as potentially deviant.

After the verdict was announced and the first flurry of reports about the end of the trial and the effect of his six years of stress died away, Kevin Taylor ceased once again to be a central figure in the drama. The document which Stalker held and which he claimed showed Cabinet-level involvement became the focus for journalistic inquiries. By the day after the trial this document and the government's reaction to the possibility of its existence was the subject of the *Manchester Evening News* lead story. This said that the government would challenge Stalker to produce the document, and reported his response that he would show it if any proper investigation were launched: 'It is a typewritten note of a meeting which took place at the time of my removal involving a number of people who are only referred to by initials', he said. 'I believe I know their identities. The note relates to the recollections of one individual present at that meeting.'[36]

The document was pursued by the press as a mystery. Who were the people at the meeting? What had transpired there? Who was the individual who had 'recollected' the meeting? The initials of those taking part became known. They were R.A., P.M., and C.S. Speculation quickly arose that the R.A. referred to the then Sir Robert Armstrong, now Lord Armstrong, the former Cabinet secretary famed for his less than felicitous aphorism that he had been 'economical with the truth'. On 20 January *The Guardian* reported that when asked by the *Manchester Evening News*, the great man had replied: 'I have no comment whatsoever to make.'[37]

The following day *The Observer* reported that 'a former senior Northern Ireland official' had said R. A. was Sir Robert Andrew who was at the time of the meeting the most senior civil servant in the province. The other initials referred to Sir Philip Myers and Colin Sampson and, according to the source, the meeting took place after Stalker had been removed from the inquiry and could not have been part of a conspiracy to fabricate charges against him, the story said.[38]

During the week that followed the Conservative MP for Barrow, Cecil Franks, pressed his campaign for a full public inquiry including a question to the Prime Minister who in characteristically unapologetic frame of mind denied the request and called on Stalker to produce his evidence. 'I do not know why he is delaying,' she said in a rare confession that there was something which she did not know. During the course of the week it was revealed that the documents were extracts from the engagements diary of Sir John Hermon, which had become available indirectly as a consequence of documents discovered during a libel action which Hermon had brought. Stalker and his solicitor Roger Pannone, attended by a phalanx of press photographers, newspaper reporters and television news teams, handed the documents over to Home Office officials on 25 January.

The issue in the press coverage became an arcane debate about the meaning of the word 'seeing'. John Carvel, David Pallister and Alan Travis wrote in *The Guardian*:

> According to Mr Stalker the extract said: 'a C.C. has seen B.S, RA and TK and that DH was au fait with developments.' This could be translated as: 'A chief constable has seen Barry Shaw [the Northern Ireland Director of Public Prosecutions], Sir Robert Andrew (the permanent under-secretary in the Northern Ireland Office), Tom King (the Northern Ireland Secretary) and Douglas Hurd (the Home Secretary) has been kept informed.' An alternative RA may be Sir Robert Armstrong, the Cabinet Secretary, and the chief constable could be Colin Sampson of West Yorkshire or James Anderton of Greater Manchester.
>
> According to the Home Office, Mr Stalker misquoted the extract, which should read: 'mentioned a C. C. seeing B. S, RA and TK and that DH was au fait with developments'.
>
> A spokesman said: 'The difference in tense is crucial. Assuming that CC is Colin Sampson who replaced Mr. Stalker on the RUC inquiry the reference to seeing BS, RA and TK must be related to the future because Mr Sampson knew nothing of these matters until the meeting he attended on May 19, 1986, the day after the date of the diary entry.'[39]

This bland civil service explanation cheerfully ignored the fact that the normal colloquial use of the present participle 'seeing' to mean 'having seen' (as in "I remember seeing him") did not attach to a later entry in the Hermon diary which Stalker produced. This read: 'I expressed concern about structure of the inquiry. Clearly collusion between P.M., R.A., C.S., and D.P.P. I must hold the line.' The spin doctors were not able to provide the press with any new and innocent meaning of the word 'collusion', nor a special civil service use of the phrase 'to express concern' which meant 'to be completely satisfied with', nor why Sir John was feeling compelled to 'hold the line'. *The*

Guardian reported that *before Stalker delivered his document* the Home Secretary David Waddington had said in the House of Commons that he would study it but that he had 'no reason whatsoever to believe that anything improper had occurred'.[40]

The following day Stalker held a press conference at his solicitor's office in Manchester where he brushed aside the quibble over the implied tense and sense of the word 'seeing'. He said: 'Whether "seeing" is past, present or future, arrangements were in hand to communicate with individuals initialled, and DH was au fait with developments, this being 10 days before my removal.' He also pointed out that the Home Office was quick to spot his error over the word "seeing", but had failed to comment on the use of the word 'collusion'. All he had ever said was that the document deserved further investigation, he stated. Interviewed by *The Guardian*, Sir John Hermon said there was no conspiracy to remove Stalker from the inquiry, and that the word 'collusion' referred to his concerns about the inquiry after Stalker had been taken off it.[41] Eventually, on 4 April 1990, in a written parliamentary statement Waddington was able to provide a complete explanation of the whole mystery. 'Seeing', he said, referred to a future meeting, and was able to reveal that Hermon regretted the use of the word 'collusion' and 'did not intend anything sinister'. A new and bland meaning of the word 'collusion' had been invented to take account of the difficulty. The occasion of this answer once again raised the issue of the shoot-to-kill inquiry and the Taylor trial, and the *Guardian* news story which reported the answer in order to make sense of it as a narrative summarized the background to the affair and included an interview with Stalker in which he said, not surprisingly, that the Home Secretary's reply did not address the central questions he had raised.[42]

Conclusion

The trial of Kevin Taylor provided an important evidential crux in the establishment of an 'authorized version' of reality in the history of the Stalker affair. The defence of Kevin Taylor was based on the proposition that he had been the innocent victim of a plot to get Stalker off the shoot-to-kill inquiry in Northern

Ireland. The success of this defence would clearly provide the stamp of judicial approval for this version of events. Evidence at the trial might also provide the means for the press to divine who was party to any plot which may have been hatched against Stalker and Taylor. Equally, if Taylor had been found guilty the whole basis of the conspiracy theory would have been undermined.

Yet the national press did not cover the trial. Only the *Manchester Evening News* carried regular reports. And these covered only the first and last weeks, and the point in the proceedings when Davenport, the prosecution witness, acknowledged that he thought that the press were out to get Stalker. Evidence which showed that prosecution witnesses were questioned repeatedly and for long hours in order to obtain appropriate statements so that Kevin Taylor might be charged, and evidence that the chief constable of Greater Manchester had been involved in the inquiry from its early stages never became public.

The reasons for this can be adduced to organizational changes in the national press, to changes in personnel and to managerial decisions taken by news executives. As a consequence, when the trial ended the coverage in the national press was heavily restricted to what had happened in the last few days. There was no attempt to examine what had happened during the trial to see what it might reveal of the way in which the Stalker affair was brought about. This was also reinforced by the way in which Stalker himself had become a reference point in the social construction of the reality of the case. His document became a new hare to chase. In this context the document also had two important characteristics of a good story: it involved a conflict over its meaning, and it could be portrayed as a mystery to be solved. To whom did the initials refer? Who had written it? What did it say?

In the final analysis the document turned out to be a damp squib. But the reason for this was not that there was anything intrinsically insignificant about what it said. The reason was twofold: first, that the government and those who had been involved in the May 1986 meetings either kept quiet or were prepared to offer in a bare faced way answers to questions which were either trivial or frankly preposterous; and, second, no source of attack with access to major political levers manifested itself to challenge this establishment blandness. In the end, the authorities have prevailed without offering an explanation for a trial result which involved evidence of police pressure on witnesses, which indicated high-level involvement in the expensive and frenzied prosecution of a man who was found not guilty, which involved the charge of defrauding a bank which had made no complaint to the police (and had made a profit of £360,000 on the deal), which had involved senior police officers in contempt of court and, earlier, in making untrue statements to a judge. The only issues the government have found it necessary to address in public are the meaning of the word 'seeing' and a new version of the word 'collusion', which implied nothing sinister. Yet none of this can be seen as the outcome of a subservient press. Despite the fact that they did not cover the trial in full they addressed most of the issues raised publicly by it both in terms of news coverage and in terms of editorials.

CHAPTER TWELVE

Conclusions

The intention in writing this book was to address the issue of whether an analysis based on the idea of a dominant ideology or on 'ideological hegemony' satisfactorily explains the way in which news is produced, as for instance, the Glasgow Media Group, the Birmingham Centre for Cultural Studies and others seem to suggest. The Stalker affair provided a case study with which to do so. The idea of a dominant ideology, exemplified by the Glasgow Media Group studies (pages 4–8) is that a system of ideas provides a framework for understanding and depicting the world in a way which explains and justifies the distribution of power by legitimizing those in power and marginalizing and stigmatizing those who oppose. This system underlies and explains the construction of social and political reality. This can be decoded from the word-usage, construction and content of the news. For instance, the use of terms such as 'militants', 'moderates', 'extremists' and their concentration in the coverage of industrial disputes would indicate the underlying pro-capital anti-trade union elements in the ideological formulations which underlie news reporting in the British mass media.

The way in which 'terrorism' is depicted in the media has also been an area in which ideological hegemony is an appealing analysis. As Philip Schlesinger, Graham Murdock and Philip Elliott have pointed out in their analysis of the television of 'terrorism' a number of arguments are foreclosed by the way in which television news production takes place.[1] At their time of writing the government had not then gone so far as to ban the spokesman of the IRA, INLA and Sinn Fein, so that although they were able to show that in most cases argument about the legitimacy of pro-republican violence as against state violence was foreclosed, in some respects that situation is now more marked. Elliott and Schlesinger's argument is much more sophisticated than a simple syllogism based on a match between the interests of the ruling class and the content of television coverage of terrorism, however, and we will return to it later.

Proponents of the dominant ideology analysis of the mass media face a problem in relation to the actual operation of the press and broadcast media in capitalist societies in that there at least appears to be a plurality of divergent interpretations of events freely available to people, and that where outlets for dissident views cease to exist it is simply because people are voting with their money and freely choosing not to read them. A number of arguments can be put against such a simple-minded version of pluralism. Most obviously, it can be shown that the press in capitalist countries is characterized by a continual secular tendency towards monopoly. This has characterized local daily and evening papers in Britain which now operate entirely as local monopolies. The consequence of this tendency has been the concentration of ownership in the hands of a few large companies, increasingly multinational and often owned by very rich individuals. Increasingly the financial empires of such enterprises and individuals involve ownership of industrial and commercial undertakings across the range of cultural production in publishing and the broadcast media as well as other forms of undertaking altogether, such as paper production or oil extraction.[2] Such an argument would be accepted here. The consequence of this position is that newspapers increasingly represent the views of such plutocrats and that news and ideas are increasingly market commodities. This is an argument about the preconditions for the production of ideology. It does not necessarily follow from this that a pro-capitalist interpretation of events is inevitably produced, nor does it enable us to infer from the products of journalistic and other cultural production the code which underlies them.

It is also important to recognize that the ideology of impartiality and balance which underlies the production of news and current affairs by the broadcast media in this country is also a construction of bureaucrats, managers and politicians and is often consciously designed to deny public debate of ideas considered to be dangerous or subversive, as Philip Schlesinger's study of BBC news[3] and Jean Seaton's analysis of the BBC have shown.[4] But it has to be recognized that while it can be shown that the management and ownership of the news media are structured to favour certain individuals and interests it does not *necessarily* follow that news and other forms of construction of reality entirely or even predominantly reflect those interests. These are empirical questions.

Given that we are not confronted by monolithic conformity in the output of the mass media then dominant ideology theorists need some way of evaluating the products of the mass media in order to explain the relative significance of conformist constructions of reality and opinions on the one hand and dissident or subversive ones on the other. One way of saving the case is to follow Herbert Marcuse's notion of 'repressive tolerance'[5] and dismiss the acceptance of divergent views as part of a means of perpetuating the myth of the free press, and therefore of maintaining the capitalist state and system. The argument here is that such a view is not an adequate means of understanding the processes of news production and that the press coverage of the Stalker affair represents a case which can only be absorbed into such a view of news production by making words meaningless.

In examining the way in which the Stalker affair was treated in the press we have not been so much concerned with editorializing policy as with the way in which newspapers arrived at a version of the facts, and the version which eventually came to be accepted was centred on the idea of a conspiracy by powerful individuals acting as representatives of institutions to pervert the course of justice. Both news coverage and editorializing (pages 256–61) raised the issue of the legitimacy of state violence in relation to 'terrorist' violence. Elliott, Murdock and Schlesinger identify the difference between 'open' and 'closed' presentations of terrorism, the former foreclosing debate about the issues the latter laying them open to question.[6] One of the ways in which the official discourse against 'terrorism' is made the dominant one is by foreclosing alternative and oppositional discourses by the use of 'closed' presentations which assume out of existence such arguments about whether, say, the state is justified in its use of violence, while, say, the IRA is not. In Elliott *et al.*'s terms an alternative discourse is one which might offer criticism of the policy of the state, while an oppositional discourse would put the views of its opponents.[7] In terms of such an analysis the coverage in the respectable press of the Stalker affair was a partly 'open' presentation of events. 'Alternative' views to those of the state, that of the 'official discourse', were thoroughly aired. These views and these versions of events entertained the idea that the agents of the state might have acted illegitimately in their treatment of John Stalker and in the killing of the six Irish Catholics. The presentation never extended to entertaining or considering the views of Sinn Fein or the IRA, however. In this sense oppositional discourses were excluded and this part of the argument was foreclosed.

In addition to their news coverage the papers did also editorialize. Thus, without recourse to inferring an underlying ideological code to know what their editors thought about the Stalker inquiry, we can consult what they actually wrote. Across the range of the press they were prepared to raise the possibility of the state having subverted Stalker's inquiry into the shoot-to-kill allegations. This is not to argue that the press accommodated an analysis of power which approves of the revolutionary overthrow of the state or that they gave a fair hearing to the arguments which might be put to justify IRA violence. But they did offer variations on the theme that the Stalker affair involved actions by those in power which probed the limits of political legitimacy and which began to make it difficult to distinguish between the moral basis of the IRA's violence and that of the state.

From the outset the press questioned the good faith of those who had removed Stalker from his duties and they drew attention to the coincidence of this having happened at the very time he was about to return to Northern Ireland to confront the RUC with his crucial demand for the hayshed evidence. The words 'stink' and 'stench' were used in a number of leading articles. Although one might expect *The Guardian* and *The Observer* to take such a line, the Conservative, pro-Thatcher *Daily Express*, which was one of first papers actively to investigate the affair, declared five weeks after his removal from duty: 'There is a stench about that is strong enough to linger through the summer, autumn, winter and spring.' This they related to what he was investigating in Northern Ireland: 'Even if all the published allegations against Mr. Stalker prove to be wholly correct he is guilty at most of trifling indiscretions. In Ulster Mr. Stalker was investigating a series of killings. Murder is more than an indiscretion.'[8] They had thus crossed the line, and raised the spectre of possible murder committed by state agents employed to maintain law and order.

In taking up this line the *Daily Express* was following on from what their sister paper, *The Star*, had declared twelve days earlier:

> There is a very nasty stench about the suspension from duty of Manchester's Deputy Chief Constable, John Stalker, and the investigation into allegations of misconduct by him . . . there are plenty of grounds for the suspicion that he could be the victim of a political witch-hunt based on a tissue of rumour and innuendo and malice . . . There is talk that he accuses senior RUC officers of covering up the unlawful killings of suspects and that the Special Branch and even MI5 are also involved. One very strong rumour now in circulation is that Mr. Stalker was 'fingered' either by a senior RUC officer or by a top Unionist politician in Belfast anxious to suppress the report . . . The silence must end. The bad smell is becoming overpowering.'[9]

The smell was also registered by *The Guardian*. On the same day it declared: 'The stink that surrounds the coincidence of Mr. Stalker's planned return to Northern Ireland to complete his RUC inquiry and his enforced leave will not go away.'[10] The *Manchester Evening News* registered a similar unpleasant odour, suggesting that if some of the suspicions about the case were proved true there would be 'more than a whiff of Watergate about the Stalker affair.'[11] A year and a half later *The Guardian* still sensed the aftermath of the smell. 'The Stalker affair', it declared, 'left a bad taste in the mouth.'[12]

Such phrases do not figure prominently in the lexicon of precise logical analysis, but they do have meaning for those writing and those reading them. They imply that something unpleasant had been done, something involving bad faith. What is more, in the context in which they were used they could only be referring either to government or senior officials in the police and the security services. News stories in the same newspapers could only be read to make sense if they inculpated such agencies. At the beginning of the affair in June 1986 the *Manchester Evening News* entertained in its leader column the suspicion of the state as an agent of the murder of its opponents. The paper editorialized: 'There have been suspicions in the past about the security services and their activities; in the Hilda Murrell case for instance.' This was a reference to the anti-nuclear campaigner who was found murdered after her home was broken into in Shrewsbury and only papers stolen. The leader did not state that she had been murdered by agents of the state but raised the suspicion as a valid issue which needed to be addressed.[13]

In the *Today* newspaper's opinion and comment section on 9 September 1986, the political editor, Sue Cameron, suggested that the circumstances under which Stalker had been removed from duty might well amount to a conspiracy by the 'establishment'. Under the headline 'Scandalous. The smokescreen that still obscures the Stalker affair', she wrote: 'When things go badly wrong in the British Establishment's machine, it is invariably because of a cock-up rather than a conspiracy,' but added that the Stalker affair could well be the exception that proved the rule.[14]

In early 1988 *The Guardian* raised the issue of the involvement of the police in covert operations and the fact that RUC men had been told to lie in the course of a murder trial. It concluded with an ironic parody of the government's position:

> In this affair the Government has always said it is not involved: it knew nothing about Stalker, did not interfere in police matters in Northern Ireland. Until the crunch, when there is a report and a decision to do nothing. Only don't for a moment suspect cover-up; take it from us that the sole determining factor is the public interest. The Government cries that one too often. It has devalued the term.[15]

There is a clear implication in these views that neither the government's good faith nor that of senior police officials could be assumed in looking at their explanations of what had happened in the events in Ulster which Stalker had investigated. Without recourse to invoking a hidden code underlying the surface of such articles it is only possible for them to make sense if the government is seen either as the source of wrongdoing or is covering up the wrongdoing of its agents in the police and security services.

One might argue that such arguments might be expected in *The Guardian* or on Channel Four where they can be marginalized to a small audience who are already predisposed to conspiracy politics. But the *Manchester Evening News* is a populist regional evening newspaper with the largest local evening newspaper sales monopoly in the provinces. It is the established commercial press for the region. Similarly, the *Daily Express* and *The Star* can only be categorized pro-Conservative in their political stance.

No established British newspaper took the view that the IRA should be supported or that there was no legitimacy in the British government's presence in Northern Ireland. The position taken was that the Stalker affair indicated probable wrongdoing by members of the RUC which had been covered up and that this threatened the credibility of the police and the security forces because it called into question the legitimacy of their actions. The papers above stressed the grounds for suspecting the government's good faith and they appeared to place no boundaries on what might have been done by the agents of the state nor covered up by ministers and high-ranking police officers. The more establishment version of the argument was to adopt a suspicious attitude to the government's actions but to stress the need for the successful fight against the IRA and the need for Anglo-Irish anti-terrorist co-operation.

While its news columns contained detailed accounts of the killings by the RUC of unarmed Catholics *The Independent* attempted to draw the line for the establishment in dealing with terrorism. Arguing for a meticulously rigid adherence to the law by the security forces in fighting terrorism the paper intoned: 'While some breaches of the law may remain hidden, others come out, conferring a spurious legitimacy on the other side.'[16]

A little later *The Daily Telegraph* leader writer put the concerns of the supporters of the legitimacy of the British state with some poignancy:

Mr. Tom King's remarks in the House of Commons yesterday about the so-called Stalker affair reflected a laudable honesty of purpose by the Northern Ireland Secretary, but also a profoundly unsatisfactory situation. We remarked almost a fortnight ago that the publication of Mr. John Stalker's book on his investigation of the RUC shootings of six men, four of them indisputably unarmed, was unlikely to help British–Irish relations. So indeed it has proved. No branch of government has found itself able to refute Mr. Stalker's claims that members of the the RUC acted with terminal ruthlessness towards suspects in 1982, and that the subsequent police investigations were conducted unprofessionally, to say the very least. Mr. King, to his credit, did not seek to pretend that the RUC's behaviour either in the 1982 shootings or the later inquiries reflected well on the force.[17]

Even later, in August 1988, the same newspaper was using the Stalker affair to draw a lesson about relations between the UK and Eire in the wake of the Gibraltar shootings:

The greatest danger for Britain and Ireland now is that the IRA's campaign to polarise London and Dublin, the British and Irish people, should gain ground. The saloon bar wisdom of Britain is that 'Gibraltar showed the only way to deal with the IRA.' Yet the Stalker affair reinforced the alienation of many Ulster Catholics from the RUC and the Belfast authorities. The British as a nation have never much liked or respected the Irish. Yet the further we allow ourselves to be driven towards treating them as racial stereotypes, the more parlous will our political predicament there become.[18]

(This was a slightly different line of argument from that pursued by the *Sunday Telegraph*, owned by the same company, whose editor, Peregrine Worsthorne, was in May of 1988 dismissing as unworthy of concern any qualms that people might have about the fact that unarmed IRA suspects had been 'shot down like dogs' by the SAS.)

I have deliberately considered the leaders and comment which appeared in the established commercial British press and have ignored comments in publications such as the *New Statesman*, the *Morning Star* or *Private Eye* where for reasons of political viewpoints or journalistic style such expressions would be regarded as atypical of the general output of the normal range of newspaper opinion. But what is apparent is a willingness to call into question not simply the wisdom of government policies or the good faith of individual politicians, but a questioning of the good faith and legitimacy of the state and its agents and of the establishment which is seen as lying behind them. Defects of a fundamental nature as well as of particular circumstances are identified as explanations of the smell rising from the Stalker affair.

The argument so far has addressed the nature of content as empirical evidence relating to generalized conclusions about the nature of ideological dominance. A more fundamental difficulty seems to me to arise from the notion of decoding the dominant ideology from representations of reality, such as news stories. If we could explain what appears in the press and the broadcast media in terms of an underlying code reflecting a dominant ideology we would expect that we could see it at work, especially in a case where the legitimacy of the state and its institutions are called into question. There is no reason to think that the coverage of industrial relations, for instance, should be more subject to the rules of encoding the dominant ideology than the coverage of police murders of terrorist suspects. In any case, terrorism as a subject has been included in analyses heavily dependent on the idea of the media articulating an underlying ideology of order by use of devices such as stereotypical representations of certain social groups and categories.

The very labelling of some groups as terrorists and others as freedom fighters as many have indicated is a way of constructing reality to give it a particular meaning. While all the established British press refer to the IRA as terrorists, the *Washington Post*, for instance, refers to them as 'guerrillas'. A nice variant of this can be seen in the *Belfast Telegraph* which refers to those Catholics suspected of IRA sympathies or membership as 'republican' while other Catholics, such as Michael Tighe, the victim of the hayshed killing, are exculpated by the term 'nationalists'. This different way of evaluating the homicides and destruction done by people with different allegiances and different uniforms cannot be used to infer, however, that some unified belief system can be used to analyse everything that is produced in the media where such labelling occurs.

There is a fundamental difficulty in the use of the concept of ideology to comprehend the way in which news is produced, and this relates both to the fundamental nature of the idea and to the way in which the empirical data are inferred. First, the nature of ideology is conceived initially as a way of explaining aggregate states of affairs – the domination of one class by another. In this, a whole state of social, political and economic relations is made possible by a set of ideas, values, norms, perceptions which logically fits the relations it sustains. The difficulty with this conception for understanding day-to-day cultural production is that it is not capable of explaining particular events, it only explains the whole.

Second, and as a consequence of this, the only way in which ideology can be inferred empirically is by deducing it from such surface manifestations as news stories by a process of content analysis. The ideology is revealed by attaching meanings to particular words which can then be decoded to reveal the underlying structure of meaning. But the only way in which we are able to do this decoding work is through the *a priori* assumption that it exists. Professional explanations by journalists, for instance, have to be dismissed as less adequate.

Both of these difficulties manifest themselves in a fundamental empirical problem – it is not possible to identify the mechanism by which such an ideological formulation leads to the journalist actually doing ideological work. We can see how certain proprietors, such as Rupert Murdoch or Lord Rothermere, use their power of brute ownership to enforce policy on their reporters and editors, but this is not the same thing. Equally, as Philip Elliott and Peter Golding[19] have shown, the policy of the broadcasting authorities produces a different sort of uniformity in their news coverage. But this again does not require any underlying explanatory device to account for it. There is a proximate cause to hand.

If the production of some examples of pro-business pro-state propaganda can be adduced to show that the press sustain a capitalist ideology, then the production of a major and continuing drama in the press which calls into question the legitimacy of the state must constitute a challenge to this view.

More importantly, it is impossible to explain the press coverage of the Stalker affair in a way which does not take into account the work practices of those engaged in the production of news. Journalists are concerned with the production of social facts and of social meanings. This is not a construction put on what they do by a sociologist but what they self-consciously do. When they manufacture news they do so by deciding whether a story is worth doing and this depends on whether it can be made to show something significant, whether it can be shown to be factually accurate and whether it is legally safe to publish it.

In examining the way in which news stories are written we showed how the sources of news and significance of news are built into the narrative structure. With much news this involves building in 'normal' perceptions of who is in authority and what institutions confer authority by simply reporting events which are constructed by those in power. This enables journalists to produce quick reliable news which is both factually sustained and established as significant by virtue of its sources in the structure of authority. In this sense it is possible to argue that the press sustain the status quo by reinforcing as legitimate given relationships of authority and that market pressures in terms of production costs cause this state of affairs. In this situation the press and the system of power relationships on which it reports sustain one another in a symbiotic relationship.

This analysis, which I have tended to promulgate myself elsewhere in attempts to analyse what journalists do and the way in which they apparently censor themselves[20] turns out to be facile when applied to the Stalker affair. It may well apply generally, but does so only because other relationships normally hold good. For instance, it normally depends on a regular system of contacts and sources which provide the raw material of news in a form which is easy for journalists to manufacture as news. This in turn relies on a system of government in which the rules of debate and the means by which reality is defined are accepted by all the players. In the case of the Stalker affair the coverage of police affairs in Manchester had not been in this state for a number of years. It was not simply that there were inter-party differences over law and order or a debate between the chief constable and the GMPA. The chief constable had challenged the authority's right to take decisions in given areas relating to policing, and the majority group on the earlier Police Monitoring Committee had habitually challenged Anderton's fitness to take decisions in other areas.

This meant that the routine coverage of police politics in Manchester had involved the depiction of a state of affairs in which the legitimacy of authority was in question, and in which the rules of debate were not agreed upon. Some of this directly involved the activities of journalists in that James Anderton had often included some journalists among those groups of people whom he identified as posing a bigger threat to society than mere criminals. The Stalker affair involved a critical increase in the level of disputed legitimacy, in that one of the planks of the police view of order and legitimacy was removed. The deputy chief constable's bona fides was now in question by the very structure of authority of which he had previously been a part.

The effect of competition in newspapers on the type of news produced is complex. In general it tends to produce in the tabloids a greater and greater stress on entertainment and presentation rather than content. But equally among reporters it generates a vigorous pursuit of the 'good story'. This notion is part of the professional culture of journalists, and when one reporter or editor sees what he or she regards as a good story in another paper they normally desire to better it. The Stalker affair had a number of elements about it which made it such a story: it could be told as a political thriller, or as soap opera and make good narrative; it could be reduced to good, simple dramatic themes. For the quality papers it posed problems about the rule of law in Northern Ireland.

The only way that it could be reported, however, was by the press attempting to decide what sense could be made of it. The meanings that it had could not be taken as read from the authority structure. This was because in its nature the story involved a contest about the truth and about the meaning of events. As it happened no official version was ever forthcoming so that the option simply to accept the government version of events was never there. More to the point, Stalker and his solicitors were able to mount a campaign to convince journalists of his version of events.

Newspapers also decided to devote resources to covering the story with a level of manpower not associated with normal routine news coverage. The fact that the *Manchester Evening*

News editor, Michael Unger, made the decision to investigate and campaign on the issue meant that there was a mainspring of local journalistic knowledge in the area that the national dailies could tap. He was able to take this decision because a big regional paper can devote enough resources to a large investigative enterprise and carry on with its routine coverage elsewhere. A smaller evening paper might find it more difficult. The local alternative magazine, *City Life*, already had a news reporting system based on covering only a few revelatory stories and leaving the routine ones alone. It also operated on taking risks in its news coverage, which tends to reduce the manpower required for a story.

National newspapers, and papers from abroad such as the *Washington Post*, often used these local papers as first sources of news and would begin their inquiries by talking to local reporters. None the less, *The Guardian, The Observer* and the *Daily Express* all entered into coverage of the affair eearly in its development and would have done so even if the start had not been made by the *Manchester Evening News*.

Newspapers were not frightened off or convinced by rumours and innuendo about Stalker and very rapidly arrived at an agenda which related his suspension from duty to the shoot-to-kill inquiry in Northern Ireland. One of the reasons they were willing to do so was that when journalists interviewed Stalker at length they were prepared to believe in him as a person. But there can also be little doubt that this was combined with the fact that he was a very senior policeman and therefore could not be so easily rubbished as, say, a convicted 'terrorist'.

The simple idea that the use of stereotypes is merely an inevitable part of the process of marginalizing and ridiculing those opposed to the established order does not bear up well in the light of the press coverage of the Stalker affair. Stereotypical notions of the honest cop, and the man in the dark from political thrillers provided a reference point for story-telling and helped to convey the narrative of a probable state plot against a decent law officer. Equally, hackneyed epithets such as 'bible-bashing' were used frequently to categorize James Anderton. Some stereotypes can be and were used subversively, and although journalists may employ them normally in a way which can be seen as sustaining the established order and marginalizing the deviant this is not always or necessarily the case. Journalists have to use stereotypical descriptions because their work is to provide short accounts of events in which each word has to convey the maximum effect.

In particular we saw how the political thriller constituted a stereotypical way of seeing the Stalker affair: the honest policeman finds the system which employs him is corrupt and it attempts to stop him by frustrating his inquiries and threatening to destroy him. The choice he faces is to capitulate or fight on. The word Stalker has now entered the language of this genre, so that it now reinforces the notion that such things happen. On 17 September BBC 1 screened a film, *1996*, in which a senior police officer is sent to Wales in the eponymous year to investigate civil unrest generated by 'terrorists'. He has to investigate the killings of a number of unarmed Welshmen by a squad of heavily armed policemen. One incident involves the shooting of two Welsh teenagers, one fatally, and the subsequent lying under oath in court by officers involved. There is a tape-recording of the incident made by MI5 . . . The screenplay was by G. F. Newman who has written a number of plays based on the work of the police in which their conditions of work, their ideology, the power structure of their bureaucracy, their relationship with government all lead to violence, corruption and a conspiracy of silence. The *Guardian* critique of the film was headlined 'The Stalker scenario'. In the course of the review the critic Hugh Herbert wrote: 'We get Stalker minced and served with Peter Wright onions . . . '[21] 'Stalker' as a word has become shorthand for the very fictional political conspiracy which helped the headline writers to locate the original Stalker news coverage in terms of its meaning for their readers years ago. It has become a proxy for its own stereotypical formulation – one which is charged with dissident rather than conformist implications. The way in which this meaning has become established is through the activity of journalists in the press and the broadcast media and through their interaction with participants in the political process.

The press coverage of the Stalker affair does not show that the press is a free agency equally available to all members of society to influence what is published. Equally, it does not challenge the view that there is only a limited gamut of meanings which can be attributed to events in the political arena: as Elliott *et al.* point out no paper editorializes on behalf of the IRA. But it does indicate that the newspapers are not simply ciphers of a hidden agenda based on a pro-capitalist ideology which manifests itself mysteriously in the reporting of events.

Normal reporting bolsters up the existing arrangements for the exercise of power only so long as the participants promulgate a system based on agreed values. Where this is not the case, and where alternative views are promulgated in such a way that they fit with the work practices and business interests of the press, alternative representations of reality are produced. The press cannot be understood simply by deriving its behaviour from a general model of society. It has to be understood in terms of the activities of people engaged in a production process under conditions which vary from situation to situation and do not necessarily produce results which conform to some universal rationality.

In his analysis of the 'rediscovery of ideology' Stuart Hall[22] identifies a whole series of empirical and conditional necessities for the production of an ideological formulation of the world, and in doing so advances the notion of ideological production to one which is the outcome of practices and not simply a by-product of a system. One of the issues he draws attention to is the need that 'The world has to be *made to mean*'. Hall is concerned with language as the means of producing symbolization – the attribution of meaning, and the relationship of this process to content analysis. But before we can identify such linguistic output, work has to have gone into its production. The construction of meaning is part of the work output of journalists and part of the means by which they achieve such output.

This process of attributing significance for journalists has two important elements. One is to show a sort of teleological meaning – that the events described mean something for society or for mankind or some other universalistic category beyond the particular incidents of the narrative. This is normally done simply by reference to the political or social context in which it occurs. This can be seen then as a situation in which news inevitably sustains the system of power relations. But such a view is wide of the mark. What may be a normal state of affairs

– the press supporting the status quo – is a conditional outcome of normal news producing practices, and when those conditions are not met, as in the events of this book, such an outcome is not produced.

The second sort of meaning is the sort which provides the story with narrative sense. The bits of the narrative system have to be shown to hold together, and the characters have to be seen to have acted as expected within the characters ascribed to them, whether that of gangland bosses (organizing crimes), bible-bashers (speaking to God en route to a seminar) or fuddy-duddies (leaving the gangland bosses at the party before the fun starts). In providing for this sort of explanation journalists do not simply apply a set of rules, they improvise and invent ways of doing what they have to do, and invoke whatever means may come to hand most effectively to do their job. For instance, to show the pressure on the Stalker family, this may mean invoking a view of the state as the originator of malpractice or borrowing the forms of the human interest story in order to clarify and explain what is happening, how it is happening and why. The trouble with ideological analysis as a means of understanding such processes is that it tries to understand what the creators of mass media output intend by looking for deep structures or rules which underlie what is produced, but not by examining the work practices of the producers, their own occupational rationality and the context in which they work.

Epilogue

Academic detachment becomes impossible when one considers some sorts of issue, even though reading press reports and interviewing people after the event may distance one from the incidents which gave rise to the press coverage – which I have tried to examine as dispassionately as possible.

In this case six unarmed civilians were shot dead by policemen in a region of the UK, and the policeman who investigated this was himself forced off the inquiry for reasons which stretched to breaking point the credulity of almost everyone who looked at the case. The press, in the person of a small number of reporters and editors, could hardly have spent more time attempting to unearth what they conceived of as the truth. And where they could not get the evidence they needed to verify their explanations and protect themselves from reprisals they still floated them as possibilities. Academics frequently bemoan the shortcomings of journalists. In this case, however, it would be hard to argue that the press had failed Michael Tighe, Kevin Taylor, or John Stalker. Stalker also had to cross his Rubicon to make sure that what others clearly wanted to suppress should be made public. Many would not have had the courage to do so. That their efforts did not produce the results they sought in the political arena needs to be explained by reference to more deep-seated and disturbing characteristics of British society. It seems it is possible for agents of the state to kill people who pose no immediate danger and to go unpunished even if this is exposed by an active press. Who cares?

Notes and references

Chapter 1

1 For instance, see Stuart Hall, 'Deviance, politics and the media', in Paul Rock and Mary McIntosh (eds), *Deviance and Social Control* (London: Tavistock, 1974), pp 261–306, subsequently revised in 'The rediscovery of ideology' in Michael Gurevitch, Tony Bennett, James Curran and Janet Woollacott (eds), *Culture, Society and the Media* (London: Methuen, 1982), pp. 56–90.
2 See Phillip Elliott, *The Making of a Television Series* (London: Constable, 1972); Peter Golding and Phillip Elliott, *Making the News*, (Harlow: Longman, 1979); David Murphy, *The Silent Watchdog: The Press in Local Politics* (London: Constable, 1976); Philip Schlesinger, *Putting Reality Together* (London: Constable, 1974); Jeremy Tunstall, *Journalists at Work: Specialist Correspondents* (London: Constable, 1970).
3 The Glasgow Media Group, *More Bad News* (London: Routledge & Kegan Paul, 1980), p. 121.
4 ibid., p. 119.
5 ibid., p. 132.
6 ibid., p. 122.
7 ibid., p. 132.
8 *The Independent*, 6 February 1988.
9 Gaye Tuchman, 'Making news is doing work', *American Journal of Sociology*, vol. 79, no. 1, 1973, pp. 110–31 quotes Helen Hughes, *News and the Human Interest Story* (Chicago: Chicago University Press, 1940).
10 Quotation by Tuchman from an address by Newbold Noyes to the American Society of Newspaper Editors, Washington DC, 14 April 1973.
11 'General quizzed by police', Ed Vale, *Daily Mirror*, 8 August 1985.
12 Granada screened *The Untouchables* on 3 November 1986 and *Scotland Yard's Cocaine Connection* on 3 April 1989.
13 Cost quoted in 'BBC exposé halted by Yard pressure', Paul Lashmar and David Leigh, *The Observer*, 13 October 1985,

and 'BBC film stopped after police requests', *The Guardian*, 14 October 1985.

14   For fuller details of this case see Andrew Jennings, Paul Lashmar and David Leigh, *Scotland Yard's Cocaine Connection* (London: Jonathan Cape, 1990). This also gives an excellent insight into the methods and thought processes of investigative journalists at work.

Chapter 2

1   George Gerbner, 'A generalised graphic model of communication', in John Corner and Jeremy Hawthorne (eds), *Communication Studies* (London, Edward Arnold, 1985) pp. 21–2.

2   Malcolm S. MacLean and Bruce H. Westley, 'A conceptual model for communication research', *Journalism Quarterly*, vol. 34, no. 4 , 1957, pp. 31–8.

3   For instance, see David Manning White, 'The "Gatekeeper", a case study in the selection of news', in Lewis A. Dexter and David Manning White (eds), *People, Society and Mass Communication* (New York: Free Press, 1964), pp. 160–73.

4   Gaye Tuchman, 'Making news is doing work', *American Journal of Sociology*, vol. 79, no. 1, 1973, p. 110–31.

5   James Aitchison, *Writing for the Press* (London: Hutchinson, 1988), p. 1.

6   ibid., p. 1.

7   ibid., p. 1.

8   ibid., p. 3.

9   ibid.

10   ibid., p. 10.

11   ibid.

12   ibid., p. 13.

13   Aitchison, p. 22.

14   See Jeremy Tunstall, *Journalists at Work: Specialist Correspondents* (London: Constable, 1970).

Chapter 3

1   *The Guardian*, 31 May 1986.

2   *Manchester Evening News*, 20 November 1985.

3   ibid., 20 September 1986.

4   ibid., 15 October 1986.

5   *The Guardian*, 2 February 1987.

6   ibid., 31 May 1986, p. 1. See previous chapter.

7   'MI5 smear scandal exposed', Neil Wallis, *The Star*, 19 July 1986.

8   'Stalker: why MI5 tried to silence him', Neil Wallis, *The Star*, 19 July 1986.

9   'My 17-year friendship', Paul Horrocks, *Manchester Evening News*, 5 June 1986.

10 'I am the "criminal" in party picture', Paul Horrocks, *Manchester Evening News*, 21 June 1986.

11 '"Weed" cleared after quiz', *Metro News*, 2 September 1988. 'Weed's £9,000 dodge', *Manchester Evening News*, 19 October 1989.

12 West Yorkshire Police, *Report of the Investigation by Chief Constable Colin Sampson QPM. Subject: allegation of misconduct against Deputy Chief Constable of the Greater Manchester Police*, (known as the 'Sampson report'), par. 101.

13 'Gangland guests saw street star's party piece with top cop. Inside story of night that cast cloud over crime buster Stalker', Nick Pritchard, *News of the World*, 22 June 1986.

Chapter 4

1   West Yorkshire Police, *Report of the Investigation by Chief Constable Colin Sampson QPM. Subject: allegation of misconduct against Deputy Chief Constable of the Greater Manchester Police*, par. 38

2   ibid., par. 1.

3   ibid., par. 3.

4   ibid., par. 2.

5   ibid., pars. 233–4.

6   ibid., par. 15.

7   ibid., par. 16.

8   ibid., par. 17.

9   ibid.

10 ibid.

11 ibid., par. 18.

12 ibid., par. 19.

13 ibid., par. 21.

14 ibid., par. 22.

15 ibid., par. 23.

16 ibid.

17 ibid., par. 183.

18 ibid., par. 184.

19 ibid., par. 185.

20 ibid., par. 186.

21 ibid., par. 187.

22 ibid., par. 205.

23 ibid., par. 373.

24 ibid., par. 396.

25 ibid., par. 397.
26 ibid., par. 87.
27 ibid.
28 ibid., par. 252.
29 ibid., par. 222.
30 ibid., pars 253–4.
31 ibid., par. 258.
32 ibid., par. 259.
33 ibid., par. 260.
34 ibid., par. 262.
35 ibid., par. 278.
36 ibid., par. 279.
37 ibid.
38 ibid., par. 264.
39 ibid., par. 265.
40 ibid., par. 266.
41 ibid., par. 271.
42 ibid.
43 ibid., par. 272.
44 ibid., par. 427.
45 ibid., par. 428.
46 'Stalker report rapped by MP', Paul Horrocks, *Manchester Evening News*, 27 September 1986.
47 Sampson report, par. 435.
48 ibid., par. 434.
49 ibid., par. 436.
50 ibid., par. 437.
51 ibid., par. 447.
52 ibid., par. 459.

Chapter 5

1 'Police chief in the dark', Aileen Ballantyne, *The Guardian*, 2 June 1986.
2 'Police silent over absence of chief', John Alley, *Daily Express*, 2 June 1986.
3 'MPs' fury at police probe secrecy', *Daily Express*, 5 June 1986.
4 'The riddle of John Stalker', Ian Craig, *Manchester Evening News*, June 1986.
5 'Deputy police chief attacks veil of secrecy: "Tell me what I have done"', John Alley, *Daily Express*, 7 June 1986.
6 'Cop is axed from probe', *The Star*, 7 June 1986.
7 'RUC men linked to Stalker claims', Paul Johnson, *The Guardian*, 9 June 1986.
8 'Mr. Stalker's odd ordeal', *The Guardian*, 10 June 1986.
9 'Stalker and police chief meet over allegations', Tom Sharratt, *The Guardian*, 10 June 1986.

10 'MI5 mystery over Stalker wrangle', *The Star*, 17 June 1986.
11 'The Stalker affair, and the questions', *The Guardian*, 18 June 1986.
12 'Let me go back to work. Plea by top cop as probe goes on', *The Star*, 26 June 1986.
13 'I'm innocent, says Stalker', Tom Sharratt, *The Guardian*, 26 June 1986.
14 'Stalker in a void', *The Guardian*, 26 June 1986.
15 'Police chief probe "won't be dropped"', *Daily Mirror*, 27 June 1986.
16 'Police chief to be told of mystery allegation', *Daily Telegraph*, 9 June 1986.
17 'Suspension on Monday?' *Manchester Evening News*, 27 June 1986.
18 'Stalker could be suspended', *The Star*, 28 June 1986.
19 'Clash over vital dates: Stalker in new riddle', Paul Horrocks, *Manchester Evening News*, 1 July 1986.
20 'Fury of top cop', *The Star*, 2 July 1986.
21 'My anguish, by Mrs. Stalker', Paul Horrocks, *Manchester Evening News*, 2 July 1986.
22 'Anguish of Mrs Stalker', Paul Horrocks, *Manchester Evening News*, 2 July 1986.
23 'MP in plea for Stalker', *Manchester Evening News*, 12 July 1986.
24 'Secret heartache of Stalker's girl', David Stokes and Frank Welsby, *Daily Express*, 14 August 1986.
25 'Stalker: I quit over Myra's trip to moors. It was the last straw says daughter', *Daily Mirror*, 20 December 1986.
26 'Sad Stalker says: I can't take any more. Embittered police chief quits force', David Wooding and Ian Fletcher, *Today*, 20 December 1986; 'Stalker leaves police force for "family reasons"', Malcolm Pithers, *The Independent*, 20 December 1986; 'Stalker quits over moors snub', Derek Hornby, *Daily Express*, 20 December 1986; 'Stalker quits to end his family's pain', *Daily Mail*, 20 December 1986; 'Stalker to quit "for sake of family"', Tom Sharratt, Peter Murtagh, *The Guardian*, 20 December 1986; 'Stalker quits "to put family first"', *Mail on Sunday*, 21 December 1986; 'Stalker quits for his family', *Sunday Telegraph*, 21 December 1986; 'The REAL story behind Stalker's shock retirement. I MADE JOHN QUIT SAYS WIFE', *Sunday Mirror*, 21 December 1986.

Chapter 6

1 'Stalker's edge of darkness', Peter Murtagh, *The Guardian*, 2 February 1988.

2   'The man who knew too much', *Sunday Tribune*, 22 June 1986.

3   'The man who saw too much', David Leigh, *The Observer*, 14 February 1988.

4   'Gangland guests saw street star's party piece with top cop. Inside story of night that cast cloud over crime buster Stalker', Nick Pritchard, *News of the World*, 22 June 1986.

5   'Police chief faces lavish hospitality charge', Barrie Penrose and David Connett, *The Sunday Times*, 8 June 1986; 'Top cop quiz over "shady pals": "He was snapped"', James Weatherup, *News of the World*, 8 June 1986.

6   'Holiday allegation against police chief', Margaret Henfield and Peter Burden, *Daily Mail*, 5 June 1986

7   'Police chief's friend denies reports', *The Daily Telegraph*, 6 June 1986.

8   'I am the criminal in party picture', Paul Horrocks and James Cusick, *Manchester Evening News*, 21 June 1986.

9   '"Masonic mafia framed top cop. His own men bid to ruin him"', Alan Hart, *News of the World*, 29 June 1986.

10 'Suspension of police chief not connected with RUC, MI5 or freemasons. Stalker is cleared to return to work', David Connett, Barrie Penrose and Heather Angus, *The Sunday Times*, 10 August 1986.

11 ibid.

12 'Stalker in dark over "vindication"', Peter Murtagh, *The Guardian*, 11 August 1986; 'The date Stalker will remember forever', Margaret Henfield and Alan Qualtrough, *Daily Mail*, 11 August 1986.

13 'Hot money link in Stalker report', Barrie Penrose and David Connett, *The Sunday Times*, 17 August 1986.

14 'Stalker may face discredit charge', Kim Fletcher, *The Daily Telegraph*, 27 June 1986.

15 'Police chief probe won't be dropped', *Daily Mirror*, 27 June 1986.

16 Philip Schlesinger, *Putting Reality Together* (London: Constable, 1974).

17 'Why the tories are gunning for Stalker', Martin Lee, *The Militant*, 27 June 1986.

18 'Stalking Stalker', Graham Stringer, *New Socialist*, February 1987.

Chapter 7

1   'Police silent over absence of chief', John Alley, *Daily Express*, 2 June 1986

2   'Stalker dropped from probe team', *Manchester Evening News*, 2 June 1986.

3   'The riddle of John Stalker', Ian Craig, *Manchester Evening News*, 4 June 1986.

4   ibid.
5   'RUC men linked to Stalker claims', Paul Johnson, *The Guardian*, 9 June 1986.
6   'RUC tried to stop Stalker's questions about senior officers', Peter Murtagh, *The Guardian*, 16 June 1986.
7   ibid.
8   'Stalker's RUC inquiry', Peter Murtagh, *The Guardian*, 16 June 1986.
9   'Killings that put public gaze on covert security', Paul Johnson, *The Guardian*, 6 June 1986.
10 ibid.
11 'Stalker's RUC inquiry', Peter Murtagh, *The Guardian*, 16 June 1986.
12 John Stalker, *Stalker* (London: Harrap, 1988; Harmondsworth: Penguin, 1989, containing new material).
13 'What CID said about boss', Paul Horrocks, *Manchester Evening News*, 17 June 1986.
14 'Mallon to raise claims over Stalker with PM', *Belfast Telegraph*, 9 June 1986.
15 Peter Taylor, *Stalker: The Search for the Truth* (London: Faber & Faber, 1987).
16 Stalker, op cit.
17 'MI5 mystery over Stalker wrangle', Frank Curran, *The Star*, 17 June 1986.
18 'Stalker may have found new evidence on RUC killing before his suspension', Peter Murtagh, *The Guardian*, 17 June 1986.
19 ibid.
20 'MI5 smear exposed', Neil Wallis, *The Star*, 19 July 1986.
21 'Stalker planned to quiz Hermon for his Ulster Police report', Peter Murtagh and Paul Johnson, *The Guardian*, 20 June 1986.
22 'Stalker planned to ask Hermon about "cover-up"', Conor O'Clery, *Irish Times*, 20 June 1986.
23 ibid.
24 'MP to quiz King on Stalker issue', David Watson, *Belfast Telegraph*, 6 June 1986.
25 'The Stalking's over', Ed Glinert, *City Life*, 6 June 1986.
26 'Masonic mafia framed top cop: own men in bid to ruin him', Alan Hart, *News of the World*, 29 June 1986.
27 '"Masonic witch hunt on top cop"', Andrew Leatham and Peter Reece, *The People*, 29 June 1986.
28 'The Masonic connection', James Cusick, *Manchester Evening News*, 25 June 1986.
29 'Mason's denial over Stalker', Ray King and Patrick Mulchrone, *Manchester Evening News*, 6 August 1986.
30 'Brotherhood on trial', Roger Todd, *Daily Mirror*, 7 August 1986.
31 ibid.

32 'Secrets of the Masons. They open their doors but not their mouths', Robert Wilson, *The Star*, 7 August 1986.

Chapter 8

1 'High-level order to silence Stalker', David Leigh, Nick Davies and Jonathan Foster, *The Observer*, 6 July 1986.
2 'Stalker rap over cars', Paul Horrocks, *Manchester Evening News*, 15 August 1986.
3 ibid.
4 'Anderton ready to defend Stalker over use of cars', Jonathan Foster and Paul Lashmar, 17 August 1986.
5 'A new blow for Stalker', Paul Horrocks, *Manchester Evening News*, 18 August 1986.
6 'Denial on warnings', Steve Panter, *Manchester Evening News*, 18 August 1986.
7 'Stalker "tried to stop key CID promotions"', Kevin Bowling and Edward Scallan, *Daily Mail*, 20 August 1986.
8 'Stalker may have to face tribunal', Peter Murtagh, *The Guardian*, 20 August 1986.
9 ibid.
10 'Send police chief back', *Manchester Evening News*, 21 August 1986.
11 'Stalker's mistake', Paul Horrocks, *Manchester Evening News*, 21 August 1986.
12 'Move to send Stalker back', Paul Horrocks, Steve Panter and Michael Duffy, *Manchester Evening News*, 21 August 1986.
13 'Stalker: why no warning?' Paul Horrocks, *Manchester Evening News*, 21 August 1986.
14 ibid.
15 'Report names nine behind Stalker charges', Peter Murtagh, *The Guardian*, 22 August 1986.
16 ibid.
17 'Mr. Stalker should return to work', *The Guardian*, 22 August 1986.
18 '"I can work with Mr. Anderton," Stalker – "I don't bear grudges"', Paul Horrocks, *Manchester Evening News*, 22 August 1986.
19 'End of the Agony', *Manchester Evening News*, 22 August 1986.
20 'Stalker and a Mitty liar', Steve Panter, *Manchester Evening News*, 22 August 1986.
21 'Stalker: the central question remains', *The Observer*, 24 August 1986.
22 'Stalker may sue police chief for defamation', Paul Horrocks, *Manchester Evening News*, 8 September 1986.
23 'Officer claims Stalker report distortion', Peter Murtagh, *The Guardian*, 17 September 1986.

24 ibid.
25 'Stalker report rapped by MP', Paul Horrocks, *Manchester Evening News*, 27 September 1986.
26 'The Irish connection. Lying pest behind Stalker probe', David Leigh, Paul Lashmar and Jonathan Foster, *The Observer*, 28 September 1986.
27 ibid.
28 ibid.
29 ibid.
30 ibid.
31 ibid.
32 'RUC officer in Stalker link to province', Peter Murtagh, *The Guardian*, 29 September 1986.
33 ibid.

Chapter 9

1 'Tory infighting led to Stalker probe', David Leigh and Paul Lashmar, *The Observer*, 29 June 1986.
2 ibid.
3 ibid.
4 ibid.
5 ibid.
6 'Citizen', Ed Glinert, *City Life*, 4 July 1986.
7 Reports, Ed Glinert, *City Life*, 18 July 1986.
8 'Stalker affair: "It was a conspiracy"', Charles Langley, *Today*, 1 September 1986.
9 'Now Anderton faces inquiry', *The Star*, 1 September 1986.
10 'Anderton tells accusers to show their evidence', Tom Sharratt, *The Guardian*, 2 September 1986; 'Top cop hits out', *The Star*, 2 September 1986; 'I did my duty over Stalker inquiry, says Anderton', Peter Davenport, *The Times*, 2 September 1986.
11 'Labour group may call Anderton inquiry', Peter Murtagh and Michael Morris, *The Guardian*, 3 September 1986.
12 'AIDS speech was inspired by God, says Anderton', John Kelly, *Daily Mail*, 20 December 1986.
13 'Anderton: I was moved by God's spirit', *Daily Express*, 20 December 1986.
14 'Anderton's girl quits college to help homeless. A quiet Samaritan among the drop-outs', Paul Horrocks, *Manchester Evening News*, 27 January 1987.
15 'GOD'S COP GIRL IS A GAY. He cries at news', Tim Carroll, *News of the World*, 20 March 1988.
16 ibid.
17 'Row over Anderton prophet claim', Malcolm Pithers, *The Independent*, 20 January 1987.

18 'AIDS outburst police chief's amazing claim. I MAY BE GOD'S PROPHET', John Kelly, *Daily Mirror*, 20 January 1987.
19 '"He needs medical help"', *Manchester Evening News*, 19 January 1986.
20 'Anderton crisis talk', Fred Hackworth and Patrick Mulchrone, *Manchester Evening News*, 20 January 1987.
21 'Prophet' Anderton is given down to earth message: Resign. HOW DO YOU TELL A CHIEF CONSTABLE HE'S OFF HIS ROCKER?', *Daily Mirror*, 20 January 1987.
22 'Jim upset as ad knocks his halo', *Manchester Evening News*, 23 February 1987.
23 'Anderton receives a second call', Gareth Parry, *The Guardian*, 23 February 1987.
24 'Time to look hard at Manchester's police', *The Independent*, 20 January 1987.
25 ibid.
26 'God's policeman', *The Daily Telegraph*, 20 January 1987.
27 'Time for quiet', *Manchester Evening News*, 28 January 1987.
28 'Anderton and Stalker', *Manchester Evening News*, 26 August 1986.
29 '"Arrogant media"', *Manchester Evening News*, 9 October 1987.
30 'Taylor launching legal action against Anderton', Peter Murtagh, *The Guardian*, 29 September 1986.
31 'Anderton accused of conspiracy', *Manchester Evening News*, 15 October 1986.
32 'Anderton pulls out', James Lewis, *The Guardian*, 22 January 1987.

Chapter 10

1 John Stalker, *Stalker* (London: Harrap, 1988).
2 'Stalker frozen out of office by Anderton', Jonathan Foster, *The Observer*, 21 December 1986.
3 'Anderton and me. The very man who spoke of being moved by the finger of God deliberately isolated me and forced me into bitter resignation', John Stalker, *Daily Express*, 5 February 1988.
4 'When the rumour mill ground out tales of free meals in Chinatown', Michael Unger, *The Guardian*, 28 January 1988.
5 Philip Schlesinger, *Putting Reality Together* (London: Constable, 1978).
6 'Manchester's police chief in fresh row', David Leigh, Jonathan Foster and Paul Lashmar, *The Observer*, 5 October 1986.
7 ibid.
8 'Bad riddance', Ed Glinert, *City Life*, 4 December 1986.

9   'Stalker quits over moors snub', Derek Hornby, *Daily Express*, 20 December 1986.
10 ibid.
11 'Stalker: I quit over Myra's trip to moors. It was the last straw, says daughter', Maurice Chesworth, *Daily Mirror*, 20 December 1986.
12 'Sad Stalker says: I can't take any more. Embittered police chief quits force', David Wooding and Ian Fletcher, *Today*, 20 December 1986.
13 'Stalker leaves force for "family reasons"', Malcolm Pithers, *The Independent*, 20 December 1986.
14 'Stalker to quit "for sake of family"', Tom Sharratt and Peter Murtagh, *The Guardian*, 20 December 1986.
15 'Stalker frozen out of office by Anderton', Jonathan Foster, *The Observer*, 21 December 1986.
16 'Stalker quits for his family,' *The Sunday Telegraph*, 21 December 1986.
17 'The REAL story behind Stalker's shock retirement. I MADE JOHN QUIT SAYS WIFE', *Sunday Mirror*, 21 December 1986.
18 '"I am not a broken man" says Stalker. Troubled police chief speaks out', Ian Fletcher, *Today*, 21 December 1986.
19 John Stalker, *Stalker* (Harmondsworth: Penguin, 1989), pp. 232–5
20 'Stalker criticised for seeing solicitor "too soon"', Michael Morris, *The Guardian*, 18 October 1986.
21 'RUC chief denies death squad blame', *The Observer*, 19 October 1986.
22 'New cash setback for Stalker', *Daily Mail*, 5 December 1986.
23 'Bad Riddance', Ed Glinert, *City Life*, 5 – 19 December 1986.
24 ibid.
25 'My top cop pal, by drag star Foo Foo', Alan Hart, *News of the World*, 23 November 1986.
26 ibid.
27 'Stalker versus his boss. He faces courtroom clash', *Daily Mirror*, 1 December 1986; 'Stalker may speak in Anderton case', *Daily Mail*, 1 December 1986.
28 *Daily Mirror*, ibid.
29 'Why they had to silence me', Peter Grosvenor and John Burns, *Daily Express*, 1 February 1988.
30 'Shoot-to-kill trials would have forced resignations. Report shelved to protect top RUC officers', Peter Murtagh, *The Guardian*, 30 January 1988.
31 'Unarmed men "deliberately shot"', Mark Rosselli, *The Independent*, 3 February 1988.
32 'MP names "men in Stalker inquiry"', Anthony Bevins, Andrew Marr and David McKittrick, *The Independent*, 3 February 1988.
33 'Haughey sounds Stalker warning', David Hearst and Joe Joyce, *The Guardian*, 4 February 1988.

34   'Decision not to prosecute was a bombshell to Dublin govern-ment', *The Independent*, 5 February 1988.

Chapter 11

1   'Police seize Stalker case yacht in drugs swoop', Margeret Henfield, *Daily Mail*, 5 February 1987.
2   'Bank fiddle by a tycoon', Alan Slater, *Manchester Evening News*, 4 October 1989.
3   'Taylor's "money go-round"', Alan Slater, *Manchester Evening News*, 5 October 1989.
4   'Bank man's cover-up' and '"United link" in fraud trial', Alan Slater, *Manchester Evening News*, 6 October 1989.
5   'Police were getting at Stalker QC', *Manchester Evening News*, 16 October 1986.
6   ibid.
7   ibid.
8   'Bank man "broke rules"', *Manchester Evening News*, 19 October 1986.
9   '"Frenetic" activity during Stalker probe: Cop denies Ulster link to Taylor', Ray King, *Manchester Evening News*, 15 January 1990.
10 'Taylor trial furore for top cop', Ray King, *Manchester Evening News*, 16 January 1990.
11 ibid.
12 'Clash on raid at Taylor firm', Ray King, *Manchester Evening News*, 17 January 1990.
13 ibid.
14 ibid.
15 'Taylor case snag. Judge calls top police to court', Ray King, *Manchester Evening News*, 17 January 1990.
16 ibid.
17 'Secret of police Taylor probe', Ray King, *Manchester Evening News*, 18 January 1990.
18 'Judge throws out fraud case. Taylor cleared', Ray King, *Manchester Evening News*, 18 January 1990.
19 ibid.
20 ibid.
21 'Mason witch hunt on top cop', Andrew Leatham and Peter Reece, *The People*, 29 June 1986.
22 'Joy after Stalker's old friend is cleared', James Collins and John Ingham, *Daily Express*, 19 January 1990; 'Freed Stalker tycoon is set to sue for £10m', Stephen White, *Daily Mirror*, 19 January 1990; 'Free Stalker pal is set to sue for £10m', David Hudson, *Daily Star*, 19 January 1990.
23 'Stalker ruined by the link that never was', Chris Ryder, *The Daily Telegraph*, 19 January 1990.

24 'Cabinet "sacrificed my friend" says ex-police chief. Stalker inquiry demand as £1m trial collapses', Nigel Bunyan and David Millward, *The Daily Telegraph*, 19 January 1990.
25 ibid.
26 See, for example, 'Stalker: the row that won't go away', Walter Ellis, *The Sunday Times*, 21 January 1990.
27 *Stalker – the Search for the Truth*, (London: Faber & Faber, 1987).
28 'Stalker: no case for a conspiracy', Peter Taylor, *The Sunday Telegraph*, 21 January 1990.
29 'How Anglo-Irish accord doomed Stalker's inquiry', Mary Holland, *The Observer*, 21 January 1990.
30 'An abscess bursts', *The Independent*, 20 January 1990.
31 ibid.
32 ibid.
33 ibid.
34 'We must see justice done in Stalker's case', *Daily Express*, 20 January 1990.
35 *The Independent*, 20 January 1990.
36 'Give us your evidence says Whitehall: Challenge to Stalker', Ian Wylie and Don Frame, *Manchester Evening News*, 19 January 1990.
36 'DPP urges Stalker case inquiry', Peter Murtagh, Michael White and Michael Morris, *The Guardian*, 20 January 1990.
37 'Stalker notes "fail to show misconduct"', John Carvel, David Pallister and Alan Travis, *The Guardian*, 26 January 1990.
38 'Stalker memo: officials named', Simon de Bruxelles and Victor Smart, *The Observer*, 21 January 1990.
39 Carvel, Pallister and Travis, op cit.
40 ibid.
41 'Stalker renews call for answer on Hermon diary', Tom Sharratt, *The Guardian*, 27 January 1990.
42 '"Nothing sinister" in Stalker affair', David Pallister, *The Guardian*, 5 April 1990.

Chapter 12

1 Philip Elliott, Graham Murdock and Philip Schlesinger, '"Terrorism" and the state: a case study of the discourses of television', in Richard Collins, James Curran, Nicholas Garnham, Paddy Scannell, Philip Schlesinger and Colin Sparks, *Media Culture and Society* (London: Sage, 1986).
2 James Curran and Jean Seaton, *Power Without Responsibility*, (London: Routledge, 1988), pp. 78–114.
3 Philip Schlesinger, *Putting Reality Together* (London: Constable, 1974).
4 Curran and Seaton, pp. 115–210.

5   H. Marcuse, *One Dimensional Man* (London: Routledge & Kegan Paul, 1974).
6   Elliott *et al.* p. 265.
7   ibid.
8   'Why this man must not be lost in the shadows', *Daily Express*, 7 July 1986.
9   'The *Star* says justice must be done: end this silence', *The Star*, 26 June 1986.
10 'Stalker in a void', *The Guardian*, 26 June 1986.
11 'Was he "Stalkered?",' *Manchester Evening News*, 15 June 1986.
12 'The veil drops over Stalker', *The Guardian*, 22 January 1988.
13 'Was he "Stalkered?"', *Manchester Evening News*, 15 June 1986.
14 'Scandalous. The smokescreen that still obscures the Stalker affair', Sue Cameron, *Today*, 9 September 1986.
15 'The veil drops over Stalker', *The Guardian*, 22 January 1988.
16 'Terrorism in the liberal state', *The Independent*, 6 February 1988.
17 'The Stalker legacy', *The Daily Telegraph*, 18 February 1986.
18 'Ulster - test of our political maturity', *The Daily Telegraph*, 22 August 1988.
19 Philip Elliott and Peter Golding, *Making the News* (London: Longman, 1979).
20 David Murphy, 'Control without censorship', in James Curran (ed.), *The British Press: a Manifesto* (London: Macmillan, 1978).
21 'The Stalker scenario', Hugh Herbert, *The Guardian*, 19 September 1989.
22 Michael Gurevitch, Tony Bennett, James Curran, and Janet Woollacott (eds), 'The rediscovery of "ideology"', *Culture, Society and the Media* (London: Methuen, 1982), pp. 56–90.

Index